NORTHAMPTONSHIRE

GUIDE TO THE COUNTRYSIDE

Edited by Ron Wilson

JEMA PUBLICATIONS

First published 1977 by County Guide Publications.
This revised edition published 2001 by Jema Publications
ISBN 1-871468-24-8

Jema Publications
40 Ashley Lane
Moulton
Northampton
NN3 7TJ

CONTENTS

ACKNOWLEDGEMENTS

As with the first edition of *Northamptonshire - A Guide to the Countryside*, the revised edition would not have been possible without the help of a large number of people. Most of the original contributors have revised their contributions, and where appropriate supplied photographs. The contributors to major articles have been named; my thanks to them for producing their material often under pressure and at short notice. There are a number of other people who have supplied information, offered suggestions, etc. These include Anglian Water, Daventry Library, Rights of Way Officer (NCC), Nene Valley Project (NCC), Cycling Officer (NCC), The Wildlife Trust, Northamptonshire ACRE, Churches Conservation Trust, FWAG, Northamptonshire Archaeology (NCC), Northamptonshire Heritage (NCC), Northamptonshire County Council - Environment Directorate (various departments), Northamptonshire Record Office (NCC), Tree and Landscape Officer (NCC), Knuston Hall, Ramblers Association, Rockingham Forest Trust, Woodland Trust, together with the many other people who have offered help and advice.

I am also grateful to Jane Long, who typed up some of the material, and to Tony Noble from Jema Publications for agreeing to publish this revised edition, and for his help and support throughout.

I apologise if I have misconstrued anything in editing the contributions. Although published under the auspices of the Northamptonshire Association for Environmental Education, any views expressed are those of the individual contributors.

INTRODUCTION

Introduction to the First Edition

Northamptonshire is a county which, although on the surface may not appear particularly appealing or productive, is rich in countryside features. With its present policies of rapid development, large tracts of land are now being given over to housing, factories, offices, shops and schools and the hundred and one ancillary activities which are necessary to keep a modern community in motion. With such expansion vast areas, once a sanctuary for wildlife and wild things, are now decreasing.

In this short book, various experts have prepared a series of articles which offer information about the county, both as it is and as it was. From these contributions, we hope that those who have an interest in, care for, and are concerned about the Northamptonshire landscape, will come to know more about THEIR county.

Armed with a copy of the book, we hope that the individual's enjoyment of the countryside will be enhanced. If this happens, then there are ways in which you can help YOUR county by joining an organisation and so assist in the urgent task of, for example, looking after its wildlife, preserving its landscape or perhaps discovering more about its historical remains.

The recently formed Northamptonshire Association for Environmental Education is concerned about the environment in all its guises, and hopes that the following pages will stimulate an interest in the county, for Northamptonshire has much of beauty and joy in its hedges and hills and its waters and woodlands. If the book should prove of interest, and at some time in the future there is a chance to reprint it, we would like to include any amendments which the reader might think appropriate.

Ron Wilson
Chairman
Northamptonshire Association for Environmental Education
Everdon Field Centre
September 1977

Introduction to the Second Edition

Coincidentally a number of people who had purchased the first edition of Northamptonshire a guide to the countryside – and who were still using the book – asked about a new edition. In the course of a conversation with Tony Noble of Jema Publications he also indicated that he found the original edition useful – and without too much arm twisting – agreed to produce a revised and updated version for the new millennium.

There are even greater pressures on Northamptonshire than when the original edition was published over 20 years ago, and all of us who form part of the Northamptonshire community have a responsibility to protect those areas, which are important for our future well-being. Computers may have 'revolutionised' our lives, but however good a CD ROM is there is no substitute for a walk in a wood, a view across a valley, or taking in lungfuls of fresh air in some quiet spot. These are fundamentals that we must preserve for future generations. We all have a responsibility for this; we must all do what we can to ensure that the opportunities are not lost.

Ron Wilson,
April 2001

IN PRAISE OF NORTHAMPTONSHIRE
by Trevor Hold

Mountains move minds; their towering heads reveal
Depths of sky. Forests too, whose aspect
Giddies the sight with unremitting vastness;
Lakes, coasts and seas: all these impress
Our disenchanted souls. We still
Respond to the grandeur of each prospect.

But it is to that unassuming shire
Where I was born that my own spirit flies,
Homing to her parks and ancient trees,
The sandstone manor and the weathered spire,
The steady river ambling to the seas.

Wherever I may live, my exiled eyes
Will seek that landscape and those gentle skies.

NATURE CONSERVATION IN NORTHAMPTONSHIRE

Matt Jackson

Nature conservation has changed considerably over the last twenty years. The Rio Conference in 1992 marked an important change in government attitudes to nature conservation worldwide. All the governments attending the Summit signed up to 'Local Agenda 21' - involving the public in their country in the process of Nature Conservation – the '21' referring to the twenty first century.

In England this led to the Biodiversity Action Plan process. The British Government produced an action plan to identify both the actions required to preserve the Biodiversity of the UK, and also to identify the costs involved. The Northamptonshire Nature Conservation and Landscape Forum produced their own Biodiversity Action Plan for the County in 1997, which details all the species and habitats which are considered to be at risk nationally and which occur in Northamptonshire, and highlighted those which are a priority for conservation in our County. The Rio definition of biodiversity is "... the variability among living organisms from all sources, including inter alias, terrestrial, marine and other aquatic ecosystems and the ecological complexes of which they are a part: this includes diversity within species, between species and ecosystems". However, Brian Evesham of the Wildlife Trust suggests that a wider, more practical and all-encompassing alternative definition may be helpful:

"Habitats, species and the systems and processes which maintain them".

Every County is unique, and Northamptonshire covers a range of natural areas each of which supports its associated wildlife. The Rockingham Forest has large areas of semi-natural ancient woodland and wood-pasture where the forest was traditionally grazed. Enough of the forest exists for English Nature and the Forestry Commission to have been able to release Red Kites in the area, safe in the knowledge that there is enough natural habitat to support them.

Along the Nene, and some of its tributaries, the otter can again be seen, and is one of the major success stories for nature conservation in recent years. But in spite of this success it needs to be emphasised that the Nene Valley has changed beyond all recognition from its original natural state. Many of the old hay meadows have now been dug up for gravel, the river has been straightened, and its banks shored up. However, where the importance of nature conservation has been recognised there are some exciting developments. Summer Leys Local Nature Reserve, run by Northamptonshire County Council, is centred around a disused gravel pit, and has now become an important site for wading birds - a good example of the planning process being used to ensure that development is sustainable.

High Wood and Meadow Nature Reserve *Photograph: Ron Wilson*

Almost certainly the most important development in conservation over the last twenty years has been the change in public awareness of the issues. In the political arena it is now usual to hear candidates stressing their 'green' credentials, because they know that the environment is now high on the public agenda.

There are still many challenges ahead if we are to ensure that the wildlife of Northamptonshire gets the best possible chance for the future. Although the number of nature reserves now managed by the Wildlife Trust and others has continued to increase, they remain refugees in an environment that is inhospitable to the majority of wildlife. Agricultural policies still promote land management which is unfavourable to wild plants and animals alike, and it is as ever vitally important to co-operate with landowners to establish 'wildlife-friendly' management wherever possible.

THE ROCKS OF NORTHAMPTONSHIRE

George Ilsley

When looking at the map of Britain, an obvious feature of relief is the parallel escarpments of South East England, which stretch from Whitby in the north east to the Weymouth/Portland area in the south. Northamptonshire sits astride one of these escarpments called by some the 'Northamptonshire Uplands'. It is a pear-shaped county, whose long axis extends N.N.E. to S.S.W. Visitors, especially in the northern half of the county, see building stone similar to that used in the Cotswolds; and this is not surprising when one considers that the rock in both areas was laid down under similar geological conditions at approximately the same period of time.

Although boreholes prove the existence of some of the earliest rocks in Britain (Late Upper Cambrian age 525 m.a. [millions of years before present] penetrated at Deanshanger 765388 and Whaddon 805341), most of the surface rocks, which are sedimentary in origin, were laid down during the Jurassic period of geological time (225 to 195 m.a.). Nowhere can be found the fire-formed 'igneous' rocks intruded into the upper layers of the earth's crust, or erupted from volcanoes of the past. Neither are those rocks, whose nature has been changed by the application of tremendous heat or pressure - and called 'metamorphic' - to be discovered in Northamptonshire.

The rocks of Northamptonshire are sediments deposited as beds in ancient shelf seas and on beaches in much the same way that can be observed today. Later rumblings in the earth's crust produced the south-easterly dip of the present layers of rock or strata. Further deposits of boulder clay and sand laid down on the top of this during the recent Ice Age, which, it is presently believed, ended approximately 11,000 years ago, tends to obscure this dipping structure of the Jurassic sediments, but something of a scarp slope can be seen from the A508 road at Lamport, where the ground slopes away steeply W.N.W. for 15 metres (49 feet). There are, however, areas where this blanket of glacial deposits has been breached naturally by rivers, the main ones are the Nene, Welland and their tributaries, which flow northwards to empty into the North Sea at the Wash. These have floored their valleys with riverine deposits called 'alluvium'. The glacial deposits, collectively called 'drift' are not continuous, especially in the south of the county around Northampton, where it is confined mainly to the tops of gently rounded hills, which are often described as 'undulating', the highest of which reaches 209 metres (690 feet).

The surface rocks of the county are Middle Jurassic in age, earlier beds, such as the Liassic sediments of the Lower Jurassic period are rarely naturally exposed in river valleys, and are best seen in quarries, if permission can be obtained, or in temporary exposures during the building of new housing estates or roads. To the naturalist, the county provides a rich variety of the major types of sedimentary rocks i.e. limestones, sandstones and clays, with their contained fossilised fauna.

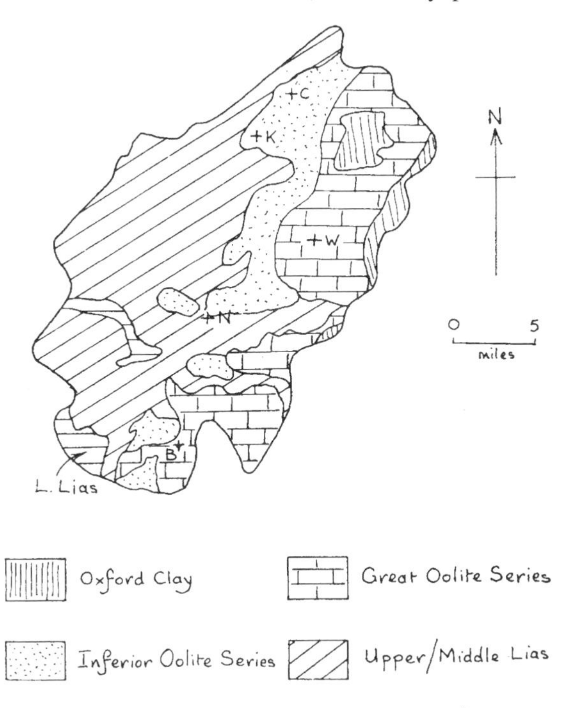

Sketch map of Northamptonshire Geology (solid)

The pattern of Jurassic deposition in the county is complex and much research still remains to be done, but an attempt can be made to examine in simple outline, the deposition sequence.

We look at any landscape today and see that in some parts, especially swamps, lakes, rivers, seas and deserts, deposits are being laid down through the work of nature; and in other areas, not only is no deposition being made, but the present landscape is also being eroded away. What is true of our time is also true of any one moment in geological time; therefore in different parts of the county the rocks represent the local deposition characteristics at a particular time. Our outline therefore only permits the mention of selected examples of rock of particular interest to the naturalist.

Deposition Sequence in Northamptonshire

Geological Period	Series of Beds	Beds
Present	____	Alluvium
Pleistocene	Glacial Drift	Boulder Clay Sands
	____	Oxford Clay
Middle	Great Oolite Series	Cornbrash Blisworth Clay Limestone (Blisworth Limestone)
Jurassic	Inferior oolite Series	Upper Estuarine Limestone Limestone (Collyweston Slate) Lowe Estuarine Northant Sand Ironstone
Lower	Lias	Upper Lias Middle Lias Lower Lias

The Lower Lias forms the lowest and earliest rock group of the Lower Jurassic Period. These clayey (argillaceous) sediments are contemporary with the famous fossiliferous clays of the Dorset coast at Lyme Regis, but lack of exposure make them less of interest to the would-be palaeontologist. They were deposited in a range of fairly shallow, rather muddy, low energy environments of the Liassic sea. Although 141.5 metres (467 feet) is recorded from a borehole near Northampton most of this clay floors the valleys to the north-west of the escarpment, where it is used for cement-making in Rugby.

Exposures of the Middle Lias are also rare in the county. The top of the Middle Lias consists of a Marlstone Rock Bed, and is made up of calcareous clay which contains iron (ferruginous): elsewhere outside the county it is exploited as an ore.

The Upper Lias is the youngest grouping of the Lower Jurassic, and is represented by 57.5 metres (190 feet) of clays, interbedded with clayey limestones, finally becoming mudstones with ferruginous and calcareous nodules.

The Middle Jurassic is a complex series of beds originating under shallow water conditions. A walk around Northampton or any surrounding village will soon acquaint the observer with the yellow-brown building stones quarried locally from the Northampton Sands. The bed in places is ferruginous sandstone, which caps the hills around Northampton such as Honey Hill 209 metres (690 feet) and Borough Hill 197.8 metres (653 feet). In the past these

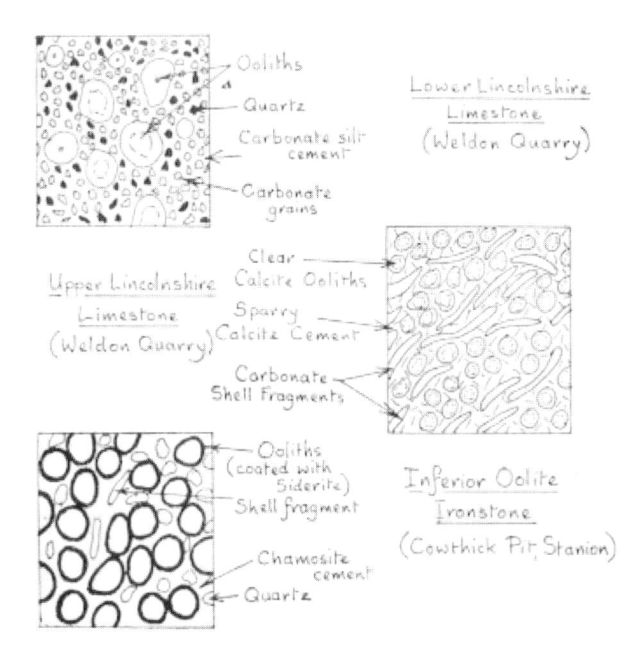

Characteristics of some Northamptonshire Rocks (all drawings magnified x 15)

have been exploited as iron ore sites e.g. Hunsbury Hill. Possibly laid down under dellaic conditions the sands can be up to 24 metres (79 feet) thick, consisting of the already mentioned yellow-brown ferruginous sandstones, calcareous sandstone, sandy oolitic limestone and ironstones. The latter have the grains coated with a thick veneer of the iron mineral chamosite (iron aluminium silicate) and could best be seen in the north of the county around Corby where they were mined by the then British Steel Corporation using open cast methods, and constituted the main ironstone mining area in Britain. The last material was taken on 4 January 1980.

The Lower Estuarine Series consists of river/sea sands, silts and clays. Sands and silts are worked for furnace linings, but near Corby, black carbonaceous shale occurs underlain by sandy silt with root markings that could indicate a fossil soil.

The Lincolnshire Limestone contains approximately a few feet of limestone (the Collyweston Slate) which splits easily into thin layers (fissile) and, although heavy, is ideal as a roofing material. This part of the county, from mediaeval times has been important for the supply of building stone from the Lincolnshire Limestone beds, providing standard 'infill' blocks, even fine-textured stone for carving and Collyweston slates for the roof. The Cambridge colleges, and cathedrals such as Peterborough, sought their natural stone from such places as Weldon, Ketton, Kings Cliffe and Collyweston. Most of this limestone tends to look like coarse fish roe (oolite) consisting in part of small spheres made up of layers of calcium carbonate possibly precipitated around a nucleus by fluctuating currents. Some of the beds contain abundant shell fragments of brachiopods and other fossils, but the purer oolite was most sought after for carving.

Uplift of the land caused a change in deposits to the sands and silts of the beginning of the Great Oolite Series. This varied from clear, shallow water to muddy waters resulting in the formation of the Blisworth Clay; the type village for this bed is just south of Northampton. This is overlain in parts of the county by a reddish-brown rubbly oolite called the Cornbrash, which was sometimes used for local road metal. It is a very thin bed with an average thickness of 3 metres (10 feet). There are, however, some deposits of Oxford Clay in the east of the county. This is a thick and very varied group of deposits but consists mainly of a grey-brown clay laid down in muddy water with lens-shaped deposits of sand. The clay is used for brickmaking over the county border in Peterborough. Fletton, near that city, is the original home of the 'pressed' brick.

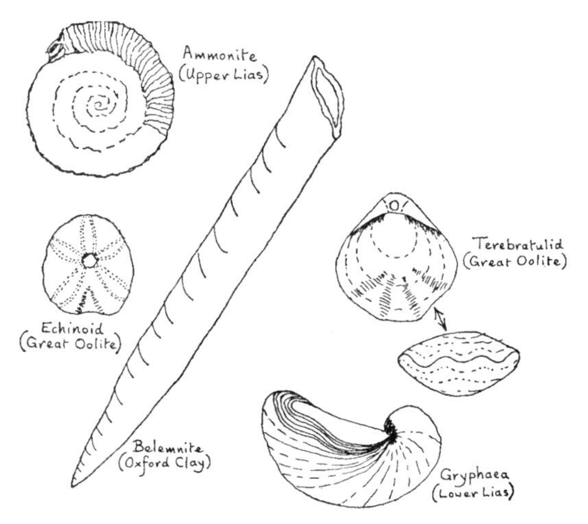

A Selection of Northamptonshire Fossils

The glacial drift deposits consist of boulder clay and, in some areas, such as Duston, pure quartz sands occur, which are almost up to glass-making quality. The boulder clay can be a source of fossils derived from the rocks beneath.

Northamptonshire's rocks are, on the whole, fossiliferous and some existing vertebrate remains have been found. This is not surprising as most of the sediments were laid down in a landscape roamed by dinosaurs. The bones of one of the largest plesiosaurs ever found were dug up at Kingsthorpe and are on display in the Natural History Museum in London. The most common fossils found in the county today are the invertebrate varieties consisting of ammonites, belemnites, brachiopods, and echinoids. The most fossiliferous rocks are the limestones, although the fossils may not be easily removed except in a laboratory as the matrix in which they are embedded is as hard as the fossil itself.

Equipped with a notebook and x10 hand lens, for rarely will a hammer be needed, and in the cause of conservation, it is to be actively discouraged, one of the many footpaths indicated on the Ordnance Survey map can be followed which passes through old quarry or open-cast mining areas. There is also much to be said for discreetly using the hand lens to examine the building stones found in villages and towns such as Brackley and Oundle. Some of the references below may help you in this pursuit.

References

Hains, B.A. and Horton, A., Central England - British Regional Geology. HMSO.
Martin R.A. Historical Geology of Northamptonshire. Northamptonshire Natural History Society and Field club.
Pettijohn, F.J. Sedimentary Rocks, Harper & Row.
Poole, E.G. and others, Geology of the country around Market Harborough. HMSO.
Purcell, D. Cambridge Stone.
Sylvester-Bradley, P.C. and Ford, T.D., Geology of the East Midlands. University of Leicester.
Taylor, J.H. Geology of the country around Kettering, Corby and Oundle. HMSO.

Maps

1:25 000 Ordnance Survey Explorer Sheets 191, 192, 207, 223, 224.
1:50.000 Ordnance Survey sheets 141 and 152.
1:63.360 Geological Survey Solid and Drift Editions:
185 (Northampton); 186 (Wellingborough);
170 (Market Harborough); 171 (Kettering);
201 (Banbury); 202 (Towcester); 157 (Stamford).

WEATHER IN NORTHAMPTONSHIRE

Marion Ilsley

The county's position, shape and relief all influence the weather experienced in Northamptonshire. Situated in the East Midlands, at a distance of about 62 miles (160 kilometres) from most coasts with their associated moderating influences, the county has one of the more continental type climates in the British Isles. Northampton itself has slightly colder winters (January 3.7°C) and warmer summers (July 17.4°C) than either Oxford to the south (4.2°C; 17.1°C) or Cambridge to the east (3.8°C; 17°C).

Highest rainfall averages are to be found in the western half of the county (fig.1), at stations on the Northamptonshire Uplands which extend north-east/south-west to the west of Northampton. On the lower land to the east, sloping from the Uplands towards the Fens, totals decrease. Much of the Nene valley is also relatively dry, with less than 635 mm of precipitation annually, e.g. Northampton 623 mm, Wellingborough 574 mm, Wollaston 543 mm and Oundle 583 mm. These contrast with Litchborough and Lamport Hall 664 mm, Sibbertoft 686 mm and Kelmarsh Hall 724 mm, all of which are on the main line of the Uplands. Lying athwart the prevailing westerly winds, the Uplands intercept the air stream, causing it to rise and cool. Thus these areas tend to receive slightly more precipitation than those parts of the county in their lee.

August is generally the wettest month of the year throughout the county (e.g. Northampton 59.4 mm, Kelmarsh Hall 76 mm). This is probably often the result of thunderstorms or areas of thundery rain. The preceding months from March have generally shown a steady increase in precipitation amounts, rising to the maximum in August. There is then a decrease in September and October but a secondary maximum, very similar to the August figure, is usually experienced in November (e.g. Northampton 59 mm, Kelmarsh Hall 72 mm). This has been ascribed to the frequent flow of westerly maritime air in November. It is noticeable that the two maxima are closer in value in the drier parts of the county than in the wetter areas.

The driest parts of the year are February, March and April, contributing about one-fifth of the total annual precipitation. February, however (and also January as well), can be highly variable. At this time of the year Northamptonshire can be part of the country dominated by anticyclones (high pressure systems) centred over Europe and Scandinavia. These give more settled weather and less precipitation than usual. Counties to the east may experience snowfall from the easterly winds off the North Sea but Northamptonshire's inland position tends to decrease precipitation from easterly winds as it does from westerlies. If winter and early spring are dominated by the unsettled low pressure systems (depressions), higher precipitation totals result. The last hundred years have seen totals for these three months in Northampton ranging from 24 mm in 1938 to 284 mm in 1976, with the average for the period being 130 mm.

The range of temperature experienced in this county has already been mentioned. Northampton having a range of 13.7°C (56.6°F) from a mean of 3.7°C (38.7°F) in January to 17.4°C (63.3°F) in July. The height of the land will obviously affect temperatures in different parts of the county. The higher land in the west rising in places to over 600 feet (183 metres) will result in lower average temperatures than in Northampton at 248 feet. (79 metres), or in areas in the north-east of the county at less than 200 feet. (61 metres).

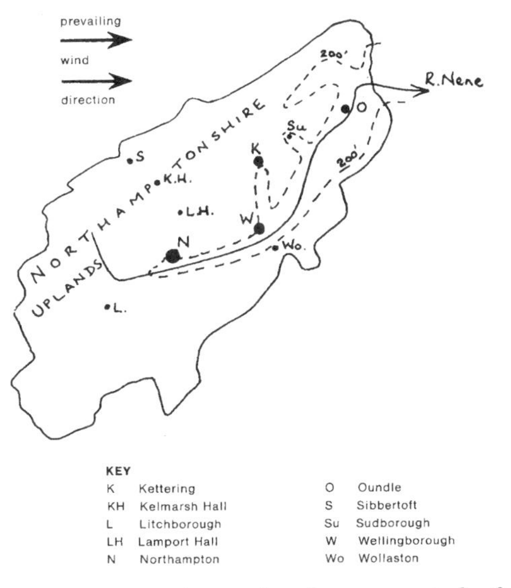

Fig 1 Location of places quoted for precipitation in relation to the major relief features in Northamptonshire.

At times, however, this contrast may well be reversed in individual sets of temperatures. Temperatures published in the Journal of the Northamptonshire Natural History Society suggest that stations in some of the valleys cut deeply into the Northamptonshire Uplands may well experience downward draining cold air in winter, thus giving them lower temperatures than the surrounding hills. Such a situation is known as a temperature inversion. If skies are clear, the valley sides cool rapidly and chill the air immediately above them. This then tends to sink towards the bottom of the valley, possibly giving frost whereas the hills above are clear. Sudborough, in a valley north-east of Kettering, frequently returns the lowest temperature of the year for the Natural History Society records.

Winter temperatures for the county can vary in the same way as the winter rainfall totals. Winters affected by high pressure systems to any extent will return lower average temperatures and greater frequency of frosts than those characterised by the prevailing westerly winds and a series of depressions or low pressure systems. Low temperatures are recorded about one year in four on average, and may fall as low as Sudborough's lowest minimum of -17°C (1°F) in 1965.

The average date of the first air frost is mid-October, the last frost, on average, occurring in the first half of May. This gives just under half of the year without frost although local patches can occur at other times under suitable conditions. The length of the growing season decreases slightly towards the north, the area immediately around Northampton having 255 days suitable for plant growth. This figure does not take into account differences in aspect.

Although on average July is the warmest month in Northampton, in some years August may have a higher mean temperature, e.g. in 1975 - July 19.1°C (66.3°F), August 20.2°C (68.3°F). In other years, the August mean temperature may fall below the July mean for any year. This variability in August reflects the fact that in some years high pressure systems with clear skies predominate during the month and thus temperatures rise to high levels, for example when 34.4°C (94°F) was recorded in Sudborough in 1968. This situation is often ended by the thunderstorms or thundery rain mentioned above. In other years cooler, cloudier, maritime air may dominate, keeping temperatures much lower.

Northamptonshire's weather is thus much as one would expect in an inland county in the southern half of Britain. It is transitional between southern and northern England and, being in the rain shadow of the Welsh Mountains, is relatively dry. Superimposed on this, however, are local peculiarities resulting from the physical form of the county.

Unfortunately it is now much more difficult to compare different areas of the County because fewer people keep consistent weather records.

In spite of all the information about global warming, records kept in Northamptonshire over the last twenty years has not altered the statistics that are presented here.

The Northamptonshire Natural History Society and Field Club has a unique collection of weather data (records) that goes back to 1870. Taylor and Chapman researched these records, and came to this conclusion about rainfall. '.... there was a period of extremely high rainfall between 1870 and 1890 in both Northampton and Wellingborough. This was followed by a period of very low rainfall between 1895 and 1910. After this major fluctuation, rainfall levels and averages have remained relatively constant at between 600 and 650 mm from 1910 to 1990, although there was a less significant fluctuation in rainfall averages between 1950 and 1979. The average annual rainfall for the 110 year period was 615mm, and this can be broken down into a spring average of 136mm, a summer average of 162mm, an autumn average of 165mm and a winter average of 149mm.'

Statistics taken from:

Anglian Water.
Northamptonshire Natural History Society.
Dury G. The East Midlands. Nelson.

Reference

Taylor, M and Chapman, M. Changes in the Weather in Northamptonshire 1880-1994. In Northamptonshire Natural History Society Journal Vol. 42. No 1. Issue 273. 1996/97. (Page 38).

Archaeologists at work in Brackmills, Northampton

THE ARCHAEOLOGY OF NORTHAMPTONSHIRE

Alan Hannan
Revised by Roy Friendship-Taylor

The archaeology of any area is the study of material remains of man's past use of the landscape, reflecting the inter-action with his natural environment. In Northamptonshire the remains of the impact of man on his environment in historic and pre-historic times were, until recent times, more conspicuous. Prior to this century human settlement and land use was dictated largely by geological and topographical factors and by the prevailing technology. Although settlement patterns inevitably altered over major historic periods, it is only in this century that man has developed across the landscape without regard for the geology.

The Natural Background

The county lies across an intermediate zone of midland England and there is a fundamental contrast between the undulating landscape in the west of the county and the broad plain into which the River Nene flows to the east. The uplands in the west have few vantage points and in the main comprise areas elevated to about 400 feet (122 metres) above sea level. The rivers Nene, Welland, and Tove/Ouse rise in this area and flow eastwards. The Nene is the most conspicuous feature and where the river has cut downwards the older formations have been exposed in the valley sides, creating spring lines, while successive depositions of sand and gravel have in turn produced light valley soils ideal for Man's early exploitation. It is the bridging points along the Nene which have served as focal points for human settlement in the county and in later periods centres of urban trade developed at Northampton, Wellingborough, Oundle and Peterborough.

The Prehistoric Period

(a) Palaeolithic Mesolithic (60,000-4,000 BC). Evidence for the great span of time covered by this era is slight and the presence of hunting bands can only be inferred from finds of hand axes (at Duston, Hardingstone, Earls Barton) and remains of extinct fauna. Old land surfaces of this period are difficult to find as they are covered by fluvial overburden or have been eroded by ploughing. Throughout this period, marked by spells of intense cold, it can be surmised that small bands of people moved over large territories, and were engaged in hunting, fishing and the gathering of vegetable foods. The characteristic microliths of Mesolithic activity are more common and indicate either an increase in the number and frequency of hunting groups or more wide-ranging movement of these groups.

(b) Neolithic (4,000-2,200 BC). The gradual adoption of new modes of subsistence brought profound changes on social and economic organisation. Agriculture, involving cultivated grasses and pastoral practices, based on domesticated animals, led to settlement sites being occupied. The construction of monuments of some size and complexity in some parts of the county, shows that there were adequate workforces available, that there was an organisation capable of mobilising such forces, and that there were strong beliefs which

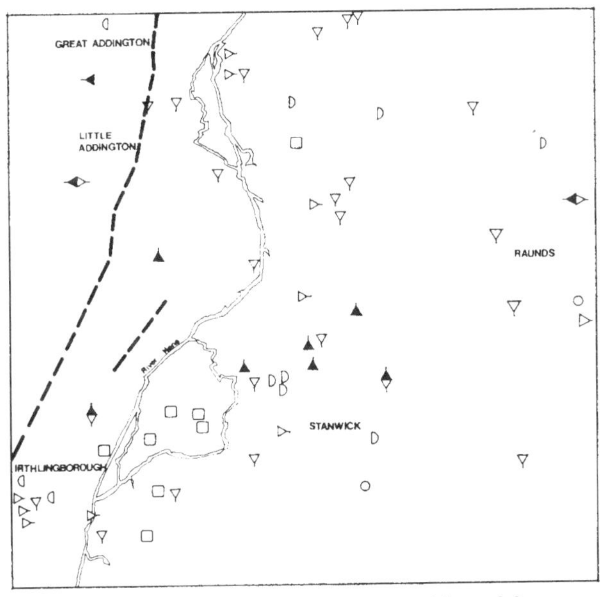

Archaeological sites in the Nene valley around Stanwick

could inspire such endeavour within the technological limits imposed by the use of wood, bone and stone. The distribution of Neolithic finds argues for settlement extending beyond the confines of the valleys. Simple rotation systems required the clearance of forested land and the clearance would have been aided by the domesticated animals, goats and cattle in particular, which followed human societies. Settlement sites with actual evidence of houses were found at Ecton and Irthlingborough and it is this period that pottery is made for regular use. There are archaeological features, mainly seen through aerial photographs, of the period, recognised in increasing numbers in southern and central England, including Northamptonshire, which could provide information about the Neolithic. These are "causewayed camps" which comprise double rows of enclosing ditches, interrupted by causeways and entrances, linking the enclosed interior to the outside. There is a causewayed camp at Briar Hill, on the southern slope of the Nene Valley overlooking Northampton to the north-east. First located from the air, the causewayed camp was then planned by geophysical survey prior to the excavation. Unfortunately this has now been built over. The function of such sites is not yet clearly understood, but the most plausible explanation is that these were the places where scattered communities of early farmers gathered for tribal assemblies, cattle markets and for the enactment of ritual. The excavations at Briar Hill concentrated on the interior of the camp, where there was much evidence for intense activity throughout the Neolithic period.

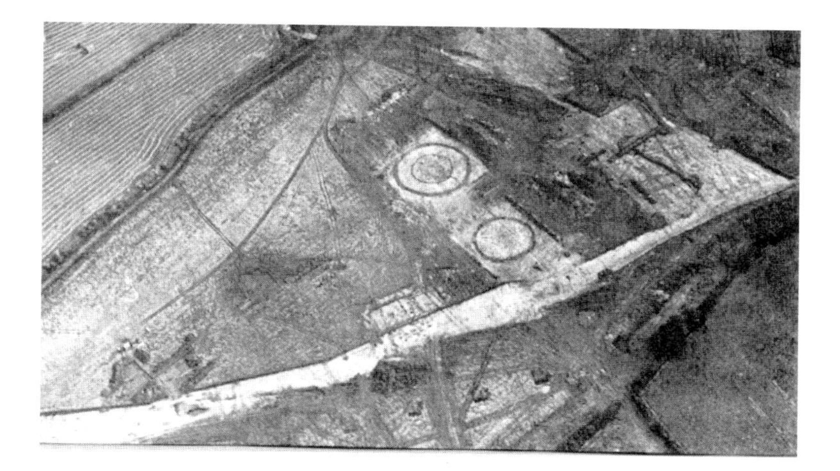

Bronze Age barrows, (burial mounds defined here by single or double ditches) under excavation at Grendon in 1974. *Photograph by NCC*

It is often claimed that for the early prehistoric period more is known of the activities associated with the dead than with the living. Unlike some southern counties of England, where there are great numbers of burial mounds (or 'long barrows') Northamptonshire has only a few sites which could have been burial mounds of this period. At Longman's Hill, Pitsford and at Three Hills, Woodford, there are the remains of what may have been long earthen mounds associated with burial in the Neolithic. It is likely that there were other funerary chambers built in the 4th and 3rd millennia BC to house the remains of the dead, but these may have been removed by quarrying or eroded by later ploughing. During gravel extraction at Aldwincle a mortuary enclosure was uncovered and sites of this type may only be found during quarrying or by the most intensive preliminary survey.

In the Neolithic for the first time there is evidence of medium and long distance routes across England. The commonest artefacts are of stone and flint and in some cases the stone has been traced among other sources to the Lake District. This suggests lines of communication along which materials and new technologies could travel. The best known of these in the county is the possible existence of a routeway. Called the Jurassic Way this ran south-west/north-east across the county possibly linking communities in Somerset with those in Lincolnshire and Yorkshire.

(c) Bronze Age (c. 2,5000-1,000 BC). The adoption of a technology based on metal working was gradual and the impact of the spread of copper and bronze metallurgy would have varied according to locality, social organisation and wealth. Apart from the changes in tools and weapons, and the adoption of new pottery forms, the most widespread feature of this period is the use of a round burial mound. Although there are many varieties of round barrows the main characteristics include a burial beneath a mound, enclosed by a ditch which provided the material for the mound and at the same time probably served to demarcate the burial area. Such round barrows rarely survive as upstanding monuments along the Nene valley, and in upland areas, but in most cases have been eroded by later agriculture, leaving no trace of their existence on the surface. From the air the ploughed-out barrows are conspicuous since the circular ditch can often be clearly seen as a soil or crop mark. The rapid spread of the round barrow as a funerary practice is probably associated with the migration and movement of the Beaker people into the British Isles c. 2,000 BC. Grave goods, including daggers, jewellery and characteristic decorated pottery vessels accompanied their burials, hence the name 'Beaker' people. The excavation of a barrow of this type at Earls Barton, besides producing a dagger and ornaments, yielded evidence of environmental changes in the landscape. It appeared that one barrow had been constructed when the soils in the vicinity were lighter and sandier than at present, prior to the accumulation of clayey sediment. Most of the artefacts that survive from this period were found during recent quarrying and although inadequate for any proper appraisal of this period, they point to a high level of metal working skill and to wide-ranging trade links, to southern England, Ireland and the Continent.

(d) Iron Age (c. 1,000-50BC). The evolution of a technology based on the smelting of iron must again be seen as a gradual process. Elsewhere in Britain the 1st millennia BC is marked by the appearance of the largest and most awe-inspiring earthworks in the historic landscape - the hillforts. Comparatively few of these were built in Northamptonshire, but Borough Hill, near Daventry is an imposing monument. Enclosing some 70.8 ha (175 acres), and it may well have had its origins further back in time, probably in the Bronze Age. The fort was constructed in two stages and the major features that survive are the banks, ditches and scarps of successive defensive arrangements. It is not known whether the interiors of such forts were continuously occupied, but in dominating the hinterland they must have played an important role in the period. The landscape surrounding these hillforts was increasingly settled by small farms. The study of the pattern of settlement in the Iron Age outside the forts is no less important than the forts themselves. Air photography, field-walking and excavation have revealed widespread settlement taking place in what would now be considered unlikely and inhospitable locations. The occurrence of farmsteads on the heaviest clay soils indicates how advanced forest clearance was, and refutes the idea of prehistoric man being assailed by primeval forest. Successive patterns of Iron Age settlement can be seen from the air, with complexes of intersecting lines of ditches, irregular, round or trapezoidal enclosures. Within these lay clusters of houses, linked to neighbouring settlements by trackways, and with a population dependent on a mixed farming economy of agriculture and stock breeding. Peculiar to this period are the pit alignments, traversing the landscape and coming to an abrupt halt, perhaps because they were contiguous with forest or with a bank long since ploughed away.

This period also saw the origins of one of Northamptonshire's major industrial activities, the mining of iron ore, with its attendant smelting and smithing to make all manner of tools and weapons. The Desborough mirror epitomises the highly developed nature of the metalsmith's skill at this time.

A century before the Roman Conquest far-reaching political changes were wrought by incomers to the area and heavily influenced by new technologies brought from the continent and the south-east. This was accompanied by new pottery forms using for the first time the wheel, and by changes in the layout of farms and fields to allow more efficient use of heavier ploughs. This meant that Britain now became part of the European and Mediterranean network.

The Roman Period

(e) Roman Britain (AD 43-c.AD 400). The impact of the Roman Conquest was immediate, and a two-prolonged advance by the Roman army crossed the area of the county along the lines of Watling Street and, to the east, Ermine Street. Only recently, evidence of military activity has come to light to the south of Northampton, where secure control of old river crossings would have been strategically imperative. The most impressive stretches of Roman road are along the course of Watling Street, which enters the county at Old Stratford and proceeds directly to Towcester. The road was carried on a broad mound, or 'agger', which has in places been removed or altered. The course of the modern A5 follows the line of the Roman road and recent re-alignment and lowering of this carriageway at Long Buckby resulted in the total clearance of nearly 200 metres (656 metres) of the silted up flanking ditch on the east side. The contents of the ditch within a 20 metre section included a human skeleton and an intact amphora. During roadworks near Corby, a section cut across the line of the Gartree Road from Leicester to Godmanchester showed a high concentration of charcoal in the buried soil beneath the metalled road surface, evidence of the scrub and forest burning which must have preceded road construction. Further east where this road crossed the River Nene, gravel extraction exposed the timbers of the Roman bridge which carried the road on a wooden framework 18 feet (6m<) wide.

Such roads formed the main routeways of Roman Britain. These were lines of communication established for military, administrative and economic reasons. They linked the other major additions to the landscape - the towns. Romanisation implied the founding and development of towns. The sites of three towns are known: Towcester, Irchester and Bannaventa. The latter two have special interest archaeologically in that they were abandoned at the end of, or shortly after, the Roman period. The site of Irchester to the south bank of the River Nene between Wellingborough and Higham Ferrers is now under cultivation, but is partially defined by the earth banks that marked the buried walls. The town was first walled with a timber and earth rampart in the second century AD. A stone wall was then inserted into the face of the rampart. Within the walls the expected dense occupation has been shown by limited excavation and by air photography. The spread of settlement beyond the walls of the town has been noted on the south side, and as the largest urban settlement in the upper/middle Nene Valley. Evidence for the conduct and organising of industrial activity can be expected. Inevitably the existence of the town raises the question of the first use of the site and the possibility of military presence from which the town developed. There is also the problem of the fate of such centres with the breakdown of Roman military authority in the late fourth century AD. There is the potential at Irchester to establish whether town life or occupation continued in the centuries following the cessation of Roman rule. At Towcester it is reasonably certain that the town was revived as a military and administration centre in the Saxon period, but whether settlement was continuous has not been established. Part of the extensive extra mural settlement has been investigated and much of the remainder has now been built over by Towcester's modern expansion.

Closely related to the towns were the villas, a type of farming unit at the apex of the rural landscape, and which depended on the proximity of town markets. The villas, numbering about 40 in the county, often had substantial stone buildings, with mosaics and central heating, and excavated examples include Piddington, Weldon, Brixworth, Thenford, Wood Burcote and Apethorpe. However, these were just part of a spectrum of intensive rural settlement in the Roman period.

The peace that came in the wake of Roman administration, and the inducement to provide corn for the army of occupation, led to the increase of land under plough, and to the multiplication of farming units. Whereas Roman influence in rural areas may have been superficial, perhaps resulting in the adoption of rectilinear house plans, the use of locally made coarse pottery and limited experience of cash economy, it can be assumed that such improvements in living standards that were realised brought an increase in population. Apart from the proliferation of scattered settlement across contrasting geographical zones, there appears for the first time a settlement type, which foreshadows the village of the medieval period. Near Nassington village a large cropmark site has features similar to that of a medieval village with a long main street with tenements on either side, marked by property boundaries.

Industrial activity, initially stimulated during the late Iron Age, seems to have flourished. Quarries were opened for ironstone and building stone and there is tangible evidence for widespread pottery manufacture. The valley of the River Nene between Northampton and Peterborough appears to have a density of pottery kilns without parallel elsewhere in the region.

The Saxon Period

(f) The Anglo-Saxons (c. AD 400-AD 1066). The movement of Germanic peoples in Britain had commenced before the migration of these people across the North Sea led to their settlement across eastern and southern England. Knowledge of these early Angles, Saxons and Jutes derives almost exclusively from the chance discovery of their cemeteries. Practising cremation and inhumation, the migrants frequently deposited grave goods with their dead. Although as many as 50 such cemeteries and burial sites are known it was only during the excavations at Wakerley and Kettering that archaeologists managed to recover evidence in any systematic way.

The settlements of the Germanic settlers are even less well known. The lack of clearly defined and recognisable Saxon villages had led to the belief that many lie beneath the villages of Northamptonshire. However, it is possible that the initial settlement pattern was dictated by the nature of settlement in the Roman period. Whereas the Anglo-Saxon settlers sought well drained sandy soil for their settlements, where water could be obtained from springs or wells, it is probable that they also required access to a variety of soil types for cultivation, coarse pasture and woodland. The initial settlements of the migrants would have been founded near existing lines of communication - prehistoric trackways, Roman roads and the rivers - whereas later expansion took place in the areas of less favourable soils and dense forest. By the eve of the Norman Conquest, it is considered that the siting and settlement of most English villages was complete. The formative influence of the Anglo-Saxons on the English landscape was profound but the nature of the process is obscure.

By the seventh century AD political cohesiveness was accompanied by the advent of Christianity. Outstanding churches of the period survive at Brixworth and Earls Barton. Brixworth Church has attracted a great deal of interest and surviving features of its original construction convey a sense of spaciousness and grandeur. Aisles formerly flanked the present nave and excavations at various times in the last one hundred or so years have exposed the foundations of this earlier construction. A basilica-like plan points to early Christian missionary activity in England, mounted from Europe and well documented in Kent. The fabric of the building shows extensive re-use of Roman tile in the construction of doorways and window openings. These tiles must have been obtained from large public buildings in a Roman town, and Leicester is the most likely source. The source of some of the stone used at Brixworth was the Charnwood Forest in Leicestershire. The early date for the foundation of Brixworth church, together with its monastic associations, indicate that it was a base for the spread of Christianity in the seventh century AD.

The Danish wars of the ninth century resulted in Scandinavian settlement in eastern England, and a line along Watling Street represents the south westerly limits of Danish settlement. This fresh influx of people, disruptive at first, later stimulated manufacturing, commercial and trading activity, resulting in the growth of urban centres and markets. Excavations in Northampton since 1969 have provided evidence of an urban existence from the ninth century. Towcester's defences were re-fortified in the early tenth century by Edward the Elder, as a base from which to bring areas of Danish settlement under the control of the English kings. The military role probably soon gave way to a commerce function and as such was recognised by the Normans when, at the Conquest, a castle motte was constructed within the defences.

There is great potential for archaeology in this period and much attention is now concentrated on the origins and development of the village as a settlement form from 500-1500 AD. There are also documentary references to persons and places that require confirmation from archaeological research. These include the monastery at Oundle, a royal manor of the Mercian kings at Irthlingborough and at Whittlebury, where Athelstan presided over an assembly in the tenth century.

The Medieval Period

(g) The Norman Conquest and the Medieval period (1066-c1600AD). The Norman Conquest wrought major changes in the apex of the hierarchy of English society in matters of State and in the Church. The major additions to the landscape were the castle and the great monastic foundations. Historians have usually accepted that William and his followers brought the castle as a type of fortification to England. At Sulgrave, in the south-west of the county, there is an earthen ringwork to the west of the church and in 1960 the site was chosen for a long-term research project to examine in detail the archaeological evidence for the founding of such castles. It has been shown that in the early eleventh century there was a timber framed hall and two-storey chamber block, within a defensive enclosure, which included a stone-built gate house. The implication is that the Anglo-Saxons were familiar with the defended stronghold before the Norman Conquest.

Only at Barnwell and Rockingham are there stone remains of castles built in the Medieval period. However, there is a rich variety of earthwork remains, from mottes to manorial sites, including the splendid example at Fotheringhay, where Mary, Queen of Scots was imprisoned until her execution. By the Tudor period the great house was replacing the castle as the residence of the magnate; Northamptonshire has some outstanding Elizabethan houses, including Fawsley Hall and Kirby Hall.

A fragment of the Priory Church at Canons Ashby is all that remains above ground of nearly 40 monasteries built during this period. One of these, Pipewell Abbey, was the only foundation of the Cistercian order in Northamptonshire. Its creation in 1143 was accompanied by the desertion of Pipewell village and in the fourteenth century there was a substantial rebuilding of the church, chapter house and cloisters. Following the dissolution of the monasteries, an inventory of 1540 provides evidence of the latest monastic buildings. In 1720, Bridges, the county historian, described the remains of the site, including 'vestiges of old buildings', but robbing of stone for use in local buildings had, by this century, removed most of the stone buildings and their foundations.

Population growth, accompanied by intensification and expansion of land-use, continued after the Conquest and led to the growth of those villages already in

Braybrooke - earthworks of a medieval manor with its associated fish ponds.

existence. Churches were acquired, rebuilt or modified and now reflect the aspirations and endowments of the communities which they served. The fostering of trade by the Normans led to the growth of towns. In many cases the formal grant of a market recognised a situation that had prevailed since pre-Conquest times. At Brackley a new town was created at the gates of Brackley Castle. The main urban centres of this period were Daventry,

Northampton, Kettering, Wellingborough, Oundle and Towcester. Since the re-development of most towns in the post-war period has been extensive it is fortunate that at Northampton at least the town has been served by a programme of systematic archaeological excavation.

An excursion in almost any area of the county serves to remind that agriculture provided the basis of medieval society and occupied fully the working life of the majority of the population. The reversion of open fields to pasture meant that sheep now grazed large tracts of land formerly ridged and furrowed by the medieval plough. The survival of medieval field systems had enabled a record of these to be made which, when allied with documentary and cartographic study, provide a reconstruction of the village at the centre of its fields. Often

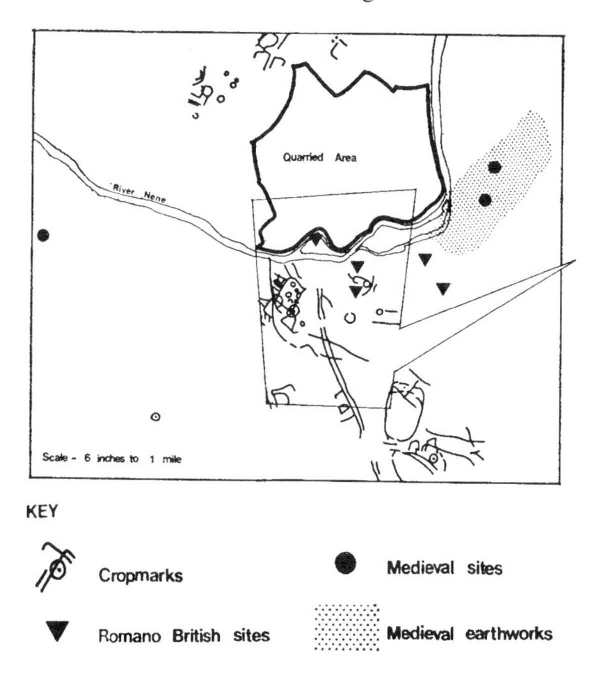

the claiming of land for the production of wool caused the abandonment of settlements and many of these still survive; shallow house platforms, separated by boundary ditches with a winding trackway between them as at Olney and Stanford, are often all that remain of sites that had been occupied for centuries.

Cropmarks at Fotheringhay - ditched trackway, enclosures and ring ditches.

Industrial activity also has its reminders; at Lamport a windmill mound has been excavated and pottery kilns are known at Lyvden, Stanion, Yardley Gobion, Potterspury and Northampton.
Medieval bridges still stand at Geddington, Braybrooke and Irthlingborough, and the Eleanor crosses at Hardingstone and Geddington mark the resting places of the body of Edward I's Queen on its journey across the county.

(h) Post medieval and Industrial Archaeology

One of the main aims of archaeology is the recovery of evidence of buildings and settlements. For the post-medieval period the most important features are the results of the great rebuilding, ranging from the grand houses to the large range of vernacular architecture. The great houses, including fine buildings such as Lamport Hall, Boughton House and Easton Neston, were just the central point of wider changes in the landscape. A variety of other buildings included gates, lodges and temples and such unusual conceptions as Tresham's Triangular Lodge at Rushton. Landscaping and formal gardens created suitable settings for the new houses and the earthwork remains of such monumental gardens can be seen at Wakerley and Harrington. One result of this was the desertion of further villages. An ordered parkland was incompatible with the activities of a small rural community and Edgecote, Overstone and Lilford are examples of late abandonment of villages.

Northamptonshire was not affected by the Industrial Revolution on the same scale as some other midland counties. The establishment of potteries in Staffordshire and Derbyshire led to a decline in a local industry and the quarrying of building stone diminished in the nineteenth century. The mechanisation of ironstone extraction however brought marked changes in the landscape, particularly where restoration was not enforced. Extraction of various materials, including a vast amount of gravel, continues on a large scale but is now followed by a remodelling of the landscape to permit the re-establishment of agriculture and the formation of nature reserves, especially along the Nene Valley. The county is known widely for its role in boot and shoe manufacture and towns along the A6 route have a characteristic mould of factory, warehouse and estate terrace, orientated towards the industry which shaped them in the nineteenth century.

The county, lying midway between London and the North, was crossed by major lines of communication in post-medieval times. The canal system, consisting of the Oxford Canal and the Grand Union Canal (formerly the Grand Junction Canal), includes much of interest, in particular the Blisworth Tunnel. The construction of a tunnel through the limestone outcrops between Stoke Bruerne and Blisworth presented great difficulties. While the tunnel was being constructed beneath, cargoes were shipped by railway employing horse-drawn wagons. Railways now complemented roads, for long a factor influencing settlement in the county. Many rail lines have been closed in recent years, and the canals now serve mainly as amenities. The role of the county as a bridging point between north and south can be seen at Watford, where the A5, the main railway from London to the midlands and north, the Grand Union Canal and the M1 all follow a course through a corridor a few hundred metres in width.

Bibliography: Northamptonshire

This list covers only the main texts and journals. For further details consult bibliographies contained within these or contact Northamptonshire Heritage, County Hall, Northampton (01604 236236), where a full county bibliography is housed. More detailed information relating to the archaeology of the county can also be obtained from the Sites and Monuments Record, also held by Northamptonshire Heritage.

Baker, G. The History and Antiquities of Northampton. Vol. I-II. 1830.
Bridges, J. The History and Antiquities of Northamptonshire. Vol. I-II. 1791.
Council for British Archaeology, Group 9. Newsletters 1-7. 1971-1977.
Hartley, B. R. Notes on the Roman Pottery Industry in the Nene Valley, Peterborough Museum. Occasional Papers No. 2. 1960.
Morton, J. The Natural History of Northamptonshire. 1712.
Nene Valley Research Committee. Durobrivae Nos 1-4. 1937-1976.
Northampton Borough Council Museums and Art Gallery. Journals 1-13. 1967-1979.

Northamptonshire Archaeological Society. Northamptonshire Archaeology. Vol. 9-12. 1974-1977.
Northamptonshire Federation of Archaeological Societies. Bulletin. Vol. 1-8. 1966-1973.
Northamptonshire Record Society. Northamptonshire Past and Present. Vol. 1-53. 1946-2000.
Pevsner, N. Northamptonshire: the Buildings of England. 1973.
Pryor, F.M. M. Prehistoric Man in the Nene Valley. 1973.
Royal Commission on Historical Monuments. An Inventory of Archaeological Sites in North-East Northamptonshire. Vol. I. 1975. HMSO.
Royal Commission on Historical Monuments. An Inventory of Archaeological Sites in Central Northamptonshire. Vol. II. 1979. HMSO.
Royal Commission on Historical Monuments. An inventory of Archaeological Sites in North-West Northamptonshire. Vol. III. 1981. HMSO.
Royal Commission on Historical Monuments. An Inventory of Archaeological Sites in South-West Northamptonshire. Vol. IV. 1982. HMSO
Royal Commission on Historical Monuments. An Inventory of Archaeological Sites and Churches in Northampton. Vol. V. 1985. HMSO.
Steane, J.M. The Northamptonshire Landscape. 1974.
Victoria County History. Northamptonshire. Vol. 1-4.
Wild, J. P. The Romans in the Nene Valley. 1972.
Williams, J.E. and Bamford, H. Northampton – the First 6000 years. Northampton Development Corporation. 1979.

Bibliography: General

This list includes some basic texts on archaeology, some recent, many in paperback, which could be of value for further reading. Grouping in by major period.

A Theory and Practice

Piggott, S. Approach to Archaeology. 1959.
Coles, J. Field Archaeology in Britain. 1972.
Duel, L. Flights into Yesterday. 1973.
Taylor, C. C. Fieldwork in Medieval Archaeology. 1974.
Evans, J. G. The Environment of Early Man in the British Isles. 1975.

B Prehistoric

Cole, S. The Neolithic Revolution (British Museum). 1970.
British Museum. Flint Implements. 1975.

Oakley, K. P. Man the Toolmaker. (British Museum). 1972.
Renfrew, C. (Ed). British Prehistory. 1974.
Renfrew, C. Before Civilisation. 1976.
Roe, D. Prehistory. 1971.
Cunliffe. B. Iron Age Communities in Britain. 1974.
Friendship-Taylor, R.M. Iron Age and Roman Quinton: The evidence for the ritual use of the site. Upper Nene Archaeological Society. 1999.
Friendship-Taylor, R.M. and D.E., Iron Age and Roman Piddington (interim report). Upper Nene Archaeological Society. 1989.
Friendship-Taylor, R.M. and D.E. Iron Age and Roman Piddington: The Mortaria 1979-1993. Upper Nene Archaeological Society. 1994 (interim report). Upper Nene Archaeological Society. 1989.
Friendship-Taylor, R.M. and D.E. (eds). Iron Age and Roman Piddington: the Faunal Remains. Upper Nene Archaeological Society. 2000.
Friendship-Taylor, R.M. and D.E. (eds). From Round House to Villa. Upper Nene Archaeological Society. 1997.
Harding, D. W. The Iron Age in Lowland Britain. 1974.
Ward, Cynthia., Iron Age and Roman Piddington: The Ceramic Building Materials 1979-1998. Upper Nene Archaeological Society. 1999
Windell, D. The Upper Nene Valley in The Iron Age and Roman Periods. Northamptonshire County Council.

C Roman

Bédoyère, Guy de la. Pottery in Roman Britain. Shire. 2000.
Frere, S. Britannia. 1974.
Friendship-Taylor, R.M. The Excavation of The Belgic and Romano-British Settlement at Quinton, Northamptonshire 1971-72. The Journal of the Northampton Museum. Vol. II. 1974.
Friendship-Taylor, R.M. The Excavation of the Belgic and Romano-British Settlement at Quinton, Northamptonshire (site 'B' 1973-7). The Journal of the Northampton Museum. Vol. II. 1979.
Hanley, Robin. Villages in Roman Britain. Shire. 2000
Margary, J. Roman Roads. 1973.
Wacher, J. The Towns of Roman Britain. 1974.
Collingwood, R. G. and Richmond, I. The Archaeology of Roman Britain. 1969.
Swan, V.G. Pottery in Roman Britain. 1988.

D Saxon and Medieval

Alcock, L. Arthur's Britain. 1971.

Allison, K.J., Beresford, M.W. and Hurst, J.G., et al. The Deserted Villages of Northamptonshire. Deserted Medieval Villages Research Group Occasional Paper No 18. Leicester University Press.
Beresford, M.W. and Hurst, J.G. Deserted Medieval Villages. 1971.
Hall, David. The Open Fields of Northamptonshire. Northamptonshire Record Society.
Hislop, Malcolm. Medieval Masons. Shire. 2000.
Northamptonshire County Council Archaeology Unit. Raunds 1979. Northamptonshire County Council. 1979.
Platt, C. The English Medieval Town. 1976.
Wilson, D. The Anglo-Saxons. 1971.
Williams, J. Saxon and Medieval Northampton. 1982. Northampton Development Corporation 1982.

E Post Medieval

Buchanan, R.A. Industrial Archaeology in Britain. 1972.
Rowley, Trevor and Wood, John. Deserted Villages. Shire. 2000.

AGRICULTURE IN NORTHAMPTONSHIRE

Robert F Smith

Introduction

The farming systems of Northamptonshire do not easily fall into any main type and examples of most of the traditional and modern systems seen throughout the country can be found within the county boundaries. The main reason for this is geographical, due to the county's position in the middle of England where we are not subject to the extremes of rainfall, temperature or altitude, factors which often restrict the type of crop grown or the species of livestock kept.

History

The forests of Rockingham, Salcey and Whittlewood at one time covered much of the county, but these were gradually cleared and by the eighteenth century the landscape had a very open appearance. The enclosure movement during the seventeenth and eighteenth centuries had a considerable effect on the county and many of the hedges planted at this time survived until the immediate post-war era when the need for large fields led to many hedges being removed. The county also includes the upper reaches of the rivers Nene and Welland, which have been responsible for influencing the early development of farming systems.

Communications

Its geographical position to the north of London has given the county a comprehensive system of communication by road, rail and water. This can be seen from the time of the Roman Watling Street and the later Great North Road, through the development of the A1, A5 and A6 trunk roads to the most recent times with the appearance of the M1 motorway and the A14. A similar situation existed with the growth of the railways. Several of the main lines to the north-east and the north-west of the country passed through the county and an extensive network of rural lines was built up in the nineteenth century, the majority of which were used for agricultural purposes. At one time there was 240 route miles (386 kilometres) of railways in Northamptonshire, and as many as 76 stations. The disappearance of these lines has, in places, led to a conflict of interests with wildlife organisations who see the deserted tracks as possible nature reserves, whereas the farmer fears that they will encourage weeds and vermin. Water transport was at one time important on the Grand

Union Canal and the River Nene was navigable from King's Lynn to Northampton. The latter only recently ceased to be used for grain transport to the flour mills at Wellingborough.

Urban and industrial effects

On the jacket flap of John Steane's book, '***The Northamptonshire Landscape***', published in 1974, the following statement appears: "Northamptonshire is a relatively unknown and thinly populated county of Midland England. In the next twenty years it will become one of the fastest growing points in the European economy, taking London and Birmingham overspill into its new and expanding towns of Corby, Daventry, Northampton, Wellingborough and Peterborough". Whereas Government policy in this respect may have changed somewhat since 1974, there is no doubt that urban development is having a considerable influence on farming in the county. In addition to the physical loss of areas of farmland for houses, schools, factories and roads, there is the increased pressure on the remaining land for leisure and recreational purposes.

Up until now the main industrial influence has been the extraction of iron ore. From the middle of the nineteenth century it was found that ironstone underlays large parts of the county and small blast furnaces sprang up in areas as far apart as Heyford, Wellingborough and Islip. The ore was extracted by open-cast methods and the land was subsequently restored to agricultural use. The observant traveller may recognise these areas by the fact that the road is often several feet above the level of the surrounding fields. Around Irthlingborough, a certain amount of mining was carried out and the later abandonment of these mines has led to problems of subsidence. From the 1930s onwards most of the smelting was concentrated at Corby and the smaller furnaces have all now disappeared. In some areas to the north of the county the quarries were planted with trees (mainly quick-growing conifers) instead of being restored to agricultural use.

The rapid urban expansion of recent years has produced a need for sand and gravel and this exists in large amounts along the Nene valley. It is now being extracted in a number of places and is producing large areas of man-made lakes. Although these may be ideal for recreational purposes, such as sailing and fishing, they represent a permanent loss of agricultural land.

Farmers

Northamptonshire was once described as the county of "squires and spires", and in the past much of the land was owned by village squires. This earlier widespread system of land tenure has now greatly declined due to various economic pressures, and has been replaced by the owner-occupier. However, there are still a number of large estates in Northamptonshire – the Spencers at Althorp, the Brudenells of Deene, the Dukes of Buccleuch at Boughton House and the Marquesses of Northampton at Castle Ashby. Current taxation policies are causing changes in the established systems. On many estates when tenant farmers either retire or die, the land is either taken over and farmed by the landlord himself, or added to an existing tenant's farm, which effectively reduces the number of tenant farmers. The so-called institutions, such as the Oxford Colleges and the London Merchants' Guilds, have been landowners in the county for some years. At the other end of the scale the County Council still maintain a number of smallholdings to be let to aspiring tenant farmers.

Farming

Whereas profitability is probably the main factor which influences the range of crops grown, soil type is also important and it is possible to see both light Northamptonshire sandstone and heavy boulder clay, often on the same farm. With the use of modern tractors and machines all types of soil are easily cultivated and do not limit the type of crop growth

Agricultural landscape in West Northamptonshire *Photograph: Ron Wilson*

Grassland

Most of the county is suited to growing grass, apart perhaps from the north-east corner where rainfall is somewhat lower. The best way to use grass is to turn it into milk or meat but the livestock sector has been in serious decline in recent years, mainly due to political decisions such as the imposition of quotas to limit over-production. Many farmers have given up milking and the sheep industry is at a low ebb due to the poor returns obtained for meat and wool production. The stability of the dairy industry was undermined by the political decision to disband the Milk Marketing Board.

The fattening of beef cattle has always been a feature of farming in the area and is still widely practised. Some of these animals originate from surplus calves from local dairy herds, but many are brought over from the marginal areas of the west and north of England to be finished on the local farms. Over the years the small local livestock markets have disappeared, but a much bigger upheaval was caused by the closure of Europe's biggest stock market in nearby Banbury, just over the county border in Oxfordshire, resulting in some of the trade being moved to the new market in Northampton. It would be impossible to leave beef cattle without mentioning the world-famous Leicestershire feeding pastures along the Welland Valley, the best of which are alleged to be in Northamptonshire! Farmers in this area exhibit great skill in the selection of suitable cattle in the right numbers to utilise these pastures to the best advantage.

Arable farming

It is in this sector that the most dramatic changes have taken place. The first of these was the change to all-arable farms with no livestock at all, followed by the move to set virtually all autumn sown crops. On many arable farms there will now be a three year sequence of cropping; first winter wheat, second another crop of wheat or possibly oats or barley, and then in the third year a "break crop" to prevent a build-up of disease. This need for, and use of, a break crop led to the rapid increase in the county of oilseed rape, the yellow flowered crop that has such an impact on the landscape from April onwards. Having reached a peak, the popularity of the crop is now decreasing due to lower prices and other break crops are being sought. One of these is the blue-flowered linseed, which has the advantage of being spring sown and so reducing the pressure on autumn cultivation. Linseed is grown for its oil content, whereas the white flowered type, known as flax, used to be grown to produce linen fibre and this was processed at the old flax mill at Billing.

Potatoes are still grown on some farms but these require specialist machinery, whereas all the previous crops can be grown and harvested with the normal range of equipment. One crop, which has almost disappeared, is sugar beet and this was mainly due to the closure of the processing factory at Peterborough, which meant that beet had to be transported to Bury St. Edmunds in Suffolk.

In some parts of the county a range of horticultural crops is grown and these are often sold on a pick-your-own basis.

Diversification

With the decline in many of the traditional farming systems which have been mentioned farmers have been encouraged to look at other enterprises to supplement their incomes. These can be very varied and may be given financial support in initiatives such as the Countryside Stewardship Scheme which gives grants to improve access to the countryside and replant and maintain hedges and trees.

Statistics	**1967 (ha)**	**1976(ha)**	**1998(ha)**
Total agricultural area	196,280	192,566	185,094
Number of holdings	3,200	2,229	2,011
Average size of holding	61.5	86.2	92
Cropping			
Wheat	33,995	43,295	63,602
Barley	50,183	35,982	12,744
Oats	4,695	5,928	2,454
Potatoes	2,711	2,115	346
Sugar beet	1,174	1,023	397
Beans (for stock feeding)	5,900	1,328	5,692
Maize (for silage)	--------	1,794	1,067
Oilseed rape	--------	5,236	23,626
Grassland	92,879	88,221	53,130
Linseed	---------	--------	1,841
Bare fallow	n/a	n/a	308
Set aside	---------	--------	8,992
Livestock			
Dairy cows	22,000	21,354	11,173
Other cattle	113,000	117,072	68,106
Total cattle	135,000	138,426	79,279
Breeding sheep	150,400	136,307	159,773
Other sheep	206,900	195,209	251,893
Total sheep	357,300	331,516	411,666

Breeding pigs	7,900	9,511	5,892
Other pigs	55,200	68,518	55,274
Total pigs	63,100	78,209	61,116
Labour force		6,218	4,765

This includes all people involved with agriculture from farm managers to part-time staff.

Figures reproduced with permission from MAFF.

THE WOODS OF NORTHAMPTONSHIRE

Barry Alcock
and
Duncan McCollin

A woodland is like an old book. Admire the jacket as a casual observer and you may be pleased by its appearance. Glancing at an odd page here and there may begin to reveal beautiful but mystifying ideas. Read and ponder, however, and you discover a whole new world of human endeavour and experience. Into woodlands you may read a history and biography of its past users, its origins and its changes, its relationships with other habitats and its uniqueness, for as every book written differs in both style and story so every woodland is unique - enigmatic and fascinating.

Evidence from pollen cores extracted from peat and lake sediments tell a story beginning with trees invading the frozen wastes left behind after retreating glaciers in the Late Glacial between 12,000 and 10,500 years ago. Cold tolerant trees, including birches (Betula spp.), aspen (Populus tremula) and willows (Salix spp.), were soon followed by Scots Pine (Pinus sylvestris) as the climate gradually warmed. Between about 7,500 and 5,000 years ago the climate had ameliorated to conditions slightly warmer and wetter than today. The land cover at this time is believed to have been continuous old-growth forest, or 'Wildwood', dominated by lime (Tilia spp.) in southern England, a tree still dominant in some woodlands in the north of the county today. Oak (Quercus spp.), ash (Fraxinus excelsior), elm (Ulmus spp.) and hazel (Corylus avellana) would also have been present as would alder (Alnus glutinosa) fringing wetter ground particularly near streams, rivers and lakes.

Whilst humans were present throughout this early period they probably had very little impact on the forest, being dependent upon hunting, fishing and gathering. However, it was in the period from about 5,000 to 2,700 years ago that Neolithic ('New Stone Age') people started to clear the forest as they modified their lifestyle to one dependent on farming. Forest clearance continued unabated until abandoned farmland 'tumbled down' to woodland after the Roman occupation. Later, Anglo-Saxon settlers brought with them ploughs to till even the heaviest of clay soils resulting in further clearance such that by the time of the Domesday Survey of 1086 AD Northamptonshire had only 8.8% woodland cover (a figure similar to the present day woodland cover of Britain).

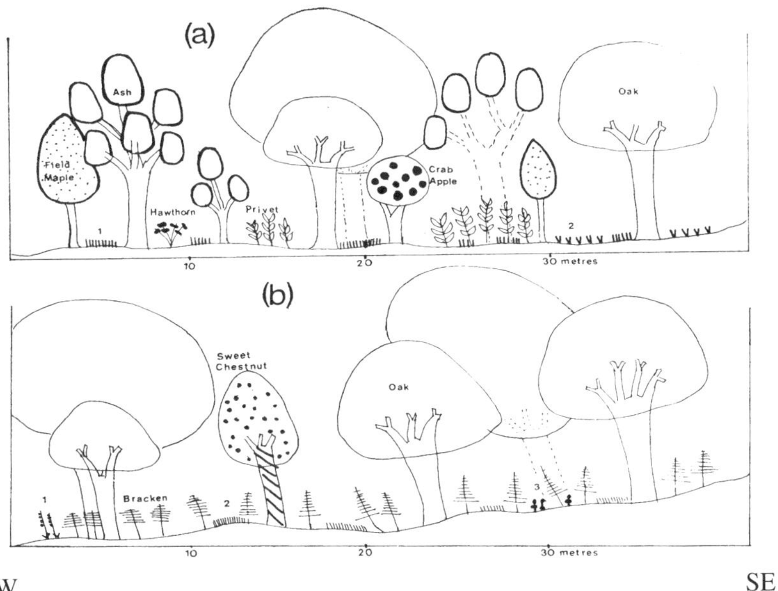

NW SE

Fig 1

a) Oolitic limestone woodland, Kings Wood, Corby. This transect shows well developed second tree and shrub layers. Herb flora, 1 slender false broom, 2 bluebell.

b) Ferruginous sandstone woodland, Badby Wood. This transect shows only primary tree and herb layers. Herb flora, 1 foxglove, 2 creeping soft grass, 3 wood sorrel.

The woods had been tamed: bear, beaver, wild boar and wolf had already been eradicated but woodlands survived because they provided a sustainable supply of fuel both for home and industry, such as iron smelting near Corby, Deene, Greens Norton, Gretton and Towcester. The traditional management practice in woodlands was 'coppice-with-standards' in which oaks and ash were grown for about 70 - 80 years to produce timber, used in construction, and hazel and sweet chestnut (Castanea sativa) were cut back to ground level at 8 - 15 year intervals to produce small wood often used by commoners to heat their houses as well as for other everyday needs such as for fencing material, thatching spars, etc.

Coppicing is a practice that is incompatible with grazing and woodlands were usually protected from animals by a bank-and-ditch and fencing. An alternative method of managing trees, which was compatible with grazing, was 'pollarding', a practice in which trees are lopped above head height to prevent animals eating the regrowth. Pollarding was especially prevalent in launds (open spaces) in the Royal Forests and in private hunting grounds such as at Moulton Park. Although these practices of regular coppicing and pollarding fell out of fashion towards the end of the nineteenth century, some of the older forest trees still reveal signs of their past management. However, large old trees, formerly prevalent in the wildwood, disappeared from the countryside except perhaps where they were retained as boundary markers on the edges of woodlands and in hedgerows.

Much of Domesday Northamptonshire was already farmland and the remaining woodland was located in the areas which are still wooded today, later to become the Royal Forests of Rockingham, Whittlewood, Salcey and Yardley Chase. Woodland cover continued to decline to about 4.4% of the land use by the late nineteenth century although planting in the present century has led to a slight increase.

Today, although there are few woodlands which can be recognised as having been continuously wooded since the Wildwood, 'ancient' woods – sites which have been continuously wooded since at least 1600 AD – cover 6,500 ha (16,061 acres) of Northamptonshire and are often found tucked away in corners of parishes. They are typified by their sinuous boundaries, banks and ditches, and characteristic relict floras. The current distribution of woodland is still very much influenced by the historical Forests and Chases, or Royal hunting grounds; most is still located within the historic confines of the Royal Forests, although occasional scattered ancient sites survive elsewhere, such as to the south of Daventry with Badby Wood, Everdon Stubbs and Mantles Heath. In ancient sites the presence of bluebell (Endymion non-scriptus), wood sorrel (Oxalis acetosella), wood anemone (Anemone nemorosa), and dogs mercury (Mercuralis perennis) are all indicators of historical continuity of woodland whilst more specific to the north east of the county indicators include lily-of-the-valley (Convallaria majalis), wild columbine (Aquilegia vulgaris), and dwale or deadly nightshadw (Atropa belladonna).

Although by virtue of its position and history, each wood is unique, two important factors have contributed most to the formation of types of woodland in the county: management history and soil type. The backbone of the county is the oolite limestone of the Northamptonshire Uplands, over which stiff glacial clay deposits occur at variable depths. In the woodlands of the

Rockingham Forest, the tree community characteristic of these basic and often thin soils includes two co-dominant species, oak and ash, with a secondary tree layer which includes field maple (Acer campestre) and occasional crab apple (Malus sylvestris). Characteristic shrubs include hazel, spindle (Euonymus europeus), buckthorn (Rhamnus catharticus), and privet (Ligustrum vulgare). Such a community is almost certainly an ancient site, and this can be confirmed if that rare and fascinating tree – the wild service – (Sorbus torminalis), is present. This species is diagnostic of the oak-ash climax woodland, which is limited to the East Midlands and East Anglia. The same is true of the small leaved lime (T. cordata).

Of woods which correspond to this type, particular mention must be made to Bedford Purlieus, Old Sulehay Forest, Wakerley Woods and Fineshade, and Kings Wood LNR, Corby. The latter is a particularly fine example with some excellent mature trees. To some extent this area of woodland has suffered from extensive use as a recreation centre for the town, but as a general area for study of this type of woodland it would be hard to find another area to surpass it. Some of these characteristics are traceable even in woods in the south west, like Hazelborough Forest and Bucknall Wood, although such areas really belong to the next group.

The second community is that on the stiff clays of the south of the county. The dominant tree is the oak and the secondary tree layer is seldom present. Hazel, hawthorns (Crataegus spp.), and blackthorn (Prunus spinosa), predominate in the shrub layer with the sallows (Salix cinerea and S. caprea) in the rides. The ground flora is similar to the woods of the north east, except that many of the calcicoles (lime-tolerant plants) are not present. The woods, which represent this community best, are Salcey Forest, Yardley Chase and some parts of Whittlebury. Here, however, the clay can be persistent enough to produce a ground flora in which the wild garlic or ransoms (Allium ursinum), and the pendulous sedge (Carex pendula) dominate, as they do in Wicken Wood.

The secondary tree layers are not clearly represented except for brambles and wild roses, including the sweet briar (Rosa rubiginosa), but the ground flora is dominated by bracken (Pteridium aquilinum), creeping soft grass (Holcus mollis), male fern (Dryopteris filix-mas), wood millet (Milium effusum), and melick grass (Melica uniflora). Also to be found, but more rarely, are calcifuge indicator species, such as the foxglove (Digitalis purpurea), golden rod (Solidago virgaurea), orpine (Sedum telephium) and ling (Calluna vulgaris).

Ash and maple in Kings Wood LNR,Corby *Photograph: B R Alcock*

In the north west of the county there are a number of areas that fall into the third group. Here the Northampton Sands exist in the form of outliers resting on the (upper lias) clays. Where woods occur on such soils, as they do at Badby and less obviously at Mantles Heath and Everdon, a calcifuge (lime-intolerant) flora is represented. Here, as before, the dominant tree is oak (Q. robur). In Badby Wood the alien sweet chestnut (Castanea sativa), undoubtedly self-sets itself in good years and, indeed, replaces the oak in the sandiest areas.

The fourth community does not readily lend itself to clearly defined description; it is not limited by soil type or aspect. It concerns those areas that have been extensively planted with soft woods. Sixty-five per cent of ancient woodland in Northamptonshire has been replanted. Until recently there was only a handful left without their stands of conifers. Perhaps the observation that strikes one most vividly about these woods is their limited ground flora. However, times they are-a-changing since the Forestry Commission has had a major rethink about their policy towards broadleaves. They have recently launched a scheme to restore 7,000 ha (17,297 acres) of woodland in Northamptonshire and adjoining counties. The aim of this scheme, called 'The Ancient Woodlands Project', is to replace conifers and to reinstate broadleaved woodlands with a type that formerly predominated before wholesale coniferisation. Such a scheme presents a massive *volte face* for the Forestry Commission and, if successful, will have a significant conservation benefit for wildlife in the region.

Everdon Stubbs *Photograph: Ron Wilson*

Little has been said about the animal communities of woodlands, but this is simply because they are dealt with elsewhere in this book. It is as well to remember that in Britain as many as five hundred species of insect are dependent either totally or in part on the oak tree alone. There is a very close match between the number of insects associated with different tree species and how long these trees have been present since they naturally colonised the British Isles after the last Ice Age. Being the natural climatic climax vegetation of Britain, woodland is remarkably good for many insect species and especially for beetles and butterflies. However, the animal that has the greatest influence on the ecology of woodlands is deer. Deer numbers in the countryside are currently at very high levels and they do much to inhibit natural regeneration. Despite this cause for concern, Northamptonshire woodlands are some of the jewels that beset the leafy crown of our county in which we have so much to be proud.

Useful Reading

Colston, A. & Perring, F. (eds.) (1989). The Nature of Northamptonshire. Barracuda Books, Buckingham.

Fuller, R.J. (1995). Bird Life of Woodland and Forest. Cambridge University Press, Cambridge.
Marren, P. (1992). The Wild Woods. David & Charles, Newton Abbot.
Peterken, G.F. (1981). Woodland Conservation and Management. Chapman & Hall, London.
Rackham, O. (1976). Trees and Woodlands in the British Landscape. Dent, London.
Rackham, O. (1980). Ancient Woodland. Arnold, London.
Rackham, O. (1986). The History of the Countryside. Dent, London.

WETLANDS IN NORTHAMPTONSHIRE

Brian Webster

There are probably more wetlands in Northamptonshire now than at any time since the end of the last Ice Age. This may seem a strange statement to make when we have been busy in recent decades straightening - canalising - our rivers and streams to prevent the formation of ox-bows, and deepening their beds to lower the water table and allow cultivation down to their margins.

Before we can investigate these areas, we have to be clear as to what a wetland is. In trying to come up with a definition we encounter problems, because there are likely to be as many definitions of the term 'wetland' as there are experts who procrastinate about it. For our purposes wetland is defined as open water, whether of large or small surface area, still or flowing, together with the surrounding land which is influenced by its dampness.

So rivers and streams, ditches and field ponds, canals, lakes, reservoirs and flooded gravel pits, are all obvious wetlands. But so too are the foetid pools that form around the base of muck-heaps, the temporary pools that fill tree hollows and even the water in the garden rainwater butt. Likewise the linear pools that lie in rutted woodland rides and farm tracks after rain also fall into wetland category.

Even the least inviting of these has a special wild animal and plant community - a true micro-habitat. A seemingly lifeless dark brown puddle close to a farmyard manure heap may be inhabited and be home to a creature which has solved all the problems of living in an oxygen-starved environment, in order to take advantage of the rich food supply provided by organic debris. The species likely to be encountered here is *Eristalis*, otherwise known as the rat-tailed maggot, a creature of the air, and a cousin of the two-winged pestiferous housefly. Belonging to the hoverfly group it pretends to be a bee, but it cannot disguise the fact that unlike this insect, it has only two, instead of four, wings. In addition it also has a fat chunky abdomen, rather than the narrow-waisted one which the bee possesses.

The female lays batches of eggs on the water's surface, and these hatch into grey maggots - the larvae - which feed on the rich organic ooze at the bottom of the water. They breathe through a long, three-segmented telescopic tube, which extends to the surface - hence the name 'rat-tailed maggot'.

Many of us have probably woken from the fitful sleep of a really hot, humid night to discover that we have been bitten by an insect. It's visit leaves an angry weal with a puncture mark at its centre. The skin itches like fury, yet when scratched it hurts, and the bite often takes more than a week to clear up. If this has happened to you, the chances are that you have been bitten by a large mosquito by the name of *Theobaldia*, which looks like a miniature cranefly, and has speckled legs, spots on its wings, and hoops of yellowish and earth-brown around the body. Its larvae develop in water rich in organic matter, and the pools that form in tree hollows are ideal.

Perhaps, like me, you have wondered why it is that our 'puny' rivers sit in such broad-bottomed valleys. For the answer we have to go back more than ten thousand years to the Ice Ages, when vast ice sheets extended from the Arctic down as far as Northamptonshire. It was at this time that mammoths and woolly rhinos roamed the land to be hunted by hyenas and the fearsome sabre-toothed cat. As the earth began to warm, the ice sheets melted and shrank away to the north. Enormous rivers carried the glacial melt-waters towards the continent to join other great streams winding their way along the land bridge - now the North Sea - an umbilical cord which joined the British Isles to Europe. As these rivers flowed they carried with them a vast burden of stones, pebbles, gravel, sand and silt, much of which was deposited along our river valleys. And as these materials were borne along by fierce currents they tore away at the land surface and gouged out the broad, shallow valleys that are a feature of the present-day Northamptonshire landscape.

The rivers shrank to their present-day size, but as is the case with all rivers they threw meandering loops across the wide valleys. Periodic vicious spates would straighten the course of the stream leaving behind horseshoe-shaped ox-bows, which are so rich in wildlife. Fresh meanders resulted in yet more ox-bows, a process that carried on until the very recent past when it was the current fashion for river engineers to become obsessed with straightening watercourses. The valley bottom was much swampier than today, resulting in the earlier oft-stated view of Northamptonshire as a county of 'Spires, squires . . . and mires', the latter making it a dangerous nightmare for those attempting to cross the river at night.

Major man-made changes were made to our wetland landscape in the seventeenth to nineteenth centuries with the creation of lakes, as features in parks of the great country house estates that were being laid out by very rich landowners. Amongst others those at Blatherwycke, Boughton, Castle Ashby and Fawsley come to mind. Doubtless they were stocked with exotic waterfowl, of which the Canada goose is a species which has escaped to become a familiar, and not always welcome, addition to our avifauna. Very soon these new man-made habitats were being colonised by a great variety of native species of plants and animals.

In the late eighteenth and nineteenth centuries the canal builders carved brown scars across the face of Northamptonshire, at the same time scooping out large holes in the ground to produce the reservoirs which served to top up the water in time of drought and heavy usage by industrial narrowboat traffic. It is tempting to think of the canals as being like rivers in terms of the wildlife that they support, but really they more closely resemble long thin lakes. In the past they have been amongst the richest of wildlife habitats, and the quietest stretches may still be thought of in these terms. But due to the tremendous upsurge in leisure traffic of recent years, the water has become turbid, allowing little light to get through to the plants upon which all else depends. The fish population has also suffered to some degree, and large fish with chunks of flesh torn from their bodies by the screws of passing boats are a common sight. Birds, like kingfishers, herons and coots, have been affected by this increased activity and also by the continual disturbance during the summer months when they are attempting to breed.

By the middle of the nineteenth century demands for clean water by the burgeoning population of our larger towns led to the damming of streams to form reservoirs. Amongst the earliest was Ravensthorpe, where the mid-Victorian buildings and slow sand filter-beds are of interest to the industrial archaeologist. Until the arrival of Pitsford Reservoir, Ravensthorpe was the major habitat for wetland birds, and it still features prominently in the pages of the annual 'Northamptonshire Bird Report'. Only 3.2 km (2 miles) to the east is Hollowell Reservoir, also important for birds, and the final link in this chain is Pitsford, which has over 243 ha (600 acres) of open water when full. It is of international importance for several bird species, and nationally important for many others.

In the early decades of the twentieth century the sewage treatment plant at Ecton, which served Northampton, sprawled over several hundred hectares (acres) of the River Nene valley. It supported a rich and diverse community of plants and animals, and especially birds, but unfortunately the information was largely unrecorded by naturalists until the 1930's. Until the early 1950's Ecton also supported a thriving colony of breeding black-headed gulls, together with nesting snipe and redshank, and it was the place to go to see waders and a number of other species on spring and autumn passage. Many gardeners also knew it as the best place to go for healthy tomato plants!

Currently it has been replaced by the chain of gravel and sand pits, which are strung out along the Nene Valley from Kislingbury to Peterborough. The earliest of these has matured and supports dense vegetation and wet scrubland around their margins. They suffer from the disadvantage, in wildlife terms, that they have steep banks and therefore have little marginal vegetation. In recent years a more enlightened approach has been adopted with these worked-out pits, and they have been graded to leave islands for shelter, and for nesting birds, and at the same time the banks have been shelved to encourage marginal vegetation. In particular the Clifford Hill complex near Northampton, Summer Leys Local Nature Reserve, near Wellingborough and the Higham Ferrers-Ditchford-Ringstead complex are all major wetland habitats. In the most recent county bird report more than forty artificial lakes, reservoirs and gravel pits were listed, together regularly supporting over 25,000 wildfowl and other bird species during the peak winter counts.

In 1996 ***'Northamptonshire's Red Data Book' species to watch in the county'*** was published. Among the mammals listed was the noctule bat, which feeds over water. It roosts in old trees, and is thought to have suffered a major decline in numbers. Fawsley Park remains a stronghold for it. The catastrophic decline of the water vole is known, but the water shrew is also thought to have decreased in numbers. On the credit side the otter, aided by reintroductions, is making a welcome comeback.

At least 20 bird species of wetlands are listed in the Red Data Book, because the county supports numbers of national, and sometimes of international significance. Even ostensibly secure species, like the black-headed gull, gets in on the act, with Pitsford Water supporting winter numbers in excess of 12,000, making it the sixth most important roost in the country. The spectacular golden plover has wintering flocks sometimes of over 5,000 birds at the Nene Washlands-Clifford Hill gravel pits. Any flock of over 2,500 is regarded as being of national importance. The sight of this enormous number in the air over the valley, against a glowing winter sky, as they wheel around alternately showing their earth-brown upperparts and their startling silvery undersides, like a cloud of drifting snowflakes, is a never-to-be-forgotten experience.

Every spring and autumn our wetlands, and especially Pitsford Water, gear themselves up for an annual event, as they take their place as a major stopover point on the world-wide flyway. In avian terms the comings and goings are like those of a major airport. The position of the Reservoir, midway between the estuaries of the Wash and Bristol Channel, and in middle England on the south-north flyway, makes it an ideal rest and refreshment locality for thousands of tired migrant birds on their way north or south to and from their breeding grounds.

We learn about the amazing journeys which birds make by ringing them. A numbered ring with a mailing address is put on one of their legs. The ring causes no distress, and from those recovered it is possible to find out about their travels. The world champion migrant is the Arctic tern, which makes the journey from Hudson's Bay in Canada to the coast of Western Australia, a round trip of some 25,000 miles, (approximately 40,000 km). Flocks of up to fifty of these birds stop off at Pitsford on their northward journey, although most of these will reach journey's end in Scotland or Scandinavia.

Cormorants are seen the year round at the Reservoir, but its close relative the shag is much rarer. However, two picked up dead at Pitsford made the trip from islets off the Gwynedd coast, at least 159 miles (256km) distant. Perhaps these were storm-driven wanderers, but the young female sparrowhawk, ringed at the Reservoir, and which was found two months later at Wansford, Cambridgeshire, and then at King's Lynn in Norfolk, was eventually picked up dead at the Isle of Grain in Kent.

The huge flock of gulls that roosts on the Reservoir is probably made up of birds that come from all over Europe and Russia. These include a black-headed gull in its tenth year, and which was ringed as a nestling near Wroclaw, Poland. Another found when I was working there as a fishing warden had been ringed in Holland. So the gulls that hang about daily on the recreation ground, taking to the skies like snowflakes when a dog approaches, may have their summer homes in any of a dozen different countries. Each night they return to the security of the gravel pits and reservoirs to roost.

Few of us are able to spend our working lives in a situation like this, but for the lucky ones the signs of migration are obvious. I remember being out on the water on a day when I seemed to have the place to myself. Literally out of the blue a flock of over a hundred terns appeared over the main dam, beating into a stiffish breeze as they made their way steadily over the water. I followed their progress with my binoculars until they disappeared into the far distance over Walgrave, their destination known only to themselves.

On another occasion fierce April winds from the north had held up migration for many days, the birds being trapped on the shores of the nearby continent.

Then as the winds relented and turned to a mild south-westerly, the birds came pouring in. Overnight the field next to the causeway car park, on the Brixworth bank was filled with exhausted yellow wagtails, little gems of green and brightest yellow, huddled in the shelter of the newly sprouted grass. I counted at least 350 of them, and many more must have been hidden from view.

The departure of the over wintering duck is often quite sudden. The vast flocks of wigeon, which track to and fro over the early grown grass, like so many avian lawnmowers, have gone overnight. Under cover of darkness they are on their way to breeding grounds that may be in eastern Europe, in Scandinavia or even in European Russia.

Perhaps most spectacular of all are the Bewick's swans, although the fashion now is to call them Tundra swans. Stiff-necked, yellow and black beaked, they are smaller than the local mute swans. They break their journey here, sometimes in flocks of twenty or more, and at other times in autumn or spring there may be no more than one or two. The return migration takes them on a transcontinental flight from the saltmarshes of the River Severn, where they may have lived in comparative luxury as guests of the Wildfowl and Wetlands Trust at Slimbridge, to the bleak tree-less tundra of Siberia, overflying the infamous Chernobyl nuclear disaster site on the way.

With the changes in our wetlands that have been described above, it should come as no surprise that the flowering plants have also had their ups and downs. Gone are the insect-eating sundews that used to be found in a tiny acidic bogland on Harlestone Heath. And along with them are several dozen other species associated with waterside and water. Along some of our lesser waterways a handful of rare plants still continues to occur. In a few places, close to the sources of rivers, that have escaped drainage, plants like the large bittercress, which resembles lady's smock, and water avens - a handsome relative of the garden geums - are still found.

An unusual little plant, which relies on the disturbed muddy margins of water, is the mudwort. It was believed to have been lost to the county but turned up at Pitsford Water and Daventry Country Park, and has subsequently been found at one or two other places. Only a few centimetres high, with long narrow leaves and minute white or pinkish flowers, it is described as gregarious, spreading by means of runners. A line of plants, spreading across the mud, all linked together, as if by an umbilical cord, is typical of this species. Nationally it is rare and decreasing.

According to the recent *'Flora of Northamptonshire'* the even smaller and rarer great duckweed, only occurs at two sites in the county. I found it several years ago in an unvisited backwater of the Higham Ferrers gravel pits, but when I went back recently to check up on it, it had gone from there.

The attractive stonewort, a plant of marshy ground, is found at a handful of locations around the county, in those few fragments of undrained wetland that remain. A good place to admire its distinctive greyish foliage and clear white flowers is Kingsthorpe Upper Mill, on the northern outskirts of Northampton, where several hundred plants are still thriving.

In common with wetlands across the nation those in Northamptonshire are increasingly under threat. At local level a document was published as part of 'Northamptonshire's Biodiversity Action Plan', with the declared aim 'Action for Wildlife'. After affirming the need to conserve existing wetland habitats it went on to assert the need to 'create wildlife rich valleys containing additional areas of grassland, marshes and other wetlands'.

This vision was to be achieved by separate habitat plans for rivers and streams, marshy grassland, marshes, reedbeds, ponds and lakes, gravel pits, canals and reservoirs. Action programmes would be aimed at restoring flood plains, *wherever possible*, to create new areas of wetland; restoring high water tables and seasonal flooding of flood plains, *wherever possible*, to sustain a variety of wildlife, restore the natural course of rivers *where appropriate*, to allow rivers to meander in the flood plain; maintain and, *where necessary*, restore high water quality standards in rivers, streams and drains; create waterside buffer zones, particularly adjacent to arable cultivation; enhance, *where possible*, bankside management to encourage more wildlife; ensure there is no further loss of existing wetland habitat and *where appropriate*, enhance the interest; enhance the wildlife value of existing areas of riverside grasslands; maintain riverside pollards as a familiar feature of our valleys and as an important wildlife haven; encourage retention and restoration of field ponds and appropriate management and excavation of new ones; ensure that the after use of gravel pits makes provision for nature conservation interests; ensure that management of canals continues to be sensitive to wildlife; increase the accessibility and availability of information on river and wetland management to land managers; and to produce action plans for nationally and locally rare wetland species.

On a national scale Biodiversity Action Plans, together with their all-important costing, have been published for the Government by English Nature, its advisory body. They will cover all those species that are deemed to be in need of help. For example, the reed bunting is amongst the wetland species of interest locally, it having declined steeply in recent years. There are also comprehensive habitat plans for fen, marsh and swamp; for standing open water and canals; and for rivers and streams; all of which are relevant to the county. They should be adopted and implemented without delay.

It is my fervent hope that this long list does not end up as somebody's wish list, and that the word 'action' really does mean what it says.

HEDGEROWS AND ROADSIDE VERGES IN NORTHAMPTONSHIRE

Ron Wilson

Additional material on new regulations Peter Bowman (formerly FWAG)

Hedgerows and roadside verges are a relatively consistent feature of the countryside pattern in the Northamptonshire landscape. Unlike some other areas, including neighbouring Cambridgeshire where hedges are virtually non-existent, those in Northamptonshire remain in sufficient numbers to provide a valuable habitat for almost the whole spectrum of the county's wildlife. However, large tracts have been 'grubbed up', although as can be seen later there is now safeguard for hedgerows. The value of a hedge depends on the role it plays in the modern farming systems. In some parts of the county, where sheep-farming is of importance, many hedges have been maintained to form barriers.

Although hedges are generally considered to be an old-established feature of the countryside, the majority have arisen as a result of the Enclosure Acts and Awards of the seventeenth and eighteenth centuries. The 'modern' landscape, as we know it, with its innumerable miles of hedgerow wending their way like snakes towards the distant skyline, is relatively new in terms of man's involvement in the county.

It is probably safe to assume that very early people probably had some kind of hedge around their plots of land in the county. However, we do not have any positive evidence to substantiate these suppositions, and the written record only dates back to Anglo-Saxon times. Even this information is, to say the least, extremely sketchy and very difficult to come by. In parts of the British Isles Roman fields probably existed, and in other areas Iron and Bronze Age field systems have been identified.

At the time of the reign of King Cnut it was common for boundaries to be established between parishes, and these very old hedges – some of which are more than a thousand years ago – now form parish boundary hedges, as opposed to field boundaries of the Enclosure period.

Dating hedges

Dr Max Hooper, who lives in the county, and who worked for the Institute of Terrestrial Ecology, came up with a method for dating the age of a hedge. When studying hedges he noted that one species of tree or shrub became established for every hundred years that the hedge had been in existence. In this way a hedge which has ten species in it is reckoned to be one thousand years old. To confirm his theories, Dr. Hooper was able to check with various historical documents, so that, for example, when he came to date an Anglo-Saxon hedge, he was able to use his dating system, and then confirm his findings with the boundary charters that existed. For later hedges it is possible to use other documents, including the large number of Enclosure Acts and Awards. Not surprisingly the Anglo-Saxon charters are very few and far between. Those for Northamptonshire include Badby, Deanshanger, Newnham, Stowe-IX-Churches and Twywell.

Hedgerow on bank *Photograph: Ron Wilson*

Although this system works, many problems are encountered when trying to actually follow the boundary, as set out in a document prepared a thousand years ago! When the boundaries were being followed, and the information recorded for the charters, reference to such features as 'a stump' would have been quite clear to our ancestors. But one thousand years later this information is often of little use when trying to follow the perimeter boundary of an earlier village. However, when local historians, who know an area well, have used the translated documents, it is possible for them to carry out careful groundwork, enabling them to trace at least part of some of the boundaries.

One parish boundary, which is of great interest, is the one that separates the villages of Newnham and Everdon. A ditch which forms part of the boundary, and which still carries water a thousand years later, can be followed. The bank, which was formed when soil was thrown from the ditch, forms the boundary, and trees and shrubs have grown up on this. Whether these grew up 'accidentally' or were planted will never be known.

In formulating his hedgerow dating theory, Max Hooper surveyed a large number of sites, many of which were in the Midlands. Although his studies showed that there were variations in other parts of the country, he worked out a simple formula that could be used. Taking a thirty metre (yard) stretch of hedge, Dr. Hooper counted the trees and shrubs, but not the smaller herbs. From his studies he evolved the following formula for determining the age.

Example:	Age of hedge	= (99 x number of species) - 16
		= (99 x 10) - 16
	Age of hedge	= 974 years

Enclosure Acts and Awards

When the idea for the Enclosure Acts and Awards, was introduced in the seventeenth century the intention was to enclose all land in the British Isles. Such a system, however, was almost doomed from the start because of the reasons behind it. These reasons included changes that had taken place in the agricultural patterns in various parts of the British Isles over the centuries. Inevitably, local communities often developed their own interpretation of particular methods. Influential people, such as the Lord of the Manor, who was usually a very large landowner, also affected the systems. We have very little idea of the actual field pattern in Northamptonshire prior to the Enclosures, because few old maps have been discovered – and perhaps not surprisingly those which had been made were probably inaccurate. The only person who could usually afford to have maps drawn was the Lord of the Manor, and quite naturally they favoured his own interests!

Although various evidence exists – e.g. the Saxon Boundary charters – which suggests that there were hedges in the county prior to the Enclosure Acts and Awards, the only other concerted efforts aimed at enclosing land which took place before the main enclosures was during the Tudor period, some 400 years ago. At this time, sheep-farming became a predominant feature in certain parts of the county, and large tracts of land were enclosed to prevent the sheep from escaping. The Knightleys at Fawsley had 4500 sheep at one time, all of which had to be kept in 'enclosed' areas. Much of the enclosure activity at this time, and most which took place in earlier centuries, was considered illegal.

The greatest period of activity, however, dates from the seventeenth and eighteenth centuries, when Parliament passed the majority of the Enclosure Acts and Awards during the sixty year period between 1760 and 1820. Legislation was put in place to ensure that – at least in theory - each parish would produce its own plan for enclosing the land. Once completed an Act of Parliament was to be passed to make it lègal. As can be imagined, it was not quite as simple as it sounds, and there was, to say the least, a good deal of 'jiggery-pokery' which, in essence, favoured the large landowners. During this period some 51.5% of Northamptonshire's land was enclosed, the greatest percentage for any county.

A condition of many of the Awards was that hedges had to be planted to divide up the land, and a fast-growing species was needed. Hawthorn, also known as quickthorn, was considered suitable, and was used for most hedges, although some blackthorn was also planted. Both species of shrub grow quickly and soon form stock-proof barriers, provided that they were managed. It wasn't long before many thousands of kilometres (miles) had been planted and a great deal of maintenance soon became necessary so that the hedges would fulfil the job for which they were intended. At that time the farming system was such that there was a slack period during the winter, and the twin activities of hedging and ditching became a common practice on most farms.

Hedges for wildlife

Although today's hedgerow, with its accompanying verge and possible ditch, is a valuable asset for wildlife, problems arise because with changes in farming methods, the need for hedges has decreased. In spite of the fact that hundreds of miles (kilometres) have been uprooted in Northamptonshire, a vast acreage still remains which can provide an important habitat for plants and animals. These areas are particularly important because vast tracts of 'natural' countryside, and in particular woodland, have disappeared. During the spring many bird species build their nests, lay their eggs and rear their young in the relative safety that the hedge affords. During summer similar species of birds search eagerly among the flourishing hedgerow vegetation for a supply of food. During autumn and winter various bushes, shrubs and trees, together with many smaller plants, often provide an abundant supply of berries, fruits and seeds for both resident and visiting species.

When the British Isles was covered with deciduous woodland this was the natural habitat for many birds. But as the woodland disappeared more and more birds have been driven out and have had to adapt to other habitats. These birds, once dependent on woodland for a combination of food, shelter and nesting sites, now look to other trees and shrubs, with many occurring in the numerous miles (kilometres) of hedgerow scattered throughout the county.

Hedges and verges for wildlife *Photograph: Ron Wilson*

This hedgerow habitat is important in a number of ways. It provides song-posts, food, nesting sites and cover. Although the hedge is of prime importance to some species, like the blackbird, it is not totally reliant on this habitat and moves out into nearby fields to feed.

As a source of food, the hedge is vitally important providing a wide range of dietary material for a large number of bird species. Grasses, which often grow profusely, provide seeds: the caterpillars, which emerge from the eggs which butterflies and moths lay, provide a source of food for other birds. Thrushes in particular search for other creatures and at certain times of the year find a continuous supply of snails, mainly in the hedge bottom, and their anvils – where they break open the shells - can be seen at various places. In some areas in autumn hips and haws, the fruit of the wild rose and hawthorn respectively, provide food for seed-eating birds. Migrant winter visiting fieldfares and redwings – relatives of our resident thrushes – eagerly seek out the vast numbers of haws.

One of our most striking resident small birds in some areas of Northamptonshire is the yellowhammer, which makes considerable use of the hedgerow. However, the variety of breeding bird species using the hedge will depend on its make up. Some birds, like the yellowhammer, make use of low herbs and brambles. Where old trees are to be found they usually have holes that encourage species which need this particular nesting site, and some owl species may take up residence.

The hedge bottom provides a sanctuary and home for many different kinds of mammals. Large numbers of rabbits live here, feeding on the verges, and taking crops from the farmer's field. The hedgehog – also known as the hedge pig because of the snuffling and grunting which it makes when feeding – has always been associated with the countryside feature. Moles, common and pygmy shrews, all insectivores, find plenty of food in most hedges. Mice, including the long-tailed or wood mouse, are relatively common. In among the interwoven and entangled plant species at the base of the hedge, many of these small mammals have their homes, and their hidden tunnels and runs will cross and criss-cross in a complicated labyrinth of passages, to which only the animals themselves have the key.

It is perhaps not surprising that, in common with other habitats, the smaller invertebrates – animals without backbones - represent by far the greatest number and variety of hedgerow species. In spring the newly formed leaves, tender and rich with food, encourage these small animals to visit the hedge. Down in the hedge bottom, where a vast amount of dead and decaying material has accumulated, there are many creatures that seek sanctuary in this particular micro-habitat – and can be discovered with a little patience. Within a relatively short stretch of hedge it is not difficult to identify as many as two to three hundred of these different animals. For many people the majority of these will never be noticed, but anyone with a keen eye will be rewarded by the diversity of wildlife to be discovered here. A simple search could reveal innumerable species, each exhibiting their own particular characteristics. Together resident and visiting species form a very important and closely woven community, in a complex interwoven food web. As night approaches predators, like the fox and the owl, make their way to the hedge, and quarter it for food, seizing unsuspecting animals with lightning speed.

New regulations
Since 1 June 1997, after considerable pressure from the public and conservation organisations, hedgerows have received greater protection. Under the new hedgerow regulations it is now against the law to remove most hedgerows without the permission of the local panning authority. Greatest protection is afforded to ancient hedgerows described above, in recognition of their irreplaceable historic, wildlife and cultural value.

So now, whereas occasional lengths will be lost, hedgerows are a valued and protected component of out countryside. Figures from MAFF and local authorities suggest that more hedges are now being planted than are being removed. Although the value of an ancient hedgerow cannot be replaced, this is to be welcomed.

It could be argued that the biggest threat to hedgerows now comes from lack of, or any appropriate management. The majority of hedges are now cut in autumn every year. Although this maintains a tidy countryside, it deprives our native wildlife of a rich source of winter berries and late summer flowers. This has undoubtedly contributed to the rapid decline in the population of many of our once familiar and common farmland birds. Lack of management can be an equal problem. Whereas in the past hedges would have been laid (see page 129 Rural Crafts of the Countryside) so as to maintain them as stockproof features this is now less often seen.

Hedgerows *Photograph: Ron Wilson*

Hedge laying is a time consuming and expensive task and the skills needed are increasingly being lost. Hedges allowed to grow on, either uncut or laid, will eventually lose their value and develop into a broken line of tall trees and shrubs.

Many organisations are keen to maintain and enhance our hedgerows. CPRE have initiated a campaign to encourage local people to survey the hedges in their parish. Local authorities often operate a small grant scheme that encourages landowners to restore their hedges. Northamptonshire FWAG employed a full time Farm Conservation Adviser since the early 1980's and giving advice on hedgerow management and restoration forms an important part of almost every farm visit. MAFF now funds the majority of hedge planting and restoration work on farms through its Countryside Stewardship grant scheme. Landowners can enter into ten year agreements and undertake a programme of work over that time to plant, lay or coppice hedgerows as appropriate.

Roadside verges

Many roads in the county have substantial roadside verges, and the policy of spraying these with herbicides stopped many years ago, mainly because of complaints made by conservation bodies (not just in Northamptonshire), although certain areas, especially close to corners and junctions have to be trimmed regularly for safety reasons.

Perhaps the most noticeable aspect of the verge is that it is 'no-man's land'. It represents a barrier between the person using the road, and the farmer whose field is behind it. But in spite of what appears to be the continuing ruthless onslaught from the ever-increasing number of motor vehicles that spray it, or perhaps ride over it, the roadside verge is an important habitat for many of the county's wild flowers. Here, in spite of continual disturbances, especially alongside busy roads, many plants still seem to flourish. In quieter areas, where there is less traffic, verges often grow high and wild, sometimes obscuring the hedge behind them. Although it is difficult to give exact numbers for the county, it is known that nation-wide these verges provide a habitat for some six hundred of the country's two thousand different wild flower species. As a habitat for animals they are also important, particularly when surrounding farmland is intensively cultivated.

There is no denying that the roadside verge, which may be several metres deep, represents a vast 'nature' reserve, providing a valuable habitat for an array of plant species, as well as for many mammals, together with an almost incalculable number of invertebrates which inhabit this seemingly unpretentious, yet in reality, very important habitat.

Poppies grow on some verges *Photographs: Ron Wilson*

Many verges also have accompanying ditches, although many of these have either been filled in, or drains put in to cut down on maintenance costs. Others become silted up due to neglect. However, there are still some that are regularly maintained, which provide a valuable habitat. Where ditches have been specifically dug to take water draining from both roads and fields, they may be quite wide, and often have a number of different habitats throughout their length. Where a ditch is particularly deep, the conditions will be similar to those found in a stream. Marshy areas may also occur, particularly around the edges, and where reeds have become established they provide cover and nesting sites for some birds, including perhaps predictably, the ubiquitous moorhen. Some ditches may provide a valuable breeding site for amphibians and especially newts and frogs, and probably to a lesser extent, toads as well. However, it should be pointed out that run-off water from roads may be toxic and so does not provide a suitable habitat for wildlife. Before their virtual demise, water voles, always opportunists, were known to colonise suitable hedge-side ditches.

And so, when the once-common countryside feature is filled in, in favour of an underground piped system, a wide range of wildlife, too numerous to mention here, will be wiped out with one quick swipe from a mechanical digger.

Hedges, verges and ditches are a very valuable asset for a wide range of our native wildlife. A number of studies have been carried out into the flora and fauna associated with hedges, and most naturalists agree that they are extremely important, particularly as feeding and nesting sites, and also as homes for many different species.

References and Bibliography

Bayer (in association with FWAG). The Good Hedge Guide. Your Pocket Guide to Hedgerow Management. Available (£5) from Bayer, Eastern Way, Bury St Edmunds, Suffolk, IP32 7AH or FWAG, National Agricultural Centre, Stoneleigh, Kenilworth, Warwickshire, CV8 2RX.

Boatman, Derrick. Fields and Lowlands. The Natural History of Britain and Northern Europe. George Rainbird.

Ellis E.A. (1971). Wild flowers of the Hedgerow. Jarrold.

Harvey N. (1976). Fields, Hedges and Ditches - Shire Album 21. Shire Publications.

Hoskins W.G. (1968). Fieldwork in Local History. Faber.

Lee, Brian. (1985). Guide to Fields, Farms and Hedgerows. Crowood Press.

Leutscher, A. (1969). Field Natural History. Bell.

Mabey R. (1974). The Roadside Wildlife Book. David and Charles.

NCSS (1971). Hedges and Local History. NCSS.

Muir, Richard and Nina. (1989). Fields. Macmillan.

Pollard, E., Hooper, M.D. and Moore, N.W. (1974). Hedges. Collins New Naturalist.

Rackham, O. (1988). History of the Countryside. Dent.

Steane, J. (1974). The Northamptonshire Landscape. Hodder & Stoughton.

Streeter, David and Richardson, Rosamund. (1982). Discovering Hedgerows. BBC Publications.

Taylor, C.C. (1975). Fields in the English Landscape. Dent.

Wilson, R.W. (1979). The Hedgerow Book. David & Charles.

MAMMALS
OF
NORTHAMPTONSHIRE

Phil Richardson
County Mammal Recorder

Mammals are rarely easy to see and most observers note their presence through the signs they leave behind - the droppings, tracks, trails, hair and discarded food items. They can also be recorded from skeletal remains in owl pellets, cat prey items and road casualties. Study of any group of mammals is rather specialised, but glimpses can be obtained by visiting the right habitat at the right time. Night-time is best for most mammals and a mixed habitat, particularly near water, is likely to produce best results. A walk around Northamptonshire's reservoirs, lakes or gravel pits will always produce signs of mammals to the careful observer. Some mammal groups need specialised equipment to locate them effectively - small mammals are best caught in live-traps (although shrew-catching requires a licence) and bats can now be identified by electronic bat detectors that make their echo-location calls audible and distinctive.

Insectivores

Hedgehogs are widespread and commonly found, although most observations are of animals dead on our roads. They visit gardens in their search for food and will take slugs so helping gardeners. Animal lovers feed many in gardens, although milk is now thought less beneficial than cat food. Hibernation requires an undisturbed place and under garden sheds is one favoured location. **Moles** do well in the rather damp soils of the county. The characteristic hills show their presence in almost all rural areas and in some urban sites. One study noted their presence in every 1 kilometre square of a selected 10 kilometre square. They are affected by changing agricultural practices, particularly deep ploughing, but numbers always survive in headlands and around hedgerows and they soon re-colonise again. **Shrews** are more often heard than seen - the characteristic high-pitched squeaking from roadside verges. The **common** and **pygmy shrews** seem to be widespread, although the former is more regularly encountered. Dead animals are often found uneaten on the surface: they can die of starvation within an hour of their last meal due to their high metabolic rate. Cats catch a large number, but prefer to leave them due to their poor taste. The much rarer **water shrew** is not found just near water and the thin scattering of records are from village centres, main roads and woodlands. Usually there is a damp ditch nearby, but the preferred habitat is small streams or ponds.

Bats

All bats are insect-eaters, hibernating in winter. Extensive surveys since 1980 have recorded eight species of bat breeding in Northamptonshire. **Pipistrelles** are the most regularly seen species which commonly feed around gardens in towns and villages and roost behind the soffit board at the gable end apex of modern houses. Recent DNA work has split the pipistrelle into two species, both of which occur in the county. One roosts in large numbers in summer (often over 400 females) and remain at the roost all summer, the other occurs in lesser numbers and often moves around between many roost sites. **Brown long-eared bats** roost in much smaller numbers (less than 30 usually) and prefer to use attics of old buildings such as stable blocks or the old vicarage in a village. They feed on moths, usually in a nearby orchard. **Noctules** are found usually over water flying high: their tree roosts are hard to find and usually only discovered when trees are felled. Their numbers have declined this century as the old trees they use are lost. **Daubenton's bats** can be seen over most of our waters, skimming across the surface feeding on aquatic insects. Most are tree-roosting, but some have been found in tunnels and under bridges. **Whiskered bats** tend to be seen feeding around lakes in old, undisturbed landscapes, such as around Fawsley Lake. They are quite rare, as is a close relative the **Brandt's bat.** This species is more often found around woodland such as the Silverstone woods. **Natterer's bats** seem to prefer roosting in stone crevices in old buildings and most of the known roosts are in church walls or roofs. Again a rare animal, with more roosts in the south of the county, probably reflecting the different farming and field structures which affect feeding opportunities. One **Leisler's bat** has been found near Northampton, and further work needs to be carried out to see if it was a vagrant or part of a small breeding pocket. Winter hibernating bats of all species have been found in disused railway tunnels, mines, ice-houses, trees and inside the structure of houses such as around window frames and in the wall cavities.

Lagomorphs

Rabbits have increased greatly in number since being almost eliminated by myxomatosis in the late 1950s. The disease still flares up so local populations wax and wane. Road casualties are common, snaring, shooting and gassing occur regularly and hunting with ferrets is still practised. Nevertheless the number living under our hedgerows, in woodlands and on farmland is huge. Over 400 were counted around one small 100 metres (300 feet) diameter copse at dusk in one area. Colour variations include pale sandy and all black. **Brown hares** can still be found, but numbers are far less than 20 years ago. Fields are used traditionally, usually near old pasture. Some hare coursing still occurs and a pack of beagles still operates across part of the county. Shoots on large farms are now less frequent and "bag" less hares.

Rodents

Grey squirrels have been our only squirrel since around the 1950s when red squirrels died out. They are found in most parks, woodlands and anywhere with mature trees. They are trapped, shot and poisoned in woodland to try to prevent tree damage, but still survive in great numbers. Some enter attics to breed or sleep. **Bank and field voles** are widespread, the latter being very common in rough grassland and a common prey item of owls and raptors. **Water voles** were once common along the waterways, but numbers crashed dramatically in the 1990s, often blamed on mink, and they are now a rare mammal, only found on a few isolated streams or water bodies. **Wood mouse** is our commonest mouse and found in woodlands, field edges, verges, gardens and attics in winter where is it often mistakenly identified as **house mouse**, a species that is now rather uncommon. The **yellow-necked mouse** has only been recorded on a few occasions and mostly in ancient hedgerows and woodland. **Harvest mice** are now recorded only infrequently - the characteristic woven nest on grass stems is now rarely found. The few recent records have been from around reservoirs, and sites where it occurred in the 1970s are no longer used. **Brown rats** are now less often seen as farms, towns and villages are tidied up. Many may still be seen where food is regularly available such as battery hen sheds, corn stores, hay stacks and feed sheds. The **common dormouse** occurs in quite small numbers in specialised habitats of ancient woodlands, mostly in the north and around Silverstone. Locating them has been successfully achieved through erecting, then monitoring, wooden nest boxes.

Carnivores

Foxes remain common even though they are still hunted with hounds, shot, trapped and poisoned. Many have successfully colonised our towns and urban foxes have become a regular sight. **Stoats** and **weasels** are widespread, the former feeding well on rabbits, the latter on voles and mice. Stoats are seen at times in winter in full ermine, but part-white coats are more usual. **Polecats** began to re-colonise the county in the 1980s, with confirmed records in the early 1990s. Since then they have spread eastwards and nearly reached Cambridgeshire. DNA tests show that they are likely to be part of an expansion of the west England population. They feed principally on rabbits and often live down their burrows. Escaped ferrets are also found, but unlike polecats, no breeding records exist in the wild in Northamptonshire. **Mink** spread into all parts of the county in the 1970s, originating from released and escaped animals from fur farms, and, through successful breeding, now may have reached saturation point. Although usually associated with rivers and canals they have been found many miles away in woodland, on farmland and in gardens. **Badger** numbers have increased in the 1990s and they have re-colonised areas abandoned in the 1970s and 1980s when the population declined. Deaths on the road are common, but have little effect on overall numbers. Testing of road casualties has shown no evidence of bovine TB in the county. **Otters** nearly died out in the 1960s, but a small and possibly transient population was recorded into the 1990s. About 12 captive-bred animals were released in the north of the county in the early 1990s and this has resulted in many more records across much of the central and northern part of Northamptonshire.

Deer

Red deer have been recorded, usually singly, in most large woodlands and originated from escaped animals (there is, for instance, a captive herd kept for venison, at Whittlebury). A few **Sika deer** have also been seen moving with the more common fallow deer, which are present in all large woodlands, and even move into small copses at times. **Fallow** are also kept in some parks as captive herds (e.g. Althorp). **Roe deer** moved in from the west in the 1980s and have since been seen throughout, but the numbers are very small. **Muntjac** (originating from Woburn in the

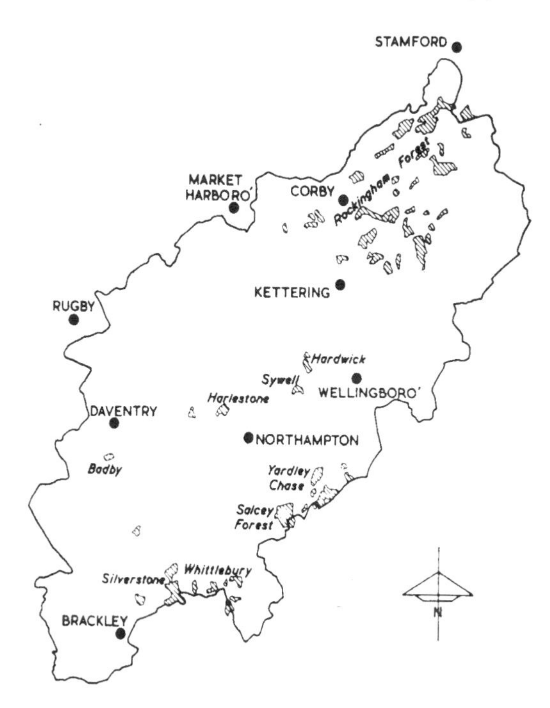

Northamptonshire Deer Forests

1940s) is common and found not only in woodlands and copses, but in large gardens and scrubland in towns as well as villages. The **water deer** has been seen only a few times and were escaped animals. All deer are culled to try to limit damage in woodland and surrounding farmland.

References

Richardson P W. (1984). The Mammals of Northamptonshire 1979-1983. Journal of the Northamptonshire Natural History Society.

Richardson P W (1999). Records of the Northants Bat Group (unpublished).

Fallow deer *Sketch by Anne Finch*

BIRDS OF NORTHAMPTONSHIRE

C J Coe

Revised by Cliff Christie, Colin Wickes and Ron Wilson

Few outsiders are really acquainted with Northamptonshire and to most people it is merely a transitional piece of terrain that is bisected by the main road and rail links - the M1 motorway, the A14, A5 and the A6 trunk roads or the Euston to Scotland main railway line. And so to the casual observer Northamptonshire probably gives the impression that it is a typical lowland county, with no particularly interesting features. It has no sea-coast, estuary or even a tidal river. It lacks mountains and cliffs, and there is a complete absence of even the smallest outcrop of rock.

In spite of what, to most people, must be a mundane - almost austere - first impression, there is a rich abundance of bird life to be discovered, which is as rich - if not richer - than in any similarly placed county. Records show that the total number of species recorded in Northamptonshire is in excess of 300, with 217 being recorded in 1996. About 130 species have been proved to nest, and at least 100 in the past ten years. Approximately 90 can be regarded as regular breeding birds.

Northamptonshire is fortunate in having more than an average share of small, moderate and large stretches of open water. These areas consist of a combination of water board and canal feeder reservoirs, flooded sand and gravel pits (some still fully operational and lacking vegetation; others disused and mature), and many ornamental lakes, some of which are of a considerable size. Several rivers either bisect or border the county, and the valleys and flood plains of these further add to the variety of habitat needed to support a diverse avifauna. Another feature of the landscape is the considerable acreage of woodlands. Many of these are managed by the Forestry Enterprise and are conifer plantations, but a significant amount is also mature semi-mature oak or mixed deciduous, some - like Rockingham and Salcey Forests - being remnants of much larger historical forests. The current tree-planting policy also ensures an ever-present proportion of infant plantations to further diversify the available habitat. With its position, the county's western edge borders the Cotswold Hills and the streams that descend from this area are fast-flowing enough to encourage a marginal colonisation of certain upland bird species. The extreme easterly part of the county touches onto the fenlands of East Anglia which has its own ornithological specialities. Locally there are several sites that are of importance for birds. These include the well established, but shallow, Pitsford Water, which with its many bays and inlets, has a variety of habitats within the perimeter fence, which was at one time considered the Mecca for Northamptonshire's birdwatchers. Pitsford has the accolade of being rated fourth most important inland water for wintering wildfowl, with nearby Hollowell reservoir in fifth position. In its own right it commands a species list of 205 birds.

However, the relatively recent establishment of Summer Leys Nature Reserve in the Nene Valley, together with an ever-increasing number of gravel pits, has provided further sites for waterfowl and waders.

All three species of Diver have been reported from the county, with the red-throated being by far the most common. As would be expected, the great northern proves the least frequent visitor, although there have been 24 sightings, with the unprecedented summer appearance of a slightly oily bird at Ravensthorpe Reservoir in June 1977. Great crested grebes are well represented as a breeding species locally, and 304 birds were counted at Pitsford Water in December 1996 and a total of 540 birds were around in the county in November of the same year. Resident little grebes are found on suitable waters, although their numbers seem to fluctuate from year to year. There is a handful of records of the red-necked, Slovenian and black-necked grebe, all of which are rare visitors, having been chiefly noted during passage months and winter.

A county as land-locked as Northamptonshire still receives a few wind-blown sea birds, particularly during autumn gales and less experienced juveniles may be carried well inland, and it is not surprising that fulmars, Manx shearwaters, storm and Leach's petrels and gannets have all been noted. And although its still a scarce visitor, the shag also features in the county's bird records annually. The cormorant being less pelagic, is a regular visitor and puts in an appearance at almost any time of the year, and as many as 300 birds have been recorded in the county early in the year. In recent years it has been breeding at many inland sites, and spends the summer in numbers on many local waters. There is one large heronry, with around forty nests in most years, as well as six or seven smaller sites, some increasing and some declining, with a once well-established site now extinct. The bittern is a rare visitor, usually encountered in the winter mainly occurring on the eastern side of the county, where it has probably strayed from the nearby fenlands.

Mallards and tufted are probably the only regular breeding ducks, but several others have done so spasmodically, including teal, garganey, and pochard. Gadwall is a steadily increasing species and now breeds regularly at several waters, with shoveler breeding at Pitsford in most years. Ruddy ducks are resident in the county, and also occur as winter visitors. These also breed regularly on many waters and over the last few years there has been a great deal of controversy because this and the white-headed ducks inter-breed. Naturalists fear that this could lead to the eradication of the white-headed species. Strategies have been put in place to remove the ruddy duck. A few other species of duck have bred from time to time, including garganey, gadwall, and other species may either be resident - shoveler, common teal and wigeon - or winter visitors. Amongst the common winter ducks are the wigeon, gadwall, teal and shoveler. Many summer duck species have their winter population increased by several hundred at the right time of the year. These include mallard, wigeon and pochard. In recent years shelduck have also bred in several areas in the county.

Although pintail, shoveler, goldeneye and gossander appear in more modest numbers, they are still a regular feature. Wanderers such as scaup, common scoter and smew are almost annual visitors, and several rarer ducks have all been seen. The Canada goose population continues to increase in numbers and the resident birds are joined by winter visitors with a December total of over 2,500 birds noted at various places, with large numbers at Daventry Country Park, Thrapston and Hardingstone gravel pits. There is an increasing population of feral greylag geese, and they breed in several areas. During the summer the population can reach a high of more than 1,200 birds. White-fronts, once a regular feature of the county when it was less well-drained, sometimes still appear as rare passage migrants or winter visitors, and flocks of more than 50 have been noted early in the year, which compares with a flock of about the same number being recorded at Stanford Reservoir just before Christmas 1976. Other geese, including pink-footed, white-fronted and brent, also occur as passage migrants and winter visitors, including feral birds.

Pitsford Water, which used to be famous for its wintering flocks of Bewicks (also referred to as Tundra) swans, which exceeded a 100 in some years, now sees the bird as a passage migrant, and rare spasmodic winter visitor. Areas such as the Ouse Washes and Slimbridge attract virtually all the winter visitors. This species, which also once seemed to favour both Cransley and Hollowell Reservoirs, now appears in other areas including Pitsford Water, Boddington Reservoir and Earls Barton gravel pits. Whooper swans arrive in small numbers as winter visitors, although most birds only stay for brief periods.

Of the breeding birds of prey the kestrel is now widespread, and is equally at home hovering over a motorway verge as a country lane. The sparrowhawk, which had almost been completely 'driven away' with the widespread use of pesticides in the late 50's and throughout the 60's, has made a complete recovery and successfully returned to the county and has probably reached its pre-pesticide levels. Several pairs are now known to have nested successfully. Other species, including the hobby and buzzard, can also be seen, but are rare breeders. Buzzards are increasing in their range from the west and are now a common sight throughout the year, with the occasional breeding bird being recorded. The rest of the raptors are rather spasmodic in their appearance, but not many years go by without reports of marsh and hen harriers, ospreys, peregrines and merlins being sited. Into the rare vagrant category fall honey buzzards and rough-legged buzzards. Red kites are seen more often since their reintroduction into the north of Northamptonshire, where they are a common sight. The birds have become well established and breed regularly.

The usual lowland gamebirds are of course present, although the fortunes of the partridge seem to fluctuate according to the amount of rain that falls during its breeding season. Quail, a spasmodic summer visitor can still sometimes be heard calling. In 'good' quail years the birds breed. Water rails are found in a number of suitable areas in winter and breed at one or two sites. Coots are found on virtually all large areas of water, their numbers being swelled by winter visitors when the population may top the 5,000 mark. Although lapwings are widespread, with regular counts of more than 1,000 birds at a couple of sites during the winter, its breeding status has declined. Others like the ringed plover (very scarce), little ringed plover (a few pairs), snipe and curlew now only occur in small numbers and as scarce breeders. However, a number of local projects should ensure their future breeding success. Other wading birds include woodcock, curlew and redshank.

As most of Northamptonshire's reservoirs are in the main shallow-sided and subject to seasonal fluctuations in water levels, we are fortunate in having an impressive wader passage, especially in autumn and the number and variety of species is very gratifying. Usually recorded at such times are ringed plover, jack snipe, green and common sandpiper, greenshank, little stint, dunlin and ruff. Although the coastal oystercatcher, typified by one naturalist as the 'pied piper of the shoreline', is now a breeding species in the county, its numbers remain small. Usual visitors also include grey plovers, turnstone, whimbrel, black-tailed godwits, wood sandpiper, curlew sandpiper and sanderling, which all turn up in varying numbers. It is not beyond possibility to expect to see temmincks stint, pectoral sandpiper, avocets and phalaropes, and even rarer ones than these have been recorded. All four skuas are on the county list with the arctic being the most frequent, and the great a close second.

At present black-headed gulls are common winter visitors, where as many as 5,000 birds have been recorded roosting at Pitsford Water, and it has also recently begun to breed here. In the 1950's, before the Ecton Sewage Works treatment plant was modernised, this site was home to a colony of several hundred pairs. Common gulls occur mainly in the winter, with roosts of around 4,000 birds having been noted at Pitsford Water, with smaller roosts of around 1,000 birds having been seen at Boddington Reservoir. The lesser-black backed gull is a winter visitor, and also turns up on passage. There have been attempts in recent years for birds to establish breeding sites, but the last birds to bring off young happened in 1969. Other gulls, including herring, glaucous, and Iceland, are winter visitors - although the latter two species usually only occur in very small numbers. Little gulls and kittiwakes are also recorded as passage migrants. Several species of tern - including common, arctic, little, sandwich and black - all pass through, and the common species is known to breed, although at only two or three sites. Specially constructed tern rafts have been put in place at sites like Sywell and Daventry Country Parks, and the birds use these, although they sometimes have to compete with other species, like the Canada goose. Most terns tend to be passing through as passage migrants pausing - usually briefly - at a variety of waters to feed before moving on. In 1996 nearly 50 arctic terns were counted in May at Daventry Country Park, and at least one pair of common terns has bred at one site in the county in the last few years. Sandwich and little terns are seen in most years and there are three records for roseate terns since 1950. Auks, represented by little auks, guillemots and puffins, have been picked up exhausted, but this is a far-from-common happening. Puffins have been recorded four times this century, the last one being released at Whitby after recovering from 'exhaustion'. In the 'Wreck-year' of 1960, a little auk was rerurned to Pitsford Water after it had been cared

Cuckoo

for for several days and others have turned up from time to time since.

Wood pigeons, and the now well established collared doves, are very abundant, with stock doves also a fairly common sight, especially in areas where older trees afford them suitable nesting sites. Although the turtle dove, a species that becomes rarer further north, is a regular summer visitor to Northamptonshire, its numbers appear to be in serious decline. Cuckoos still make landfall to spend the summer in the county, and mainly parasitise reed warblers and dunnocks in the virtual absence of their favourite host, the meadow pipit, which occurs in more upland areas.

Among the owls, the true status of the tawny is not fully understood. The barn owl declined rapidly through the 1970's and 80's, but a recent survey carried out in the east of the county tentatively suggests that the bird may be on the increase. Reports also suggest that although the numbers may still remain relatively small the bird occurs over a large area because it is thinly distributed. One of the claims to fame of Northamptonshire is undoubtedly the first successful introduction into Britain of the continental little owl as a breeding species. In the 1880's Lord Lilford made concerted attempts to introduce them into the east of the county, and breeding birds had reached Rutland in 1891 and Woburn (Beds) in 1982. The little owl is at present used as the emblem for both the Northamptonshire Bird Report Committee and the Northamptonshire Bird Club. Long-eared owls are difficult to see, being extremely nocturnal and their exact distribution is unknown, but it breeds regularly at six or seven sites. Short-eared owls are winter visitors in very varying numbers.

The nightjar, now a rare summer visitor, is no longer thought to breed in the county. In the 1970's it was restricted to only one known regular breeding area in Northamptonshire, and even this has disappeared because rapid conifer growth is quickly rendering the habitat unsuitable. Swifts are a common sight in towns, and they use reservoirs as feeding areas. After hard winters kingfishers disappear altogether as breeding birds, and often do not recover fully for many years, when populations may return to earlier levels. The bird is subjected to the vagaries of the winter, and numbers seem to seesaw. When feeding places are frozen over the bird is unable to dive for fish and starvation follows.

The three woodpeckers - great spotted, lesser spotted and green - all breed in Northamptonshire. Although the green woodpecker has been recorded at more than 120 locations, it is an amber alert species and all sightings are needed to monitor its status. The lesser spotted, which benefited from Dutch Elm

Disease, is now a local species, and although its courtship displays have been noted in recent years, breeding is not always confirmed. The wryneck, a relatively of the woodpeckers, bred at one time, but is now strictly a passage migrant.

The skylark is the only regular bird of its family, the woodlark having been lost to the county as a breeding species, probably finally in the early 1950's. Skylarks, like many other once common farmland species including tree sparrow, yellowhammer, corn bunting and linnet, show a decline that is extremely worrying. However, there have been two recent reports of woodlarks which were presumably passing through. The usual Hirundines, feature in the county's fauna, the sand martin taking full advantage of various sand and gravel pits for nesting, although only two large colonies have been identified in recent years. Both the summer-visiting swallows and house martins breed in the county, although their numbers have undoubtedly declined in recent years.

All the common crows are abundant, and the magpie seems to do well wherever it scavenges, and it can also frighten away other species, especially when it lands in the garden. Rooks, jackdaws and carrion crows are all common and the jackdaws have been recorded feeding in large numbers - sometimes in flocks of more than 500 birds - at various locations. Rooks, too, congregate in similar-sized flocks, and nearly 250 nests were counted in one of the county's largest rookeries. Hooded crows sometimes put in an appearance in winter.

All species of common tits are represented. However, other birds, like the nuthatch are now more local, and a feature of older timbered areas, although the distinctive treecreeper occurs more generally.

Of those species termed ‘occasional vagrants’, a few dippers sometimes 'wander' in from the west, and once or twice the black-bellied continental sub-species has been reported from the eastern side of the county. In 1975 a pair raised young on the county border in the extreme west and this was the first documented evidence of breeding dippers in Northamptonshire, although local reports showed that the pair had been recorded in the area for several years. The bird is now a rare vagrant, and no breeding birds have been recorded in recent years, with the latest birds turning up in 1985, 1994 and 1996. In 1965 four bearded tits were discovered at Ecton sewage farm, and now the Norfolk and Suffolk breeding population is up to strength, as an eruptive winter visitor birds have appeared in several years since then. Prior to 1965 there had been no occurrences since 1849.

Among the thrushes, mistle thrush, song thrush and blackbirds are frequent residents to be joined by winter visitors. These winter visiting relatives, the fieldfare and redwing, vary in their numbers; some years they may be common: in other winters less so. The stonechat is a scarce passage migrant, but is also a local winter visitor. Ring ousels and black redstarts are uncommon passage migrants, although the latter raised young in Northampton town many years ago, and has been suspected of doing so on other occasions. Although the redstart has bred in the past it is no longer believed to do so. With some areas managed for them, nightingales have become established in certain areas, and breeding sites have been recorded from a number of places and their populations have become stabilised over the last ten years. The wheatear is an abundant passage migrant and in recent years has been recorded from over thirty localities. Young were reported at Borough Hill Country Park (Daventry) and it is assumed that they either bred in the locality or close by.

Goldcrest

Most of the common warblers are fairly general, although the grasshopper warbler and the lesser whitethroat tend to be somewhat localised. In the mid 1970's the wood warbler was our rarest breeding warbler, raising young at sites, but it now no longer breeds, although some birds have been heard singing in various places. Goldcrests occur in quite large numbers in coniferous woodlands, and passing birds and potential winter visitors each autumn swells their population. Our smallest visitor, the firecrest has seen its numbers decline in recent years, and it is now an irregular visitor that used to breed in the county.

Another once familiar summer visitor, but now also in decline, is the spotted flycatcher, and the pied flycatcher is now a rare passage migrant only. Pipits are represented by the tree pipit, although once a local, but regular summer visitor, it has now serious declined. However, the meadow pipit is still quite a common passage migrant and winter visitor, although it does not often breed. The rock pipit is a passage migrant, with a tendency to winter around some of the larger waters, like Pitsford and Hollowell. The water pipit is a scarce passage migrant and winter visitor.

Pied wagtails are a common sight and roosts of around 500 birds have been reported, and at one time the most 'famous' of these was in the Carlsberg Brewery in Northampton! Yellow wagtails breed with large numbers passing through in spring and autumn. Grey wagtails are extending their range from he west, and now occasionally breed in the county. A few waxwings manage to penetrate into Northamptonshire during invasion years, and were last really numerous in the early part of 1996. Great grey shrikes winter in several localities, although their presence is declining, but the red-backed shrike has not bred with us since the early 1950's, although a pair returned to within 100 metres (100 yards) of the county border in 1971 and raised young.

Finches are well represented by the most common members of the family, although linnets virtually disappear in hard winters. The presence of hawfinches is regularly reported from several areas throughout the year, but it is so secretive that only a few instances of breeding have ever reported. At one time during the 1970's the redpoll increased its range from the south-east to become both a resident and winter visitor, but having established itself extremely well, it has suffered a dramatic decline over recent years. And the siskin makes an appearance either as a winter visitor or passage migrant. Flocks of between 40 and 50 being reported during the early spring and as many as 100 in the winter. It is possible that some birds may breed. The twite may make an appearance at Pitsford Water in winter, and summer birds have been reported from a small number of other sites. There are periodical invasions of crossbills, and the odd pair may remain to breed in the spring. The brambling is reported regularly during the winter months, and sometimes parties reaching almost a hundred birds may be seen. The declining ‘strange’ resident bird the corn bunting is regularly seen in its usual restricted pockets, and flocks of between 30 and 80 birds have been reported from several places in autumn and early winter. A few years ago reed buntings became less particular about their choice of territory, but they are now in decline. The occasional snow bunting sometimes shows up, mainly during the latter part of one year and the beginning of the next.

With the existence of so many areas of water, it is inevitable that a remarkable list of rare sightings has been built up over the years. Pride of place probably belongs to an eye-brewed thrush that appeared at Oundle in 1964, and at the time was the first of its kind to be recorded in the British Isles, and so for a few weeks, Northamptonshire held the honour of having the only record for this species. Although the ‘Rarities Committee of British Birds’ did not accept a short-toed lark reported on Pitsford Water in 1973, the greater short-toed lark at Sywell Reservoir in 1977 was the first and only record for Northamptonshire.

An ornithological highlight of 1977 was the arrival of an adult pied-billed grebe at Ravensthorpe Reservoir in April - a new species for the county.

During 1998, Pitsford Water received an award from the British Trust for Ornithology (BTO) for recording 159 bird species on a commercial water during the year.

However, with this success, there is also serious concern. A recent survey carried out by the Royal Society for the Protection of Birds, in conjunction with the British Trust for Ornithology, suggests that the sight of lapwings in Northamptonshire could soon be nothing more than a memory. There is grave concern that these once-common wading birds will be extinct within a relatively short time. Since they were first surveyed in the county in 1987, lapwing numbers have plummeted by a staggering 60% in eleven years. It is believed that the main reason for this decline is due to changes in farming practices. There has been a move from spring to autumn sown crops, coupled with an increase in land drainage and the continual use of pesticides and herbicides, all of which has an effect on this species. The shift from spring to autumn sowing has decreased the number of nest sites, since lapwings prefer either well-drained short grass or cropped fields. More and more traditional grassland is being lost, and especially lightly grazed damper areas. Here the once abundant supply of insects, which provided the adult lapwings with food for their chicks, is no longer available. The use of pesticides only exacerbates the problem. It is believed that since 1987 the number of lapwings found in Britain has halved from between 200 and 250,000 to around 120,000 birds in 1999.

Records for various species show that they have only occurred on one occasion. Among these are little bustard (1858), roller (1859), woodchat shrike (1869), golden eagle (1894), razorbill (1920), great reed warbler (1943), icterine warbler (1947), greater yellowlegs (1948), sociable plover (1951), buff-breasted sandpiper (1952), Wilson's phalarope (1959), black-winged stilt (1965), Richard's pipit (1966), crane sp. (1968), black-winged pratincole (1969), lesser grey shrike (1972), collared pratincole (1973), pomarine skua (1976), sooty tern (1980), broad-billed sandpiper (1984), European storm petrel (1989), two-barred crossbill (1990), long-billed dowitcher (1992), brindled tern (1993) and black kite (1995).

Great crested grebe

Species with several occurrences, but which are nonetheless extremely rare, include purple heron, night heron, little bittern, white stork, spoonbill, American wigeon, ferruginous duck, crane, Kentish plover, great snipe, lesser yellowlegs, dowitcher, white-winged black tern, Caspian tern, pallas's sandgrouse, nutcracker, and rose-coloured starling.

Northamptonshire Bird Report is published annually and is an independent publication that receives no outside financial support. For those people interested in the bird life of Northamptonshire, the Bird Report is an indispensable guide, containing records for the previous year, as well as articles and notes from contributors. Interested parties can contribute to the bird report by submitting their own records.

Further information, and copies of the current and past Northamptonshire Bird Reports, can be obtained from R Bullock, 81 Cavendish Drive, Northampton, NN3 3HL. Telephone 01604 627262.

WILD FLOWERS IN NORTHAMPTONSHIRE

G M Gent

Northamptonshire, bordered by the Fens at its north-eastern end and by Oxfordshire at its south-western extremity, is almost 70 miles (112 kilometres) long. Such an extensive distance gives rise to many varied types of soils and habitats within the county. Between 900 and 1,000 plants have been recorded in Northamptonshire, but space here will not allow for a complete list of these, which include non-flowering species like horsetails and ferns, as well as flowering plants. Although there are varieties within the county, there is no plant that is specific to Northamptonshire, that is to say which does not grow elsewhere in the British Isles. The main groups of plants are either those which prefer lime soils, or those which grow on neutral soils. Acid-loving plants are chiefly restricted to those soils directly derived from the Northamptonshire ironstone beds.

Meadow Cranesbill on roadside verge *Photograph: Ron Wilson*

Woodland

The county is rich in woodlands, which are remnants of the once extensive forests of Rockingham, Whittlebury and Salcey, and it seems logical to begin with a description of woodland plants. In spring primroses (Primula vulgaris) and bluebells (Endymion non-scriptus) are very commonly seen in most woodland, along with the less noticeable species of barren strawberry (Potentilla sterillis), wood sorrel (Oxalis acetosella), both species of wood violet (Viola riviniana) and the smaller (V. reichenbachiana), greater stitchwort (Stellaria holostea), bugle (Ajuga reptans), and the less common early purple orchid (Orchis mascula) and goldilocks (Ranunculus auricomus). A few woods have patches of wild garlic or ransoms (Allium ursinum) and yellow archangel (Lamiastrum galeobdolon), a dead nettle with beautifully marked flowers, the latter species being a good indicator of ancient woodland, as is Herb Paris (Paris quadiifolia), a rare plant and very easily overlooked amongst the general vegetation. In the north-east of the county an early woodland species is toothwort (Lathraea squamaria). Having no green leaves it is a parasite, occurring on the roots of hazel (Corylus avellana). This and other special plants favour the high alkaline content of the soil in the old Soke of Peterborough. Lily of the valley (Convallaria majalis) and wild aquilegia/columbine (Aquilegia vulgaris) may be found, and the fly orchid (Ophrys insectifera) has been recorded.

Following the early flowers of the woodland rides, other species which can be seen include common spotted orchids (Dactylorhiza) and common twayblade (Listera ovata): both species are fairly common in woodland and old quarries. Other summer flowers of ridings include common valerian (Valeriana officinalis), meadowsweet (Filipendula ulmaria), hedge woundwort (Stachys sylvatica), meadow vetchling (Lathyrus pratensis) and honeysuckle (Lonicera periclymenum), to name but a few. Hedgerow species are well represented particularly on alkaline soils, with dogwood (Thelycrania sanguinea), wayfaring tree (Viburnum lantana), guelder rose (Viburnum opulus), spindle (Euonymus europaeus) and wild clematis (Clematis vitalba). The latter is a very good indicator species for calcareous soils. One of the saprophytic orchids, the birdsnest orchid (Neottia nidus-avis), occurs in a few woods in the county and the greater butterfly orchid (Platanthera chlorantha) and broad-leaved helleborine (Epipactis helleborine) are also locally common. A woodland plant, which just about reaches its northern limits in the county, is the wood spurge (Euphorbia amygdaloides).

In contrast to woodland growing on calcareous soils, there are a few areas in the north-west which are on lighter, sandy soils, and here vivid patches of red campion (Silene dioica) are a feature, accompanying the bluebells in springtime. Where foxgloves (Digitalis purpurea) occur they indicate a more acid soil. Bitter vetch (Lathyrus montanus), a plant which is common in the west and south-west of the British Isles, is found in some areas in the west of

Northamptonshire. In early spring in western areas of the county, town hall clock (Adoxa moschatalina), an interesting small plant with four flowers arranged on four faces around the stem (hence the name), may also be found. In wet patches in woodlands in the west, opposite-leaved golden saxifrage (Chrysoplenium oppositifolium) is quite a feature during the spring and, as its name implies, makes golden splashes of colour.

Limestone grassland

In complete contrast to the woodland areas, the limestone grassland in the north-eastern corner of the county carries a very rich flora. Here the roadside verges and old limestone quarries provide habitats that are particularly suitable for many of our more interesting species. In summer these areas are bright with common rockrose (Helianthemum chamaecistus), horse-shoe vetch (Hippocrepis comosa), clustered bellflower (Campanula glomerata), dropwort (Filipendula vulgaris), small scabious (Scabiosa columbaria) and purple milk vetch (Astragalus danicus). Both pyramidal orchid (Anacamptis pyramidalis) and the fragrant orchid (Gymnadenia conopsea) occur in one or two localities along with the man orchid (Aceras anthropophorum). The beautiful pasque flower (Pulsatilla vulgaris) now only occurs in one locality. Later in the summer the very small autumn gentian or fellwort (Gentiana amarella) is quite common in old quarries. Some of the more spectacular plants of this habitat are deadly nightshade (Atropa belladonna), dark mullien (Verbascum nigrum) and tall broomrape (Orobanche elatior), the latter plant being parasitic on great knapweed (Gentaurea scabiosa).

Meadows

Meadows which have not been "improved" are a fast disappearing feature of our county, and along with them we are losing many of the species once very common in such areas. Meadow saxifrage (Saxifraga granulata) and green-winged orchid (Orchis morio) were much more common at one time. Indeed the latter species has declined all over the country, due to changes in farming practice. Cowslips (Primula veris), adderstongue fern (Ophioglossum vulgatum) and other plants typical of old pastures have rapidly declined since the last war, when large areas were ploughed up and, although the flowers still seem to be fairly common in odd places such as railway banks, they are generally thought to be decreasing in numbers throughout the county.

Water plants

Although many of our ponds have vanished, and with them we have seen the demise of many aquatic species, nevertheless there is still a rich flora alongside rivers, canals and gravel workings. Of the marginal species yellow iris (Iris pseudacorus), purple loosestrife (Lythrum salacaria), common skull-cap (Scutellaria galericulata), ragged robin (Lychnis flos-cuculi), meadowsweet (Filipendula ulmaria), marsh woundwort (Stachys palustris) and the water forget-me-nots (Myosotis caespitosa and M. scorpioides) are fairly common, together with the great hairy willow-herb (Epilobium hirsutum) and the great water dock (Rumex hydrolapathum). In contrast the attractive flowering rush (Butomus umbellatus) is less common than it used to be. Two plants that have spread along our waterways in recent years are the balsams (Impatiens glandulifera and I. capenis). The most common species of water-lily in the county is the yellow water-lily (Nuphar lutea), with its flask-shaped fruits, which gives it one of its alternative names of brandy-bottle. Although the white water-lily is encountered it is much less common than its yellow relative. Another frequently recorded aquatic plant is arrow-head (Sagittaria sagittifolia), which often grows in mid-stream, along with some species of pondweed, including Potamogeton natans, P. perfoliatus and P. pectinatus, together with amphibious persicaria (Polygonum persicaria), water milfoil (Myriophyllum spp) and the water crowfoots (Ranunculus spp).

Many of these aquatic species may be found along the fen ditches in the north-eastern part of the county, where the beautiful water violet (Hottonia palustris), once much more common, is still to be found. Small marshy areas which occurred throughout the county in the past, few of which survive to this day, provided suitable habitats for such species as grass of parnassus (Parnassia palustris) and marsh helleborine (Epipactis palustris), but they are no longer with us. Those small areas which still remain have some of the plants typical of such habitats, including marsh valerian (Valeriana dioica), marsh pennywort (Hydrocotyle vulgaris), red rattle (Pedicularis palustris), marsh arrow-grass (Triglochin palustris) and the marsh orchids (Dactylorchis praetermissa and D. incarnata).

Ironstone quarries and railway lines

Many of the disused Ironstone quarries, with their dumped calcareous overburden of estuarine clays, carry an alkaline type flora with such species as carline thistle (Carlina vulgaris), ploughman's spikenard (Inula conyza), bee orchid (Ophrys apifera), woolly thistle (Cirsium eriophorum), common centuary (Centarium erythraea) and blue fleabane (Erogeron acer). Disused railway lines have a similar type of flora where the soil is alkaline, together with such species as the mustards, including eastern rocket (Sisymbrium orientale) and tall rocket (S. altissimum). Where some ballast remains on the track thale cress (Arabidopsis thaliana), yellow toadflax (Linaria vulgaris) and the small toadflax (Chaenorrhinum minus) occur.

Man-made habitats (including gardens, walls and arable fields)
Many of our familiar garden weeds also occur in arable fields, but it is from the latter that many of our more attractive cornfield weeds have disappeared. Corn cockle (Agrostemma gigatho) has not been seen for many years, along with the corn flower (Centaurea cyanus). Such plants as the little umbellifer shepherd's needle (Scandix pecten-veneris) have become very scarce. In limestone areas it is still possible to find venus' looking-glass (Legousia hybrida), the two fluellens (Kickxia spuria and K. elatine) and night-flowering catchfly (Silene noctiflora). On the lightest soils corn marigolds (Chrysanthemum segetum) and poppies (Papaver rhoeas and P. dubium) are often a feature of cornfields in late summer.

In villages where stone walls have been neglected, they often support a surprising number of small plants. The attractive early forget-me-not (Myosotis hispida) and rueleaved saxifrage (Saxifraga tridactylites) occur in such habitats, often accompanied by small ferns, including wall rue (Asplenium ruta-muraria) and maidenhair fern (Asplenium trichomanes), together with other species such as spring whitlow grass (Arophila verna) and biting stonecrop (Sedum acre). No area of waste ground in towns and villages is without its quota of rose-bay willow-herb (Senecio squalidus), a plant that has been steadily spreading throughout the county over the last forty years or so. These are often accompanied by two species of mallow (Malva sylvestris and M. neglecta) as well as by white and red deadnettles (Lamium album and L. purpureum). A new element of our flora, now creeping in, is that of salt marsh plants colonising such road verges which are constantly sprayed with salt water from road gritting during the winter. An attractive little species is Danish scurvygrass (Cochlearia danica) which is spreading along the edges of our dual-carriageways and this has been recently joined by sea spurrey (Spergularia marina) and buck's horn plantain (Plantago coronopus) and other species are bound to follow in time.

The flora of the county is constantly changing, and although we may lose plants, perhaps through the destruction of a particular habitat, nevertheless new plants are being introduced in various ways. The overall picture of Northamptonshire's flora is never constant, but changes continuously due to a multitude of factors, too complex and too numerous to discuss here.

References

Druce, G.C. The Flora of Northamptonshire.
Gent, Gill, Wilson, Rob. Flora of Northamptonshire & The Soke of Peterborough. 1995. Robert Wilson Designs.
Lousley, A.E. Flora of Chalk and Limestone, Collins New Naturalist.
Salisbury, Sir J. Weeds and Aliens. Collins New Naturalist.
Perring, F. and Walters, M. Atlas of the British Flora. BSBI.

AMPHIBIANS AND REPTILES IN NORTHAMPTONSHIRE

Kenneth Blackwell and George Twisleton

Amphibians and Reptiles are poikilothermic/exothermic/cold-blooded vertebrates dependent upon the temperature of their environment as to whether they are active or torpid. Occupying a position on the evolutionary timescale between the cold-blooded fishes and the homeothermic/ endothermic/warm-blooded birds and mammals. Amphibians have naked skins and most go through an aquatic larval stage (tadpole) before metamorphosing into the adult animal. This is the case with the British species. Reptiles have scaly skins and begin life as miniature replicas of their parents. Some species develop from eggs deposited by the female in such places as compost heaps, where the rotting vegetation provides the temperature necessary for development and hatching. This is so with the grass snake. In other species development takes place within the female's body and the young emerge as tiny, independent, creatures.

The British Isles have thirteen indigenous Amphibians and Reptiles, albeit one of the amphibians may be on the brink of extinction, together with a number of introduced species, two of which are now included on the British list. Out of these possible species Northamptonshire can claim nine. One of the reptiles is retaining a precarious foothold, occurring only in the north-eastern tip of the county, some of its distribution being lost to Northamptonshire when the political boundary changes took place.

Records from the past indicate that Northamptonshire was never well endowed with either amphibians or reptiles compared with some other counties of Britain, and there has been a noticeable decline in the numbers of most species. This is largely due to the increasing expansion of the human population and modern farming methods.

The dependence of amphibians on water bodies for breeding has been adversely affected by the filling-in of ponds on new housing estates and on farms. Susceptibility to the effects of herbicides and pesticides has also led to a decline in numbers since their only food consists of invertebrates, which may have been in contact with these chemicals prior to being ingested.

During the last twenty plus years there has been a noticeable change in the habitats of both frogs and toads, with many natural ponds being destroyed (albeit there is now a move to create new field ponds). The greater populations of frogs and toads now occur in town and village garden ponds rather than in wild habitats. Although there is now an indication that the natural ponds that remain, together with disused gravel pits, are showing an increase in the numbers of tailless amphibians spawning there. Perhaps the next twenty years may see these animals recolonise their original habitats.

In the following species accounts, an attempt is made to indicate the present status of the animals in the county, together with pointers relating to their identification.

Tailed amphibians

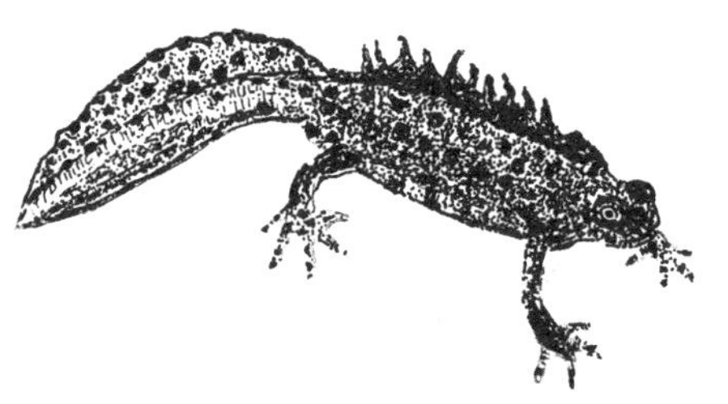

Great crested newt (Triturus cristatus). The largest of the three British newts. Distinguished from the other two species by its larger size, darker coloration, dark brown, greyish sometimes almost black, and the warty appearance of the skin. More aquatic than the other species. Local in distribution, but occurring throughout the county.

Since the introduction of The Wildlife and Countryside Act, this newt now receives complete protection in law, of the animal itself and its habitat. To legally handle the species a licence is required and its ponds are protected from development in cases such as town and industrial expansion.

It has been determined over recent years that groups of ponds within a limited area are important for its survival and that habitat fragmentation can lead to a colony dying out.

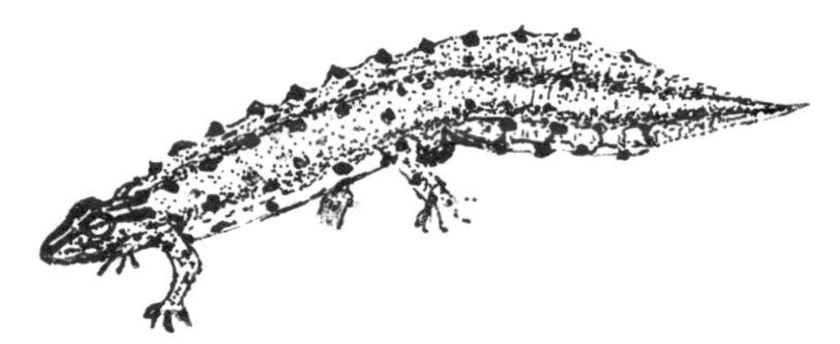

Common or smooth newt (Triturus vulgaris). This newt has a smooth skin, lighter coloration, light or dark olive green or brown, and is smaller in size than the crested newt. It is found in most water-bodies both natural and man-made, from deep vehicle ruts, garden ponds to reservoirs and flooded gravel pits. Only aquatic in the larval period and when adult during the breeding season. It is often found in gardens living a terrestrial life-style at other times of the year. The male at this time resembles the female, having no crest, which only develops during the aquatic phase of the breeding season. Both male and female are often mis-identified as lizards during the terrestrial phase. It is common throughout the county.

Palmate newt (Triturus helveticus). Very similar to the smooth newt, but smaller in size. Distinguished by lack of pigmented spots on the throat and by the abruptly truncated tail of the male, which in the aquatic phase ends in a thin black filament. The hind feet are dark and noticeably webbed. Previously believed to have been introduced into the county, recent research shows that this was incorrect and that it had escaped detection due to its small size, similarity to the smooth newt, and local distribution. Some six or seven sites are known.

All three species of newts have interesting breeding displays with the males attracting the females by an elaborate dance with much tail movement. Each of these displays terminates with a male depositing a sac of sperm which the female moves over and takes up into her cloaca. When the eggs are laid, individually, they are attached to, or wrapped in, the leaves of aquatic vegetation.

Tail-less amphibians

Common frog (Rana temporaria).
Distinguished from the toad by smoother skin, lighter coloration and pointed snout. More agile than the toad and often displaying a more nervous disposition. Its mode of progression is by hopping.

Spawn/eggs laid in clumps. Tadpoles lighter in colour than those of the toad and having more pointed tails. Once widespread in distribution in the countryside it is now mainly found in association with garden ponds. Naturally preferring damp meadows and open deciduous woodland. Numbers declined for reasons already noted plus the recently recorded mass mortality due to bacterial and fungal diseases. This problem is not confined to Northamptonshire, or for that matter, Britain, but is worldwide. Transferring spawn and adult animals is discouraged to reduce the risk of the spread of infection.

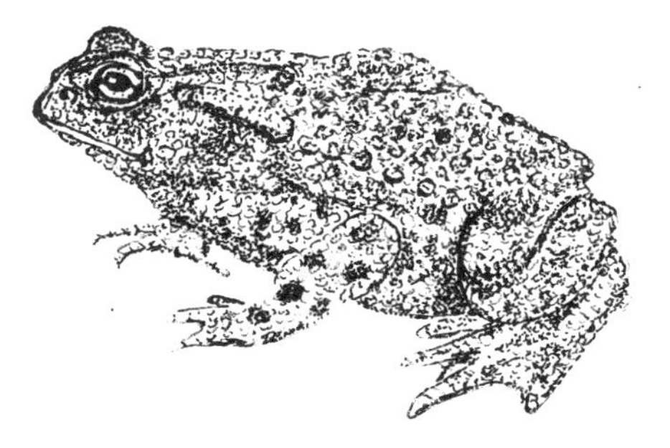

Common toad (Bufo bufo).
Darker than the frog with coarser, granular, warty-looking skin. Appearing less agile than the frog, with more deliberate movements. Crawling more often than hopping, but good at climbing. Often found in gardens whether ponds are present, or not. Tolerates drier conditions than the frog. Spawn/eggs laid in long twinned strings. Tadpoles darker than those of the frog with rounded tails. As with the frog, it is now under threat from diseases. Now quite often found in association with garden ponds, but because of pond preference still uses traditional spawning sites.

Reptiles

Common or viviparous lizard (Lacerta vivipara). Unlikely to be confused with any other reptile native to the county (but see note re smooth newt). Variable in coloration. More widely distributed than generally assumed, as shy and fast moving, unless in areas where there is constant movement of people, when it can become indifferent. Occurs throughout the county in small populations, in areas ranging from sunny banks, disused railway lines, woodland rides, and old stone walls to builder's yards. Actually occurring in Delapre Park (Northampton). The scales covering the body are noticeable when one is able to watch the animal. Produces live young.

Slow-worm (Anguis fragilis). A legless lizard, which should not be mistaken for a snake, but often, is. Eyes are small and lidded (snakes do not have eyelids). Occurs in small numbers in most woodlands of reasonable size throughout the county; rarely in large populations. Largely crepuscular spending daytime under stones, pieces of wood, etc., or buried in loose soil, emerging to feed at dusk. Can sometimes be seen basking in the early morning sun. Produces living young, which are golden in colour.

Both lizards feed on invertebrates, the slow-worm having a preference for slugs of the genus Deroceras.

Grass snake (Natrix natrix). Distinguished from the adder by it's generally lighter coloration, olive green or brownish with no prominent dorsal pattern other than a few small dark markings. Dark bars often occur along the sides of the body. A collar of yellow, which varies from pale lemon to almost orange in colour, is present immediately behind the head. A further black collar lies behind this and is commonly mistaken for the V-marking of the adder, but the dark zigzag dorsal marking is absent. Adults grow longer than adult adders and are more slender. The eye is large with a round pupil. The snake tends to occur in damp areas near lakes, rivers and ponds, since amphibians form its diet. It is still the most commonly recorded reptile despite the decline in numbers over the past forty years. It lays its eggs in decomposing vegetation such as manure heaps where the constant temperature aids incubation.

It is quite harmless, releasing its cloacal contents together with the secretion of the anal gland when handled. Apart from a disgusting smell it is also distasteful to predators. A further means of defence is 'death feigning' where it allows its body to become limp with mouth open, tongue extruded.

Adder (Vipera berus). Variable in coloration, but distinguishable from the grass snake by zigzag dorsal stripe and lack of yellow collar. It is sexually dimorphic with the male having darker/blacker markings, which are usually brown in the female. The eye is large, but the pupil is elliptical instead of round. It is a heavier looking snake than the grass snake and adults are shorter in length.

It produces live young. It feeds on lizards and small mammals. The presence of lizards being, seemingly, essential for its occurrence.

The political county boundary changes meant that part of its original distribution was lost to the county. Only known, with certainty, to occur in the north-eastern part of Northamptonshire. It is frequently reported from other areas but investigation leads to grass snakes, so far, that is. It is venomous and if seen should not be handled.

Suggested Further Reading

Smith, Malcolm. The British Amphibians and Reptiles New Naturalist Series No. 20. 1951 Collins.

Frazer, Deryk. Reptiles and Amphibians in Britain New Naturalist Series No. 69. 1983 Collins.

INSECTS IN NORTHAMPTONSHIRE

A B Drane

The geology of Northamptonshire's landscape dictates our flora, which in turn creates the rich diversity of the county's invertebrate fauna. For the most part, Northamptonshire's landscape is dominated by the rolling undulations of the heavy Boulder Clays laid down during the period of glaciation. Underlying this relatively recent deposit are limestones and ironstones which, when they are close to the surface or outcrop, create rich calcareous grasslands. These can be seen particularly well around Corby and in the Collyweston area in the north-east of the county. In the few remaining derelict quarry sites and unimproved grasslands scarce calciole plants and associated insects can be found and they are some of the county's natural treasures. Improved pasture and arable fields, which do not support a great diversity of insects, dominate much of the landscape and this may, in part, account for the under-recording of many groups in the past.

The Victoria County History list of insects, and particularly of beetles, is one of the shortest when compared with those of other counties. It has been unfortunate that many of the earlier entomologists have considered the county to be, albeit undeservedly, dull with regards insects. The county has some important old woodlands such as Salcey Forest, the remnants of the old Rockingham Forest in the north and the woods in the Silverstone area. However, coniferisation and removal of hardwoods have been major threats to Northamptonshire's deciduous woodland mosaic. Two habitats, which have been the focus for surveys in recent years, however, are indicating great interest in terms of their insect fauna. The first is the developing wetland along the Nene valley and the other is the fauna associated with old parkland and woodland trees. Many of our rarest insects are associated with dead wood and ancient trees and the work of the author in the county's large estate parks has shown that Northamptonshire has a rich saproxylic beetle fauna of national significance.

The group that has been best recorded, as is so often the case, is the Lepidoptera (or butterflies and moths) and the records show an interesting though declining population. Gent (1977) stated that there were "about 30 species (of butterfly) in the county, although this number would seem to be on the decline". Although the local Wildlife Trust has been successful in securing an increasing number of reserves, and has managed to preserve many key species, e.g. the Black Hairstreak at Glapthorn, agricultural practices and loss of habitat are still major obstacles to increased diversity and recovery of populations. Some, like the Chequered Skipper that used to be found in the woods near Oundle and Ashton, are probably gone forever. The large and beautiful Purple Emperor is currently reduced to a single definite site. However, Northamptonshire is one of the country's strongholds for the Wood White. Each year there is the arrival of a small number of migratory species and there are still old established favourites to be seen each year - the early Brimstones, Painted Lady and Red Admirals around buddleia bushes, with Speckled Woods flitting along woodland rides.

Left: Wood White on Ladies' Smock Right:Ringlet (female)
Sketches by P J Gent

A group that have been largely over-looked in the past, but which is becoming increasingly significant, particularly in their use for habitat assessment, is the Coleoptera (or beetles). Gent (1977) highlighted three kinds - the bark beetles largely responsible for the spread of Dutch elm disease, ladybirds and the glow worms. In brief a reflection on these: the country's elms are still in decline although young growth can be seen in hedges and woods. However, it will still be a long time before we will see again the stately elms, which graced our landscape forty years ago. Ladybirds abound and rare species have been discovered in the last few years. Glow worms are relatively widespread, although much more often found as larvae than as glowing flightless females or drab flying males. Any new review would want to focus on some of the nationally scarce species which have been discovered recently and which are documented in Northamptonshire's Red Data Book produced by the Wildlife Trust in 1996. For example, the county is a stronghold for two RDB1 bark beetles, one of which is associated with old lime trees in estate parklands, and the other with coppiced limes. The derelict quarries in the north of the county contain an interesting range of ground beetles including an RDB1 species, and the Collyweston Quarry grassland reserve is the only current site of a small cryptophagid, which lives on Genista. Hay refuse near Helmdon produced a staphylinid (or rove beetle) new to Britain as well as an RDB3 colydiid beetle. Increasingly, Northamptonshire's beetle fauna is emerging as rich and important, although the small and obscure appearance of many of the rarer species does not allow them to be readily appreciated by the general naturalist. The key issue is one of the conservation of the habitats where they occur if the county's bio-diversity is to be preserved. With the pressures from expansion in building programmes, conversion to arable land use and the filling of quarry sites, the need for environmental protection and conservation has never been more crucial.

Unlike our neighbouring county of Cambridgeshire, Northamptonshire is not rich in relict (primitive) wetlands and fens. The development of flooded gravel workings along the Nene, is however producing a valuable habitat for invertebrate exploitation in the future. As with so many counties, Northamptonshire has lost many farm ponds, and the drive to return disused quarries to usable land in the 1970's and 80's led to a loss of important water bodies which were rich in amphibians and invertebrates. The old quarry at Newton contained in excess of fifty species of water beetle. The straightening and channelling of rivers, as in parts of the Welland, reduces annual flooding of marginal land and increases water flow to the detriment of invertebrates. The occasional pollution of some of the smaller rivers, such as the Ise, has also affected invertebrate populations. Against this background of threat there is increasing evidence that where aquatic habitats are preserved they support a flourishing and important population of flies, dragonflies, damsel flies, beetles and aquatic bugs. Through the work of the Wildlife Trust, awareness of the importance of these habitats is growing, both with the water companies and many land owners.

Flower-rich meadows, hedgerows - unfortunately declining through their grubbing out to make ever large fields - and woodland rides are an important but threatened habitat which contain a wealth of invertebrates. One of the marvellous sights on a summer walk is to see the jostling throng of wasps, bees, flies, beetles and butterflies on the flat white umbels of hogweed and wild angelica. The abundance and diversity is directly related to the richness of the flora and the minimal influence of agro-chemicals and road-associated pollutants. Similarly influenced are the grasshoppers and crickets, bugs and leaf hoppers and the moths and butterflies of unimproved grasslands. One of the other groups most sensitive to changes in land use and chemical application are the meadow and field ants which often host other scarce invertebrates and modify floral patterns. Conversion to arable land has been very detrimental to such populations, which 'set aside' has only partially ameliorated. Frequently re-colonisation does not take place once the habitat has been fundamentally changed, especially where there are no adjacent stocks to aid recovery. Nationally, unimproved grassland is one of our most threatened habitats.

Despite the threats posed from past and present activities, Northamptonshire's invertebrate fauna is still diverse and contains elements of national importance. With the increased knowledge and recording co-ordinated by the Wildlife Trust declines may be halted and improvements made to populations which are currently precariously placed. The more detailed work on precise habitat requirements and the consequent implications for site management is making conservation efforts more effective and scientific. There are productive partnerships between conservation bodies, local authorities and landowners. Forest Enterprise is much more concerned with deciduous forestry rather than the creation of the arid dark coniferous plantations of the past. Water companies are concerned about water quality and often work together with wildlife organisations. Farmers are looking critically at the high usage of chemicals with many being willing to leave areas to develop naturally. Estate owners are starting to appreciate their heritage of the invertebrates associated with their veteran trees and coming to understand the importance of leaving dead wood in situ. The pressures on Northamptonshire's environment are increasing with little 'wilderness' to form a rallying point for public support. However, the pockets of woodland, grassland, wetland and parkland are of paramount importance if they, and their rich flora and invertebrate populations, are to survive to enrich our county's countryside.

FOOTPATHS IN NORTHAMPTONSHIRE

Maurice Tebbutt

To spend a complete day, or even just an hour or two, exploring the rights of way in the county is a pastime that is well worthwhile. Northamptonshire cannot hope to compete with the open moorlands, wild mountains or rugged coastlines of other parts of the British Isles; nevertheless the county offers a wealth of variety in interest and scenery best viewed from our rights of way network.

An autumn afternoon on the old footpath to Geddington Station (now closed and redundant).
Photograph by Bob Coles

What are rights of way and what can we see on them? There are three categories, viz. footpaths (1341 miles/2158 kilometres), available to pedestrians only; bridleways (506 miles/814 kilometres) for pedestrians, horse riders and cyclists (cyclists must give way to riders and pedestrians), and a strangely-named category, by-ways open to all traffic (65 miles/105 kilometres). Historically, the latter were unmetalled roads used by horse-drawn carts and carriages and referred to as 'green lanes', 'drift roads' or 'white roads'. In Northamptonshire alone there is a total of 1912 miles (3077 kilometres) of rights of way! Each stretch is waiting to be used as often as any interested person wishes to venture forth. It is worth remembering that these rights of way are highways in law, and enjoy the same legal status as any other public road.

How many times have you seen a green post with a green arm attached bearing either the words 'public footpath' or 'public bridleway' standing in the hedgerow - sometimes almost obscured by vegetation - and pointing across the fields to some distant settlement? And have you ever paused to wonder why it is there? These signs are called fingerposts and mark the start of all public footpaths and bridleways from the metalled road.

Why not be adventurous and set off to find out more? Cross the stile or pass through the gate by the fingerpost and immediately you will enter a different world. Follow the path and you may be able to see the way others have walked. Maybe you can see the next stile or gate, and your route may be waymarked with black and white discs. Care must of course be taken not to cause damage to crops or allow stock to stray (see the Country Code page 143) because you are now entering the world of the farmer. As the footpath crosses the fields you will be able to see the way in which the farmer utilises his land. Some fields will be down to grass for his animals; others will be set with crops at various stages of growth. Walk slowly and quietly and the wildlife can be observed. Look at the ground, in the hedgerows and at the trees, and at the enormous variety of flora and fauna which is not found within our towns.

Between Rothwell and Desborough
Photograph by Bob Coles

The county's network of rights of way goes from north to south, east to west, and is generally denser towards the south and west of the county, but every parish has some public rights of way.

In addition to short routes, the county has introduced some named local long distance routes, during the last thirty years. The first of these was the Knightley Way, dedicated in the early 1960's. This delightful 12 mile (19 kilometre) route, between Badby and Greens Norton, passes through Badby Woods and Fawsley Park. The Grafton Way, also 12 miles (19 kilometres) long, was opened shortly after the Knightley Way, and links with it at Green Norton, taking the walker on to Cosgrove. On the Cosgrove Aqueduct over the Grand Union Canal the Grafton Way joins the North Bucks Way.

Since these early paths were established others have followed including the Nene Way (Badby to Wansford - and joining up with the Sir Peter Scott Way to the Wash), the Jurassic Way (Banbury to Stamford passing across the 'spine' of our county south west to north east), and the Brampton Valley Way (Northampton to the outskirts of Market Harborough using the bed of the former railway), and are the most significant of the county's other long distance routes. In addition two national long distance routes pass through Northamptonshire - the Midshires Way (Chequers in the Chiltern Hills to Stockport) and the Macmillan Way (Boston to Abbotsbury in Dorset). The first of these is the only long distance route to cater for walkers, riders and cyclists, and because of this the route splits in places in order to afford a more suitable way for horses and cyclist. The Macmillan Way, opened in 1996, is the second longest path in the whole of the United Kingdom. All of these routes are well signed and distinctly marked throughout Northamptonshire.

Equally important is the network of local paths, and you will find that many of these have been waymarked throughout with black and white discs at strategic places. It was the county's aim, in accordance with Government directions, to have ALL paths open and in good order by the end of 1999. Sadly, the target was not be fully met, but strenuous efforts are being made to meet it early this century.

One type of path that is easily overlooked, but which should not be forgotten is the town path. By exploring the 'backs' of Northampton, Kettering or Wellingborough by footpath the history of each town soon springs to life. These town paths shed new light on the old towns and show how earlier residents would have seen it as they went about their business.

Why have we got this network of rights of way and do we still need them? The answer to the second part of the question is a resounding 'yes'. These paths form an important part of our heritage and provide a wonderful and healthy escape from the hustle and bustle of the town. How else can we get to know what is happening on the other side of the hedgerow? These footpaths and bridleways, which are such an important part of our past, are not peculiar to Northamptonshire. In England and Wales their total length is in excess of 140,00 miles (225,302 kilometres), and all are available to the general public. There is no need to go abroad for your holidays! Many of these rights of way are steeped in history, and were the ancient routes for travellers and pilgrims heading for distant markets and ports. In our county the Banbury Lane - a green lane - was a drove road and was used to drive cattle from Wales to the rich pastures of Northamptonshire for fattening before slaughter and the markets before the railways came. In other counties the Welsh Road and the Salt Way come to mind. However, the majority of footpaths were used for local purposes - workers getting to farms or factories in nearby towns, children going to school, the housewife bound for market, and people going to church and chapel. For others it was sometimes the most direct way to the nearest inn, and in the last century often the quickest way to the railway station.

In earlier times, when the main mode of transport was by foot, the footpath network grew in extent as villages began to spread and hamlets sprung up. In many instances the original needs for these routes have now gone, outdated and outmoded by the advent of the motor car and other means of transport. But the emphasis now is on recreational use. The Government's latest general household survey shows that 4 in 10 adults regularly go for a walk of two miles (3.5 kilometres) or more for pleasure.

Walking is recognised as being a very cost-effective way of enjoying recreation, available to all ages in a non-competitive way. To make the best use of the rights of way network, it is a good idea to purchase maps published by the Ordnance Survey, and the most useful ones when walking are the Pathfinder and Explorer maps, at a scale of 2.5 inches to the mile. These maps show all public rights of way, the information being regularly updated from the county council that holds complete and accurate definitive records.

Having set the scene, and put these rights of way into their historical context, it is now time to follow the path that maybe we have often wondered about. Predictably we know where it starts, where it goes and how to get there, but what we will see on the way remains something of a mystery.

Further information on rights of way, walks and groups organising rambles will be found in the Countryside Directory section of the book on page 143.

Taking a break on the bridge over the River Ise at Arthingworth.
Photograph by Bob Coles

INDUSTRIAL ARCHAEOLOGY OF NORTHAMPTONSHIRE

Geoffrey Starmer

Introduction

Industrial archaeology is concerned with the study of the physical evidence of past industrial activities. These include the provision of raw materials, the production of all kinds of goods and commodities (from pins and machines to clothing and footwear, food and drink) transport and services such as gas, electricity and water supply. This evidence often has an all-too-obvious effect on the environment but in many cases the environment will have influenced the siting of these activities as, for example, watermills and windmills. The environmental factors can be grouped into three main categories: (a) those remaining below the normal ground level, e.g. quarries and mines; (b) those more or less at the normal ground level, e.g. watercourses to a former mill; (c) those which are above the normal ground level. Usually these will be buildings but this group will also include bridges and railway or canal embankments.

Before giving examples of these features occurring in Northamptonshire it must be emphasised that industrial archaeology is concerned with more than these environmental features. The machinery, equipment, tools, other artefacts and, if possible, the processes performed on sites and inside buildings must be studied if full advantage is to be taken of the evidence and this must be complemented by a study of the documentary sources and of people. Although a significant proportion of industrial activities have been sited in urban areas, this short chapter will focus on those which were to be found in the countryside or the smaller towns of Northamptonshire.

Raw materials and basic processes

The extraction of materials for building stone, clay (for bricks, tile and drainage pipe making) and, since the 1850's, iron ore, has left a number of significant features on the Northamptonshire landscape.

Stone

There is documentary record of quarrying building stone at Weldon, near Corby, in the Rockingham Forest accounts of 1275, and since the mid-fifteenth century the stone was used for several colleges in Cambridge, including

King's College Chapel. Until the 1970s there were impressive remains of both open and underground quarries at Weldon, either side of the Kettering Road, south-west of the village. These were almost entirely obliterated by subsequent iron ore extraction but a reminder of early building stone quarrying is to be found in the early fourteenth century stained glass figure of a stone mason in the head of the Y-tracery of one of the windows on the north side of the nave of Helmdon church. Stone from the Helmdon quarries was used for buildings at Easton Neston, Blenheim, Woburn and Stowe but quarrying had virtually ceased by the nineteenth century and little physical evidence survives after filling in the deep quarries in the late 1950s.

At one time Duston, on the north-west side of Northampton, had several important quarries for building stone and some idea of the depth of working is obtained from the sunken fields on the south-west side of the Upper Harlestone road from New Duston (SP 712629).

Stone slates for roofing have been obtained from Collyweston since the fourteenth century. Although some stone has been dug from open cast workings the usual method has been by means of tunnels (known locally as 'fox-holes') from the bottom of an open shaft. Some of these are still to be seen in the series of long, narrow, stone-walled plots running west from a trackway heading north from the A43 road about half a mile towards Stamford from the centre of the village. (TF 001034). The fissile stone was quarried only during a period of about six weeks in December and January, so that the stone could be laid out on the surface to allow the winter frosts to accelerate the natural cleavage. Keeping the stone damp helped the process and hand pumps for supplying the water may be found at the site of some of the former stone yards. A pump for a similar purpose can be seen at the rear of the Blisworth Stone Works, a pleasing stone building having this title carved across the side it presents to the Stoke Bruerne road about half a mile south of the main A43 road in the village (SP 730529). This is one of the few examples of above-the-ground remains of the county's stone quarrying activities.

In the past limestone was quarried extensively for burning in kilns for agricultural or building purposes. In the early nineteenth century there were extensive lime-works at Kingsthorpe and Duston, supplying an area almost to the edge of Leicestershire. Other large lime-works were at Abington (then in the country), Blisworth, Hardwick and Moulton and it was said there were a great many private kilns kept by farmers for their own use. In 1922 in a survey of lime resources he made for the County Council, Beeby Thompson listed about 180 kilns. Sixty five of these were along the Grand Junction Canal for easy supply of coal, but only three of these were still in use. Twenty eight were at work elsewhere in the county including eleven on one site at Wakerley (SP 961 996), many of which survive although very overgrown.

Clay and brickmaking

A large number of geologically different clays have been used for brickmaking in Northamptonshire but the most widely used strata was that of the Upper Lias, on which the majority of the larger brickworks, and many small yards, were located. There were extensive works in open country at Corby, Irthlingborough, Kettering, Northampton, Rushden and Wellingborough but the sites are now covered by urban development. In making bricks, the clay is dug from the ground, calcareous nodules are extracted by washing and settling, the clay is made homogeneous in pug mills, and then formed by moulding, pressing or extrusion with wire cutting into 'green' bricks or tiles. After drying these are burnt to give the hard and relatively durable bricks or tiles. In early times the bricks were burnt in clamps but later, kilns of various types were used.

Despite the identification of over 130 brickmaking sites in the county, there is little surviving physical evidence. Even very extensive clay pits such as at Blisworth and Gayton have been used as landfill sites for urban rubbish. One survival, although flooded and providing a facility for various water recreation activities, is at the site of the former Easton Neston Estates & Mining Co. Ltd. (SP 705 510). Remains of the circular clay washer are to be found west of the footpath heading south from river end of Wharf Lane, Higham Ferrers (SP 951 686). Of the large brick kilns, nothing is to be seen but there is a ruined updraught kiln at Denford (SP 999 769) and derelict downdraught kilns at Great Doddington (SP 883 646) and Harlestone (SP 695 641)

Iron ore

The greatest below-the-surface effects in the county have come from the exploitation of the Northampton Sand Ironstone for iron smelting. Although iron had been smelted in the county in Pre-Roman times, it was the search by Black Country ironmasters for fresh supplies to replace their dwindling local resources that led to the nineteenth century development of the Northamptonshire iron ore industry. Initially The Black Country industry seemed unable to smelt the ore satisfactorily, and the furnaces in Derbyshire and Nottinghamshire were amongst the first to take supplies from the county.

Iron ore working was closely linked with developments in transport, and it was the cutting of the then Grand Junction Canal, near Blisworth Tunnel, at the beginning of the nineteenth century, that seemed to reveal the existence of iron ore there. The outcrop of these early pits was conveyed to Stanton Ironworks, near Ilkeston, by canal.

For most of that century, the iron ore was extracted entirely by hand methods. The top soil, and then separately, the overburden, was removed by hand-shovelling into barrows which would be pushed precariously along planks supported on trestles across the quarry, for filling into the area from which the iron ore had been taken. The men would then level the overburden, and smooth out the soil on top so that the ground in the worked out area was level and ready for agricultural use. The only sign that the iron ore had been removed was the surface of the land being some distance below adjoining fields or roads. Many of the early pits worked shallow deposits near to the surface so that the relatively small difference in levels is now hard to distinguish. Some of the deeper workings have left groups of farm buildings isolated on small "islands" rising above the surrounding land from which the iron ore had been taken. This is particularly noticeable at Slipton, near Thrapston, where the buildings at the north of the village, east of the road to Sudborough, are at road level, whilst the land behind them drops steeply as the result of the Islip Iron Company's operations. (SP 951 795).

In 1895 Lloyds Ironstone Co. at Corby put the first steam-powered machine to work in a Northamptonshire iron ore quarry. Supplemented later by steam engine driven transporters to take the overburden from the excavator at the working face across the quarry to drop it into the worked-out pit, the machines made it uneconomic to level and restore the land. The result was the hill and dale formation on which it became the practice to plant conifers as the only way of using the spoilt land. Instances of this exist near Corby on both sides of the A43 Stamford road, north of Stanion. The most easily accessible example is in the County Council's Irchester Country Park, which is located in an old ironstone quarry on the north side of the road running west from Irchester to the A509 road south of Little Irchester. Since the Second World War, legislation has ensured that the land behind working quarries is restored as soon as possible. Subsequently, many of the quarries left derelict since before this legislation have also been restored.

Although most of the iron was obtained by open-cast working, there have been a number of underground iron mines in Northamptonshire. All appear to have been entered from horizontal adits. The cuttings or gullets from which these adits were driven can be seen in a number of places: to the east of the lane north of Slipton, near Thrapston, and to the south of the track leading south-east from the southern area of Finedon. The most extensive, and also the most modern underground mines in the county, were started in 1918 by the Ebbw Vale Steel, Iron and Coal Co Ltd at Irthlingborough. The workings are 80-100 feet (24- 30 metres) below the surface and the tunnels, laid out on a rectangular pattern, gradually extended to more than 45 miles (72 kilometres). The entrance was from an adit about 0.25 mile (0.4 kilometres) south east of the Irthlingborough to Wellingborough road. The mines closed on 30 September 1965, the surface buildings demolished and the adit blocked for safety reasons as at other mines, but a circular brick wall in the middle of a field between Irthlingborough and Finedon is a reminder of the ventilation shaft serving the underground workings.

By the 1920's Northamptonshire's ores accounted for almost 25% of the total British output, and reached a record 10.5 million tons in 1942, just over half of the entire output from British mines and quarries. By the mid-1970s most of the iron ore workings had closed and when the last of the British Steel quarries around Corby closed on 4 January 1980, the Northamptonshire iron industry came to an end. A few of the quarries have survived because of alternative uses for recreational purposes. Mention has been made of the Irchester Quarries and part of the former Richard, Thomas and Baldwin Ltd's workings at Finedon has become a pocket park (SP 913 723) with access from the recreation ground. The workings on Hunsbury Hill, which closed as long ago as 1921, were virtually undisturbed until taken into the Country Park of that name. Although the Northamptonshire Ironstone Railway Trust now operates trains in the park, hardly any of its line corresponds to the course of the tramway for the Hunsbury Hill Iron Co. However a small part of the original course may be followed as a footpath north of the gardens of houses in Hunsbury Close and leads to exposed faces of Northampton Sand Ironstone and the end of the worked face close to the Towcester Road (SP 742 581). Another significant survival is the 70 - 80 feet (22 - 25m) deep Twywell pit of the Islip Iron Co. that ceased production early in 1948 but was recognised by the 1980s as a Site of Special Scientific Interest.

Ironmaking

Reference has already been made to the smelting of iron in the county in earlier times, and evidence for this occurs in scatters of slag in many places. Excavations have revealed the bases of primitive furnaces and small iron working hearths. In these early small furnaces, the ores were reduced to iron by smelting with charcoal. The charcoal burning from the local timber made such inroads into Rockingham Forest and other areas that during the reign of Elizabeth I, laws were passed forbidding the making of charcoal in this and other areas of the country. This brought to an end the small-scale production of iron in Northamptonshire, and when the industry was re-started after an experimental furnace was opened in Northampton in 1851, the production of iron was concentrated at a number of ironworks in the county. At various times there were twelve of these, with several others proposed, but not built. The twelve were at Corby (SP 896895), Cransley (SP 849776), Finedon (SP 895732), Heyford (SP 654578), Hunsbury Hill, Northampton (SP 731593), Irthlingborough (SP 907677), Islip (SP 969782), Kettering (SP 860802), Stowe (SP 652578), Towcester (SP 693503), Wellingborough, East End (SP 895682) and Wellingborough (SP 902694).

The Corby furnaces were the last to be in blast and were closed down at the end of 1979 and the site cleared. Little is to be seen of the county's other iron making sites. Possibly the most significant survivals are at Heyford where the bases of three furnaces are in a line across rough ground between the railway and the canal ((SP 654578). Passing the site, the buildings alongside the road, show their industrial origin by the windows. Furnace Lane in the village is another reminder of the iron smelting here between 1857 and 1891. The furnaces were eventually dismantled in 1898.

Processing the products of the land

Although farming and forestry are embraced by the description of industrial archaeology given in the introduction, space here is too limited to discuss their archaeology. Nevertheless, the processing of four products of the land: wheat, barley, hides and skins, and timber have led to significant features in the landscape: flour mills, maltings, tanneries and saw mills.

Milling

Milling involves crushing the grain to break away the bran coat and make the endosperm (or inside of the grain) into fine particles, often followed by separating the bran from the flour. The traditional method was to pass the grain into the eye of a horizontal stone rotating over a fixed stone, so that the grain was ground into a mixture of bran and flour as it reached the periphery of the stones. Rotating the upper stone and driving cleaning and separating machinery could be by animal, water, wind or, later, steam power.

The Domesday survey of 1086 records 161 mills in Northamptonshire but it is believed that some of these were animal powered. Over 170 watermill sites have so far been identified, the majority being along the River Nene. In 1885 there were 80 watermills still in commercial operation but the number dwindled until there was none at work after the Second World War. Many have been demolished or converted to an extent that they show nothing of their original purpose, even of the man-made watercourse that provided their livelihood. Although the county now has no preserved water corn mills

(Ashton Mill, near Oundle, is described later under Services) there are a number of examples where alternate use has not made significant changes to the external appearance: Holdenby Mill, alongside the road to Spratton (SP 703 689); Kislingbury (SP 694 594) where the later brick mill adjoins an older stone building adjacent to the river; Wadenhoe Mill (TL 013 834) with its long straight leat from the River Nene and the pattern of tie plates on the downstream side; and Warmington (TL 074 916) an example of the very large mills found as one goes further downstream along the River Nene.

Wadenhoe Mill *Photograph by Geoffrey Starmer*

There are a number of mills with some machinery but these are in private hands and there is no public access, except at the Billing Mill (on the outskirts of Northampton) (SP 814611), now a public house, where the water wheel and transmission machinery may be viewed behind glass.

Windmills came later. One of the earliest in the country, if not Europe, was erected at Drayton, near Daventry about 1165. Nearly 200 windmill sites have been identified in Northamptonshire although not all of these would have had a windmill at any one time. Windmills are of two basic types: the post mill where the building housing the milling machinery and carrying the windmill sails, rotates on a post; and the tower mill where the sails are carried on a rotating cap to enable them to catch the wind whilst the machinery is in the tower. There now are no remains of post mills in the county, the last being at Bozeat, which collapsed early in 1949 after having ceased work about 1918.

There are upstanding remains of twelve tower mills although most have been so altered by additions for house conversions that they are hardly recognisable. Making a visible contribution to the landscape are those at Hellidon (SP 519 578), and Braunston (SP 538 662), still six storeys high despite being reduced in height from its new-built condition of about 1810.

In 1788 a Boulton & Watt steam engine was installed in the water mill at Sulgrave (SP 556 4570. This was the very first steam engine in the county, pre-dating a similar engine installed in the Northampton Cotton Mill by nine years. Although the Sulgrave mill had reverted to water power by 1800, other water mills began to use steam engines as supplementary power. By 1885 eighteen of the watermills and windmills in commercial operation were also using steam power whilst seven mills were entirely dependent on steam engines. One of these was the large mill built by the canal at Blisworth by Joseph Westley and now converted into residential units (SP 724 533). The following year the Victoria Mills were built at Little Irchester (SP 902 666), a site chosen for water, road and rail transport, and from the start used steam power for its roller milling plant. Such large mills not dependent on water or wind for power, using modern milling methods instead of the traditional horizontal stones, and having easily accessible transport routes, caused the decline of the smaller local mills. The 1886 Victoria Mills are still at work, but using electricity instead of steam engines.

Victoria Mills, Little Irchester, Wellingborough
Photograph by Geoffrey Starmer

Maltings

Although barley was milled for animal food, it was also converted to malt for brewing by steeping in water, laid out on floors to cause rapid growth and then heated in a kiln. The long building for the 'growing' floors, and the pyramid roof capped by a cowl over the kiln, gave a distinctive appearance to maltings and records show there were a considerable number in operation throughout the county during the nineteenth century. The increase in size of the common brewers in towns led to the development of large maltings there, as can be seen at Northampton either side of the river at West Bridge, although now used for other purposes. This led to the closure of the small rural maltings and the proportions of the main buildings lent themselves to easy conversion to houses and the name 'The Maltings' is a frequently met on houses in the county's villages. Unconverted maltings might be used for barns or stores and then the main features for the malting process may be distinguished inside the building. Such was the case with the malting at Astrop (SP 505 364), on the west side of Kings Sutton, where the continuous roof line gives no hint of a kiln, yet inside was the steeping cistern, and the furnace with perforated kiln tiles above. A glimpse of a traditional kiln, although topped by a cylindrical brick chimney, may be had by looking to the right as one enters Oundle from the south (TL 037 879). This was part of the maltings at the Anchor Brewery in South Road but is on private property, preventing closer public access.

Leather

Leather is produced from the skins and hides of animals. The aim is to stop the skin putrifying, but at the same time to preserve the flexibility and durability of the material. Most early leather was made by drying and salting skins, but by the eleventh century oak bark was being used to produce a tannic acid based 'liquor' for treating the hides of cattle. Tanning operations took a long time, using a lot of water and requiring a lot of pits. In the excavation of the Saxon site south of St Peter's Church by the Northampton Development Corporation's archaeologists, a series of these early tan pits was discovered.

The main requirements for the production of leather were: (a) Plentiful supply of skins and hides; (b) Oak bark for preparing the tanning liquor; (c) Adequate supplies of pure water. The wide lowland areas of the Nene Valley provided for large numbers of cattle grazing on the long rich grass. Nearby were ample oakwoods to yield the bark, and the river itself gave an adequate supply of water. With the additional advantage that the clay subsoil made the construction of tan-pits easy, the Northamptonshire environment was peculiarly favourable for the development of tanning and the area rose to a leading position in the seventeenth century.

The movement of hides in the pits, and the subsequent activities by the currier working in oils and grease to produce the finished leather, were all manual operations until the nineteenth century. The only use of power was in grinding the oak bark and there is reference to a Leather Mill on the River Nene near Ecton, in the eighteenth century. In Wellingborough in 1869 Jotto Page erected a building for leather production on the site of Little Mill on the River Ise, at the end of Mill Road (SP 905685). This housed a waterwheel driving overhead shafting for the machines although in 1918 a new chimney was constructed, presumably for a newly installed steam engine.

In the late nineteenth century it was found that leather could be tanned by using chromium salts. The process of chrome tanning in rotating drums took about two weeks instead of the old method of 'a year and a day'. The process was introduced into Northampton by the firm of Petits in 1898. Gradually the new process took over from pit tanning and was concentrated in a smaller number of tanneries. The rural and village tanneries closed, although street names sometimes recall the vanished industry, for example Skin Yard and Hyde Park, side by side in Earls Barton.

Saw mills

The presence of extensive wooded areas in some parts of Northamptonshire led to the exploitation of this for various purposes, ranging from fuel for domestic fires to use in furniture and building and even ship building. Cutting down trees, and reducing the trunk to usable wood, for example, in the form of planks was all by human muscle and the census returns of sawyers in places such as Syresham, Wappenham and Silverstone show a peak in 1851 as the demand for wood in the towns had increased but before the general use of steam engine-driven sawing machinery. The cost of this moved the saw mills to the larger towns but some of the county's estates with extensive woodlands set up their own saw mills, as at Geddington for the Boughton Estate, alongside the road to Grafton Underwood (SP 897 827) where the yard was provided with a steam-powered reciprocating horizontal saw. Since World War II the saw mills in the large towns have closed down whilst those in the rural areas such as Silverstone and Brixworth, and on the edge of Brackley, have flourished.

Manufacturing

For many centuries some food and drink needs of those living in the country were met by the local butcher, baker and, after domestic brewing declined, by the brewing victualler to sell only from his own premises. The blacksmith, carpenter and wheelwright met the need for ordinary artefacts. All of these could be described as craftsmen employing none other than their own family except for a single journeyman or apprentice. Their premises had few distinguishing characteristics, for example windowless walls around the baker's oven, or unusually large windows at the workbench of the carpenter or blacksmith, as can be seen at the Culworth Forge (SP 543 470) and the former blacksmith's shop at Yardley Hastings (SP 866 568). During the nineteenth century there was an increasing tendency for these manufacturing activities to be carried on by larger businesses, the 'industrialist' having specialised premises, using machinery and employing large numbers of people, as has already been described with the move from the village mill to the large steam mills. The main manufacturing industries in Northamptonshire have been for textiles and clothing, footwear, engineering and brewing.

Textiles

Until the early nineteenth century the textile industry was important in Northamptonshire, as in many other counties. Since this was mainly domestically based there is little to be found of this aspect. However, almost the final stage of the woollen industry was the process of fulling where the woven cloth was first cleaned and then pounded in water so as to bring the fibres closer together. This 'fulling' process was initially done by human effort, such as stamping on the immersed cloth but it was an operation that lent itself to mechanisation to be powered by water wheels. An early reference to a fulling mill in the county is in 1274 at Billing. There were at least fifteen fulling mills in the county, including one at Ashton, near Oundle (TL 051 882) where in 1602 there were three corn mills and a fulling mill all under the same roof. Another was at Woodford near Thrapston, the building of which still stands by the side of the road to Ringstead (SP 973 752).

Woodford Upper Mill was one of several of the county's fulling mills to be converted to a paper mill as the woollen industry declined. In the seventeenth and eighteenth centuries paper was made from rags, made into a pulp by pounding in water and the water-powered machines for fulling could be adapted to papermaking. There were at least nine paper mills in Northamptonshire, including Rush Mills on the River Nene, in Hardingstone parish, where in 1840 the paper for the first 'Penny Black' postage stamps were made. The site (SP 777 593) was just north of the Britannia Inn, on the Bedford Road out of Northampton.

Another first in the county was the first water powered cotton mill in the world, which was set up at Northampton in 1742 but eventually was a commercial failure, and the industry developed in Derbyshire and then Lancashire.

Clothing

The clothing industry developed in the county during the latter part of the nineteenth century. This centred on Kettering and Wellingborough but the large companies there established branch factories in nearby villages. Surviving buildings remain at Cottingham (SP 848 903) and the surprisingly narrow factory at Brigstock (SP 945 856). A number of local co-operative societies had clothing factories but the large former corset factory in Desborough (SP 801 828) was owned by the Co-operative Wholesale Society.

Footwear manufacture

Until the seventeenth century boots and shoes were made in Northamptonshire on the same scale as everywhere else in the country. The numbers of shoemakers in each town or large village would be sufficient to serve only their own community or its periodic market. In 1642 Parliament ordered 4,000 shoes and 600 boots for the army from Northamptonshire, which meant making shoes wholesale. By 1726 Daniel Defoe, when referring to regional products, quoted shoes from Northampton, but during the eighteenth century shoe manufacturing in the town was on a smaller scale than the production of regional goods elsewhere. The supply of footwear to the army and navy during the American War of Independence (1775-1783), seems to have brought about an increase in the number of shoemakers in the county, and there was a boom in the shoe industry following the increased demand for shoes from Northamptonshire after the outbreak of war with France in 1793. After the end of the Napoleonic Wars, the Northampton shoe industry entered a period of growth, which continued until the end of the nineteenth century. This was partly due to the London shoemakers demanding such high wages that the London dealers placed orders outside the capital. Victor Hatley, in a statistical survey of shoemakers in Northamptonshire, published in 1971, notes that by 1831 a third of the men living in Northampton were shoemakers, and by 1871, this proportion had risen to just over two-fifths.

Former clothing factory, Brigstock. Photograph Geoffrey Starmer

The development of the shoe industry elsewhere in Northamptonshire followed a similar pattern. The industry was established in Wellingborough before 1760, and between then and 1780 spread to Earls Barton, Higham

Ferrers, Rushden, Raunds and Wollaston. Shoe manufacturing was established in Daventry in the late eighteenth century. At Kettering, Thomas Gotch established a shoe manufacturing business in 1778, and developed this on army contracts. Although this firm passed to his son in 1806, it remained the only footwear firm in the town until 1857, when the firm collapsed through the family's bankruptcy. A number of small firms were set up to produce shoes to fill the vacuum left by the demise of the Gotch business, and the footwear industry in Kettering began to grow.

In the early years of the industry, shoe making was entirely a hand process. The main operations in making a shoe are: Cutting out the uppers from leather (clicking); Stitching the upper parts together (closing); Drawing the upper over the last to give the three dimensional shape of the foot (lasting); Stitching it together to the insole (welt sewing); Cutting the sole: stitching on the sole (sole attaching); Trimming, scouring and colouring the edges, soles and heels (finishing). The 'master' of the business cut out the leather, and the making of the shoe was done by journeymen, helped by an apprentice on minor operations. Since this could be done in a single room of the premises where the master lived, shoemaking on this scale would have little effect on the environment. With increase in production, a 'domestic' or 'outwork' system evolved in which the uppers were cut and sometimes closed at the manufacturer's premises and then sent out with the necessary 'stuff' to the hand-sewers working in their homes. Therefore, in the early stages of its development, the buildings associated with the shoe industry were unlikely to make any more impact on their surroundings other than small medium-sized 'warehouses' for the manufacturers.

During the time of the 'domestic' system there developed in certain parts of the county, the use of sheds or workshops (often known simply as 'shops') at the bottom of the outworkers' gardens, rather than working in the house itself. Outside the towns, outworkers shops can be seen in a number of places, for example, the range of outbuildings behind a row of houses on the edge of Burton Latimer, running east from the Cranford road (SP 905 752); in Sunnyside, Earls Barton (SP 848 636); whilst at Long Buckby there are two-storey as well as single-storey 'shops'.

In the 1850's the first sewing machines were introduced from America, and with some modification could be used for stitching together the upper parts of the shoe, i.e. closing. The first phase of mechanisation of shoe manufacture had begun. There was considerable opposition from the workers to the introduction of machines for the closing process, but by 1859, these machines were being used extensively in many other centres of shoe production, and the

Northampton manufacturers adopted them after the collapse of a strike by shoemakers in the town and county against the introduction of closing machines. By the late nineteenth century all the basic footwear making processes could be performed on machines some of which needed power which was provided by steam or gas engines and production was concentrated in factories. These were usually in the towns but Earls Barton had 16 factories in 1901. Long Buckby also had several footwear factories including the Castle Factory in King Street (SP 627 676). This three-storey building was constructed in two stages between 1885 and 1890, and has recently been restored to a splendid condition for new use.

Engineering

Many of the county's engineering businesses developed as a result of the increased use of machinery in footwear manufacture and consequently were situated in the towns. On the other hand, some blacksmiths involved with farming implements developed into agricultural engineers as more machinery was used on farms. Two notable examples are Balls at Rothwell, whose premises in the High Street, opposite Fox Street (SP 815 810) were demolished but the housing development built on the site is called Plough Court, a reminder of the main product of Balls; and Roberts at Deanshanger whose products extended from farm equipment to wind pumps. Despite the closure of the business in 1929, and the subsequent use of the site for the manufacture of oxides, a building with elaborate cast-iron framed windows survives at the entrance to part of the later oxide works on the north east side of High Street. (SP 764 397)

Services

Provision of water supply, gas and electricity are usually associated with urban public utilities but owners of country estates often made their own provision of these services. On the Castle Ashby estate, the Engine Pond and Engine House, for water wheel driven pumps and later used to house hydraulic ram pumps (SP 856 594) provide evidence of this, as does the architecturally embellished water tower adjacent to the house (SP 863 593). The gas house, but not the equipment, survives near the stable block at Courtenhall (SP 761 529) and at Ashton, near Oundle, the former corn mill and fulling mill was converted to a Victorian 'power' house in 1900 by the first Lord Rothschild. Water turbines and oil engines were installed, driving through overhead shafting electric generators and pumps for water supply. All of this remains and is open to the public at summer week-ends.

Ashton Mill, Nr Oundle   Photograph by Geoffrey Starmer

In earlier times, the county's towns looked for water supply within their environs but with the increase in their population during the latter part of the nineteenth century they looked further afield and the reservoirs then constructed are still significant features in the countryside.

Ravensthorpe Water Works - photographed in 1966 but built March 1936.

Photograph by Geoffrey Starmer

In 1890 Northampton completed construction of a reservoir and the still standing pumping house (SP 682 704) at Ravensthorpe, followed by Hollowell reservoir in 1938. Kettering constructed reservoirs at Cransley and Thorpe Malsor whilst Higham Ferrers and Rushden Water Board created Sywell Reservoir and erected the surviving engine house (SP 833 651) there to house internal combustion engine driven pumps to get the water to its towns. No longer required for water supply, the reservoir, surrounding land and the works form one of the County's Country Parks providing a haven for wild life and recreation for its visitors.

Unfortunately, there are many other fascinating aspects, particularly the archaeology of transport in the county, which it has not been possible to cover in so short an article. However, we hope that the information here has whetted your appetite, and if it has why not join the Northamptonshire Industrial Archaeology Group, by contacting: Geoffrey Starmer, 34 The Crescent, Northampton, NN1 4SB. 01604 713244.

RURAL ARCHITECTURE IN NORTHAMPTONSHIRE

Paul Woodfield

The study of rural buildings is relatively new and its literature has only become prolific from about 1960. At this time the influence of the allied discipline of archaeology freed vernacular studies, the name by which it is now known, replacing the former, more stereotyped, framework of architectural practice.

Vernacular architecture is the study of traditional building forms in town and country; buildings erected largely independently of current fashion, not so much as a direct response to requirements freshly evaluated each time, but as part of a long standing tradition, passed on from generation to generation. In this way the evolutionary process only works slowly to modify traditional solutions to changing needs.

Building is indeed one of the most conservative of occupations, for who is so rash as to take a chance with what must always have been the greatest investment a man has ever made? Or who would gamble with the hard won lore residing in each craftsman's breast concerning the nature and behaviour of materials?

In Northamptonshire, as everywhere else, vernacular buildings bear a direct relationship to the area in which they stand, and as such they can tell us something about the social circumstances into which they were born. It is surprising how little is documented about the details of everyday life, even in the comparatively recent past, because doubtless these details seemed too commonplace to be worthy of record. Paintings and drawings record rural life only incidentally much of the time, and legal documents, the petitions, terriers and probate inventories, can only rarely be physically related to a standing building.

Northamptonshire is fortunate among Midland counties in having a diversity of good building materials. The major structure in the county is the band of Jurassic age limestones, giving the beautiful Lincolnshire limestone in the north, formerly quarried at Stanion, Weldon, Kings Cliffe and many lesser places. At Collyweston there is a fissile limestone which has been split by numerous winter frosts into what is perhaps the most attractive roofing slate in England. Weldon disappeared into the maw of the British Steel Corporation's giant ore draglines, a sad end for a fine free-stone. Further north, the oolites are softer and more muddy in appearance, and influence buildings around Towcester and Brackley, whereas in the eastern parishes the honey-coloured stone continues the vernacular of north Buckinghamshire. In the heartland of the county, from Chipping Warden to Rockingham, and to Irchester in the east, the earlier lias yields a rich, dark brown iron enriched marlstone. Areas within reach of both, such as Blisworth, have exploited the contrast between stones from both Norman and Victorian times to achieve architectural effect.

Figure 3 Typical Northamptonshire Smaller Houses

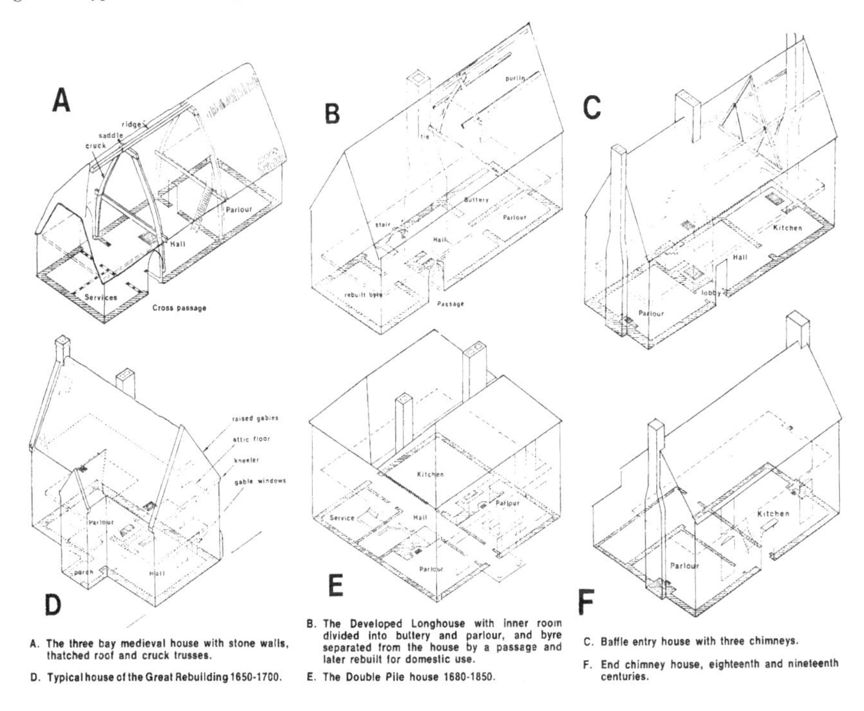

A. The three bay medieval house with stone walls, thatched roof and cruck trusses.

B. The Developed Longhouse with inner room divided into buttery and parlour, and byre separated from the house by a passage and later rebuilt for domestic use.

C. Baffle entry house with three chimneys.

D. Typical house of the Great Rebuilding 1650-1700.

E. The Double Pile house 1680-1850.

F. End chimney house, eighteenth and nineteenth centuries.

Northamptonshire, however, has more than good stone. To the west, where the land descends to the Warwickshire-Leicestershire plain, the traditional timber framing of both counties spills over into our border villages, in places like Braunston and Yelvertoft. It persists too in towns further afield, as at Towcester and King's Sutton. Construction in unfired clay became common in the eighteenth and nineteenth centuries and probably earlier in the Northamptonshire heights (Fig.1 page 123). At Clay Coton, for instance, a cottage survives which combines both timber framing and cob construction. Outside the area served by Collyweston slates the commonest roofing material was long wheat straw, often laid with lime, and at a characteristically steep pitch. After about 1800, however, Welsh slate became common, until it dominated over the straw and plain tiles, after completion of the railway network in the Victorian period.

Although materials may differ, the form of the rural house remains similar over a wide geographical context. The simplest form, and no doubt the basis of the peasant cottage from earliest times, is the single roofed dwelling, often without fireplace. It is this type of building which appears as cottages on the Bayeaux tapestry, and around 1300 AD cost between 15s (75p) and 25s (£1.25) to build, the equivalent of a man's wages for six months. The inadequacy of this type of house for any period of continuous use, combined with the empirical nature of its construction, has ensured that no early examples survive, and they are known almost entirely from archaeological research.

Side by side with these simple cottars and bordars dwellings existed the medieval house of the freeman or small yeoman farmer. In much of the country these appear to be longhouses, combining family dwelling and housing for cattle all under one roof, and sharing one access. All of these have now been altered to the exclusion of animals (Fig. 1B). Such houses differ from the simple cottage in that they represent some investment in building, the capital coming from a surplus to everyday needs. Not only does such investment represent a degree of prosperity, but also a conviction that there will be a reasonably settled life ahead. It has been claimed that building for the next 400 years is a form of conspicuous waste, and as such is a major step away from subsistence economy of earlier times. Above this social level comes the standard medieval house (Fig. 1A), usually consisting of three bays, a central open hall and service and parlour ends. In these it is often possible to identify such features as the cross passage, and thus deduce the position of the hall. The location of the open hearth can also sometimes be ascertained from the heavily smoke blackened timbers surviving in the roof space. In these the arrangement of the smaller house differs little from the houses of the gentry, except in scale, and features present in such great houses as the Hastings Manor House at Yardley Hastings, can be recognised in smaller houses, as for instance, The Old House, Stoke Albany.

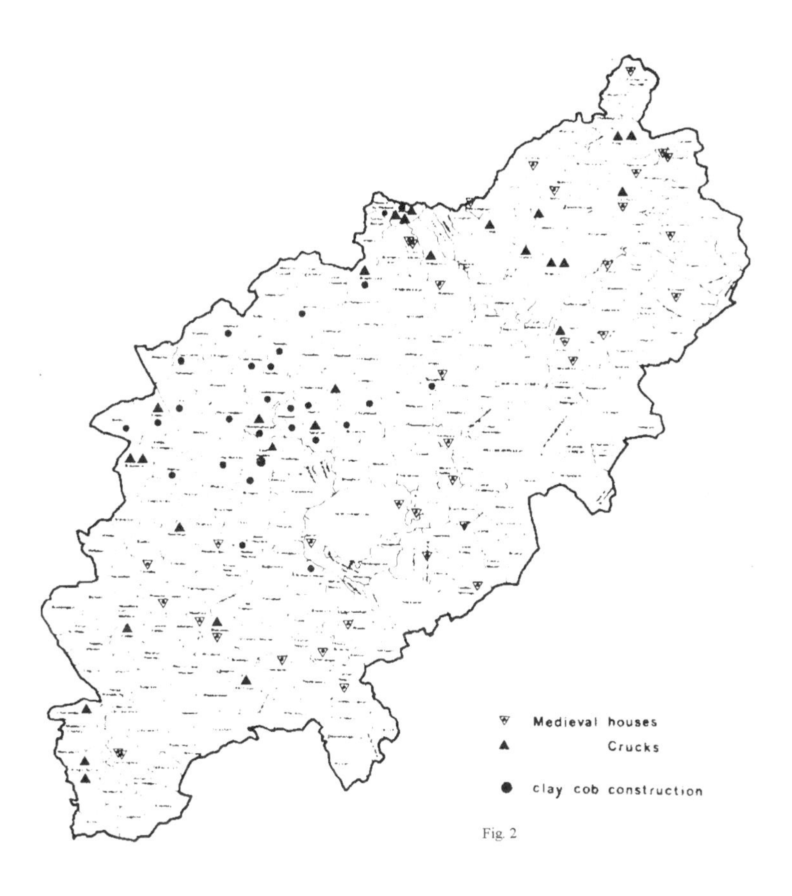

Fig. 2

Below this social level, however, come the houses built on cruck frames, the first identifiable peasant houses of the area. Twenty-nine of these are known in the county, and no doubt there are many more still unrecognised. Crucks are pairs of timbers originally standing on the ground and jointed at their apex, which forms an "A" frame, providing direct support to the roof covering. Much discussion has centred on their origin, and some experts have reluctantly conceded that, for want of more convincing evidence, they must be of very early, perhaps pre-Roman, origins. Northamptonshire lies on the eastern fringe of the cruck area of England, and the distribution of the examples within the county follows the hills, eschewing the lands beyond the River Nene (Fig.1). A national survey is at present being conducted into details of their distribution, and it has shown that many cruck trusses in the county are coeval with the stone walls of the house. Indeed, the feet of the crucks are frequently raised well above floor level in the wall, and the joints at the apex are, with few exceptions, versions of the East Midlands technique of jointing the blades into a short horizontal piece, the saddle, which carries the heavy, square sectioned ridge.

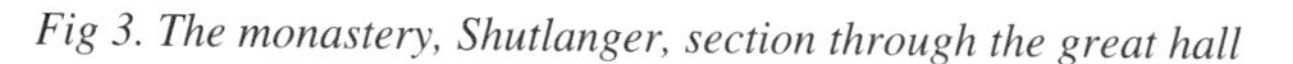

Fig 3. The monastery, Shutlanger, section through the great hall

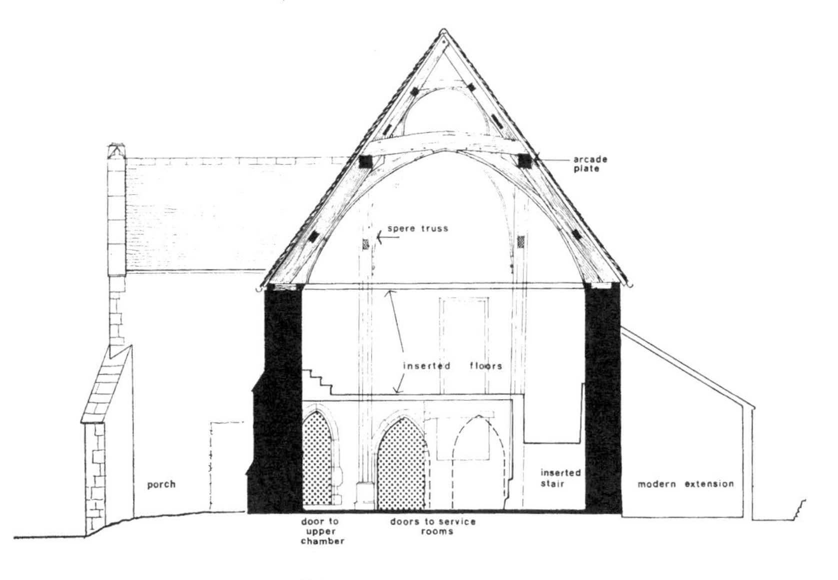

The larger medieval rural house of manorial status.

This native form of construction, in which the roof frame carried the ridge and heavy purlins, contrasts with the rather more sophisticated tradition of European origin spreading up from the southern counties. The second school of carpentry, adopted by many grander houses, used smaller, more uniform sized timbers in straight lengths, without either purlins or ridge piece. In Northamptonshire, this incoming school meets and fuses with native tradition, and houses like The Monastery, Shutlanger (Fig. 3), of a similar date to Yardley Hastings (c. 1330), have absorbed both purlins and heavier timbering into the new school, although the ridge piece is still missing. The amalgam of traditions can also be seen in the numerous examples of clasped purlin construction, where the purlin is gripped between rafter and collar, instead of being mounted on the back of the principle rafter as in the native cruck tradition. Shutlanger, like Yardley Hastings, exhibits another point of evolutionary interest. The centre truss of the Great Hall clearly demonstrates its origin in the earlier aisled hall, because here the purlins, in relationship with other members, become arcade plates. The supporting posts have been swept aside as heavy principal rafters, in order to clear the floor. The thrusts so generated are carried into external buttresses. In this process the arcade post struts have moved over too into a wind brace position but have firmly retained their strut scantling. It would appear that by 1330, arcaded walls were no longer acceptable in our area, and the carpenter was being asked to modify his traditional methods to provide a clear, uninterrupted hall.

As the medieval period closes, the box frame, whereby timbers are assembled piece by piece, has gradually replaced cruck construction, although features of the latter linger long in the county. In Braunston High Street an exposed gable end has rafters mounted in the tie beams in the usual sixteenth century manner, but at their apex a cruck saddle carries a heavy ridge. Curved principal rafters in fact are common, which points to their desirability in the cruck tradition. In the sixteenth and seventeenth centuries they were normally carried on a tie beam and cross halved at their apex. Here the ridge pole was set diagonally instead of square to the ground (Fig. 1B). This type of truss has been found in association with an open hall in nearby north Buckinghamshire, and thus it may occur as early as 1550.

During the reign of Elizabeth, prosperity reached down to the lesser orders of society, and the freeholder and villein were, for the first time, in a position of having surplus cash, and were in such a social position as to need to exhibit their wealth. In this period sheep farming tended to produce a better return than arable and the lighter soils of Northamptonshire favoured sheep. Coupled with a dramatic increase in population nationally, this was a major factor leading to the phase now known as the "Great Rebuilding". In good times - and sheep farming tended to have seven good years at a run - a house, with an area of sixty square metres, could be built out of as little as three or four years profits. Arable farming in the right place could occasionally do as well, and so from 1575 onwards whole villages began the process of translating the poor cottage of the subsistence farmer into more substantial and comfortable dwellings. It is these houses which form the backbone of the majority of the county's villages today.

In 1557, Parson Harrison describes the greater comforts, which were universally introduced into houses of his day. There were chimneys to take away the smoke from open fires, glass to keep out the wind and rain, beds of feathers instead of straw, and he also noted that stone construction was rapidly replacing timber. His remarks, derived largely from Essex, apply perhaps less pertinently to Northamptonshire, but generally the price of timber construction overtakes that of building in stone everywhere by the end of the Civil War. At this time, therefore, when timber appears, it is an ostentatious show of wealth.

In the county earlier houses were usually modernised first. A good example of this is Abbey Lodge, Farthinghoe, where a medieval longhouse was modernised by the insertion of a floor over the hall, the building of a fine Elizabethan fireplace and stack, and the introduction of a newel stair to gain access to the new upper chamber. Extensions are often added, including such rooms as a dairy or kitchen. Kitchens in separate buildings away from the main house, like Yardley Hastings, were now being generally abandoned in favour of more convenient arrangements. New buildings of this date, however, were still placed parallel to the street, and were not more than one room thick, in the same way as their medieval predecessors. Walls were better constructed using squared stone, the thickness being reduced from the medieval 750-900 mm (29.5-35 ins) to around 560 mm (22 ins). The internal planning of new building reflects a greater interest in privacy for those who could afford it, and a corresponding decrease in the relative size of the hall. The hall fireplace is frequently located in the traditional cross passage, and on entering one finds oneself in a lobby, the masonry of the stack forming a baffle to the hall (Fig. 1C). In Northamptonshire there is a tendency not to build a back-to-back fireplace, which would serve the adjoining room, but to place the hearth and chimney axially at the farthest end of the parlour and inner room, which gives rise to the characteristic Northamptonshire and north Buckinghamshire three-chimneyed house.

The Civil War brought dislocation to Northamptonshire at least as serious as anywhere else and building activities virtually ceased between the years 1640 and 1650. With the unprecedented mobility of all orders of society, and the re-allocation of land, there was a reassessment of traditional methods and values, and with the restoration of more settled times, an enormous increase in building activity took place. Houses of this phase of the Great Rebuilding, which extended to about 1720, may be found throughout the county, and are often easily identified by the common practice of placing datestones in gables or over doors containing the initials of the occupier and his wife, a practice incidentally which was passed across to America. The accommodation is often extended into the roof space of the house and lit by either a gable window or by raised dormers. Under the influence of polite architecture, itself strongly influenced by Renaissance ideas modified by the Royal Court's sojourn in Holland, vernacular buildings became more symmetrical in elevation, and the practice of placing windows symmetrically in end gable walls also became common. The windows themselves were usually of stone, with flat hood moulds in the medieval tradition, and with stone mullions with simple chamfers or ovolo mouldings. Due partly to the Dutch influence, brick became fashionable further away from the east coasts, where it had previously been used for lack of choice, and, after a period of delay, fashion is usually reflected in the vernacular. Brick floors and ovens, projecting as a conspicuous bulge in the outer wall, indicated improved standards of comfort and convenience. Plans of vernacular buildings after the Civil War tend to move towards two large rooms, instead of the traditional three and central hall and, after about 1680, include gable chimney stacks, in fact representing the standard form of cottage which was to persist into the first decades of the twentieth century (Fig.1F). Dutch influence again appears in the arrival of the "double pile" plan, a second range of rooms behind the first with a central hallway, and tucked away stair, a radical departure from all that had gone before (Fig.1E).

From about 1700, traditional vernacular building changes radically, most builders having at least a nodding acquaintance with the fashion of the day through the publication of numerous books. Brick was the preferred material for the well to-do, and sash windows replaced timber cross windows, which themselves superseded the stone mullioned windows early in William and Mary's reign.

The enclosure of common land was almost completed by 1700, resulting in dwellings on enclosed land being erected in isolation away from the cluster of the village, a practice which continued into the Victorian period. Later in the century, farm workers grew in number and instead of residing in the farm house as hitherto, they were housed in rows of cottages either erected on the periphery of villages, or nearer the farm itself.

The nineteenth century generally saw a drift from the land, and apart from the erection of brick farm cottages, peripatetic labour was frequently housed in dismal conditions in the farm buildings. However, attempts were made to improve farm design, and the Grafton farms built around Towcester in the 1840's have a double pile house with farm buildings laid according to model plans.

Vernacular tradition is not dead, it has simply moved, and the constraint upon experiment and innovation is no longer the countryman's wish not to depart from his father's footsteps, but the nervousness expressed by the Building Society. The speculative houses and council dwellings now surrounding many of our villages are equally conservative in plan and construction, as they have always been; what is lost is the sense of locality arising from local materials and the direct contact between the occupants and the land around them.

The study of vernacular buildings in Northamptonshire is still in its infancy. Some areas, like the south-west, have been studied in some detail, but large areas still remain ripe for the researcher.

By its nature, vernacular architecture can be appreciated in most of rural Northamptonshire. However, the following places stand out as being notable:

Great Houses	Fawsley; Drayton; Apethorpe.
Manorial Houses	Hardwicke, Hyde Farm; Roade; Southwick Hall; The Monastery; Shutlanger.
Cruck Houses	Yeoman's House; Ashley; Chinners Farm; Chacombe Eydon; Hall Farm; Kings Cliffe.
17th Century Houses	Rockingham; Eydon; Helmdon; Aynho; Blisworth; Blakesley; Easton on the Hill.
Timber Framed Houses	Yelvertoft.
Clay Cob	Clipston; Welford.

RURAL CRAFTS OF THE COUNTRYSIDE

Hedgerow and woodland crafts

Ron Wilson

Before the days of mechanisation on the farm the annual round of activities included ditching and hedging. Hedging was important, not only because it provided a habitat for wildlife, but also because the end result was an effective stock-proof barrier. Nowadays not only are there fewer and fewer stock kept, which means that hedges are either 'neglected' or grubbed out, but in their place mechanical barriers are used.

With the arrival of new and more efficient farm machinery the number of people employed on farms decreased and the slow, laborious, but effective, process of traditional hedge-laying became less and less viable, and hedge-cutting was left to a man on a tractor with a mechanical cutter. In recent years in some places there has been a move back towards traditional techniques for managing hedges, which not only results in an attractive feature of the countryside, but also enhances the hedge for wildlife.

As in the past, the ideal time for hedge laying is during the autumn and winter, although periods when heavy frosts are prevalent are avoided because the low temperatures are likely to affect the plants - and damage them.

Prior to the widespread planting of hedges in the eighteenth century as a result of the Enclosure Acts and Awards, hedge-laying may not have been widely practised. But hedges still had to be managed and coppicing was used. Every twelve to fifteen years the trees and shrubs would have been cut back to almost ground level. The timber products that resulted from this activity included material for producing hurdles, together with products for fencing, and thatching spars and firewood. Using this method left the field exposed and it is likely that any animals would have been taken to other sites, and the 'pasture' ploughed and planted with crops.

With an increase in the interest in traditional crafts, hedge-laying is being used more and more, and not only by farmers, but also by other groups, including the Wildlife Trust, the Woodland Trust and the county's country parks.

The Midland counties are well-known for their own style of hedge-laying and this area, together with Wales and the south-west - and to a lesser extent The Weald - still feature traditional hedge-laying activities. The methods used by a farmer will depend to some extent on the animals being kept in the field. Sheep and cattle demand different types of stock-proof hedges.

With the Enclosure Acts and Awards it was vital that a boundary grew quickly. Hawthorn, and to a lesser extent blackthorn, were used for this purpose. During hedge-laying hawthorn provides less valuable timber than in the longer established hedges, and much of what came out was used for firewood. Where hedge laying has been continuously practised, additional barriers are not necessary. To cut down the time needed to manage hedges a technique known as brushing was used. In this the top and sides of the hedge were trimmed at regular intervals - in most cases once a year. Sometimes coppicing was used with this method to prevent hedges from encroaching onto paths, roads and tracks.

Hedging takes place during winter because the sap is low, the hedgerow plants have died back and leaves have fallen from the trees and shrubs. This makes it easier for the craftsman to work, and also because activities on the farm at this time used to be less hectic than they are now. Normally the hedgerow shrubs are allowed to grow to a height of some 6-7 feet (2 metres) before cutting and laying is carried out.

A competent hedge-layer works slowly and methodically. The tools which are used vary slightly from area to area, but have changed little over the last two hundred years or so. These include a long-handled slasher, a billhook and where there are thick stems, an axe. In many places the latter has been replaced by a chain saw! Thick gloves are also a part of the kit, especially where the predominant species includes either hawthorn or blackthorn - not to mention brambles - which are not particularly kind to the skin! Kneepads will also be worn by most seasoned hedge-layers.

The hedge layer begins by clearing out the weeds, undergrowth and any dead wood from the bottom of the hedge. A great deal of debris - blown leaves, dead plant and in the twenty first century paper and bottles - accumulate. The side of the hedge is then trimmed to remove surplus stems, together with any which have grown 'out of line'. The worker strikes these off with a deft stroke of his billhook, which avoids splintering the wood, and leaves a clean line.

Elder, brambles and any other material unsuitable for the hedge will also be removed.

Although there is a style for hedge laying in this area, each craftsman will put his own individual stamp on his work. Nevertheless his operating mode will be similar to that which his ancestors have practised for hundreds of years. The initial work completed, hedge-laying proper can start. Most hedge-layers work from left to right - and where the hedge is on a slope, working up the gradient is preferred.

With his billhook the operator chops through half the thickness of the first and subsequent stems, about 0.5 metres (18 ins) above ground level. He then bends these stems over at an angle of between 45 and 60 degrees. It is important that the stem is only partially severed, so that there is still a link with the roots to enable the shrubs to obtain their nutrients in the following and subsequent years when growth takes off again. At intervals of between 45-60 cms (1.5 and 2ft) he puts in upright stakes, so that he can weave his bent-over branches around them. Sometimes these stakes are produced from suitable saplings already established in the hedge, and these will be trimmed to around a height of 1 metre (3ft). If living stakes are not available in the hedge, others will be brought in. These are usually removed after a few years once the hedge becomes established.

The bent-over branches are known as plashers, and these are interwoven around the uprights in a process known as plashing or pleaching. Each of these plashers is bent to roughly the same angle before being intertwined. To give it a neat finish hazel is often used to bind the top of the hedge. These strips, known as 'heathers' also help to hold down the newly woven branches, which often get out of place because of the springy nature of the hawthorn. Where the hedge-layer has done his job well, the branches - and especially those at the bottom - will 'tiller out' shooting strongly to quickly make the fence stock-proof.

Hedges often have trees incorporated within these. These may have been planted by the landowner to provide shade for the animals - and in the past for timber - and are left. Others will have arrived as seeds and again are generally left. Apart from providing shelter many also act as a windbreak if crops are grown in the field, or to provide shelter for animals.

Woodland crafts

Charcoal burning

As with many other countryside activities, charcoal burning has been superseded by more modern methods. However, in the past charcoal was important for every ironworker and smith. With the increase in the use of barbecues, charcoal is again in demand. British produced charcoal lights more easily than imported material. Charcoal is a by-product of woodland management. Where trees are being coppiced, the wood is used in the manufacture of charcoal, which happens in several places in the county. The wood to be used is cut roughly into 2-4 foot (60-120 cms) lengths and stacked for several months to season. In the traditional methods of charcoal burning this was done without any modern oven, but nowadays charcoal ovens are often used - and help speed up the process and take the problem of wind, etc. out of the process.

In the traditional method the seasoned timber was brought to a hearth - a circular area either in a clearing in the wood or on waste ground. With the timber stack being built, a six foot (2 metre) stake was placed in the middle and a chimney of split logs built around this. The wood was then built around this in layers sloping towards the chimney. Once completed the wood pile resembled a dome - rather like a very large inverted basin. The wood was then covered with a layer of plant material - grass, bracken, leaves, turves, straw, etc. On top of this a layer of earth or ashes was placed, the purpose being to exclude almost all the air.

Charcoal is produced when wood is heated with the exclusion of most air to allow combustion to take place. Although some charcoal burners insist that they have a secret formula for starting the process, the technique used is similar in most cases. Having removed the central stake, the chimney or flue is left up the centre of the pile. Red hot burning charcoal is then dropped down the chimney and a few dry sticks put in on top if this. Once alight soil is used to seal the flue hole, which allows the fire to spread gradually through the heap.

The charcoal needs watching. On a still day it burns evenly, but if it becomes windy the fire will be blown to the side. If it breaks through the earthen barrier the whole pile goes up in smoke and the charcoal is lost. The charcoal burner needs to be on his guard. He will ensure that he has canvas screens - called loos - on the windward side, moving these as necessary. The burning process takes from between two to ten days.

Modern charcoal makers use either brick kilns or portable metal ones. These are much more efficient and effective than the earlier methods. These modern kilns produce a ton of charcoal from every seven tons of wood, the process generally being completed in one day.

Coppicing and coppice products

Coppicing, already mentioned, provided timber for a variety of purposes. In some places sycamore is still used on the old foot-operated pole lathes. Because sycamore timber is white and has no smell, it was used for such items as kitchen utensils, including rolling pins. The word coppice comes from the Norman French word 'couper', which means to cut. In this the timber is cut close to the ground - the wood being cut at an angle so that water does not collect on the stool. In some instances brushwood is used to cover the vulnerable exposed wood in the form of a roof, until the cut section seals. The coppice stool quickly sends up new shoots that can be coppiced again in 12-15 years depending on the species. In theory the process can be practised ad infinitum.

In some Militia Lists of 1777, besom-makers appear. These were people who collected brushwood from birch and made this into rough brooms - besoms. However, any twigs can be bundled up to produce a besom. The twigs are usually cut in winter and left to season for several months. Having 'dried out' the bundle of twigs is compressed and bound onto some kind of handle, produced from the same coppicing method in the wood. The whole brush material is tied onto the handle, and in the past pliable stems from the wood would have been employed for this purpose.

Hurdle making

In the past wooden hurdles were useful on the farm, although most have been replaced by modern materials, including iron and steel. One activity in which hurdles featured prominently in the past was in sheep farming. Nowadays modern methods of sheep farming have cut out the shepherd, the guardian of the flock, who used to spend his time away from home - across the fields and far away - during the lambing season. But in the past hurdles were constantly needed to construct temporary pens, which were used to produce temporary pens to divide up the fields to keep the sheep together in bad weather and during lambing.

They were also used for smaller livestock, and as temporary structures to contain cattle when the farmer needed to ensure that smaller areas of grazing were used.

There are two main types of hurdles, by far the most common of which is the bar hurdle, made from either ash or hazel. The finished product is not unlike a small gate, without the accompanying hinges and posts. The second kind is not unlike the first, but the hurdle-maker employs withies or hazel twigs, which he weaves into a 'sturdy' framework consisting of either ash or hazel poles. This is often called a wattle hurdle.

In the past most hurdle-makers would have literally 'lived on the job' and would have spent much time living in huts or shelters. It was here that they also kept their hurdle-making tools, and when the weather was too wet to work outside would work in there.

The bar hurdle is the simplest of the two types, and consists of seven horizontal bars, with a vertical bar at each end and in the middle and two further bars at angles, going from the centre bar to the bottom of the hurdle close to the uprights. The two outer uprights were longer, and had sharpened ends for pushing into the ground.

A different method is employed for making wattle hurdles. The maker would have a mould, which was about the length of the hurdle being produced, and which would have a number of holes drilled in it. This piece of wood was fastened to the ground with pegs, and nine or ten uprights - called sails - inserted into these. The rods used at either end were slightly thicker to give the hurdle support. Thinner rods, called withies were then interwoven around the uprights. The hurdle-maker always started at the bottom, and the last - or top rod - is called a finisher. To ensure that the material was secure, a special technique was employed to make sure that the rod at the end of each line was bent in such a way that it did not break. Most hurdle-makers ensured that there was a small aperture about half way up the hurdle. This is not for keeping an eye on the animals - although it can be used for such - but is known as a twilly hole, and used when carrying the hurdle. Using a stake, it is possible for a man to place several of the hurdles on this using the twilly hole, and then the stake can be placed over the shoulder. The final hurdle is around a metre (3ft) or so deep. The end posts are sharpened so that they can easily be pushed into the ground.

Thatching

As a covering for a range of buildings 'thatching' has its origins back in prehistory. However, the word 'thatch' is of Old English derivation, and comes from thacke - or thaec - and means 'roof covering'. A variety of materials was used for this, including reeds, sedge, straw, rushes - or similar material which would keep out the water. In prehistoric times, a range of materials was used, including turf and heather. Thatch was an important material because it was easy to come by, and provided good insulation. The thatcher was an important person and found in most communities. Sadly, in recent years there have been a number of problems, including the cost of insurance and the fact that thatch needs replacing regularly. However, it is still to be found in Northamptonshire, and some houses, which were covered with other more 'modern' materials, are now reverting back to thatch. Although the thatcher was a master of his craft when it came to covering roofs, he was also in great demand during the late summer and early autumn when he would be dealing with the ricks - the stacks of straw which were built in the fields from the stooks brought in from the harvest.

Apart from the material with which the thatcher covers the roof, he needs a number of other items. Once again hazel coppice comes into use here. Thatching spars - lengths of hazel - are used by the thatcher to drive into the roof to hold the thatch in place. These thatching spars are usually around 30cm (2ft) in length. Each spar is cleft from a green hazel rod, which is no more than 5cm (2 ins) or so in diameter. The woodman cutting the spars uses a billhook to split the wood. Each rod is then sharpened' to a point, so that it can be driven easily into the thatch.

The different materials used for thatching have different life spans, and the preferred material used to be Norfolk reed. Long straw lasts for between 10 and 20 years, combed wheat reed has to be replaced after 24 to 40 years and reed may survive anything up to 80 years. Sedge, which is used on the ridge of 'traditional' thatched roofs, has be renewed every 20 to 25 years

The thatcher uses a number of tools, most of which were hand-made in the past. These include a legget for dressing the reed into position, mallet for driving in the spars, needles for holding the bundles of reed in position, knife for cutting the bonds, etc, long eaves knife for trimming the sedge and reed, shears (the old fashioned type used for shearing sheep) for trimming the reed.

The material to be used is graded according to bunch length before the thatcher begins. He then places this in three heaps made up of short, medium and long material. The bunches - usually six at a time - are taken onto the roof. The first of these is placed at the eaves and the thatcher uses his legget to dress the material into position. He then uses a needle to hold these in place before he fixes them with a hazel spar - each of which is positioned about 45cm (18 ins) apart. He may hold these in place with either an iron hook or tarred twine. A long needle is used to push the twine through the reed and around the rafter. The work continues until the thatcher reaches the roof ridge. Once here he fashions a 10cm (4in) diameter ridge roll from coarser reed. This is then secured with twine at intervals of about 30cm (12 ins) before it is attached to the ridge. The final bundles are trimmed with a long eaves knife. The thatcher usually stamps his individual mark on the roof when he completes the ridge, often decorating it with a unique pattern.

Using thatch has always posed a number of problems from fire, birds - and to some extent - small mammals. However, wire netting is now employed to cover most thatched roofs to prevent 'deterioration'.

RURAL HANDICRAFTS IN THE COUNTRYSIDE

Members of the Crafts Committee of the Northamptonshire Federation of Women's Institutes

The WI Movement in Northamptonshire takes pride in helping to keep old crafts alive and encouraging new ideas. It strives to maintain a high standard by teaching beginners basic skills, until they have the experience to create for themselves.

The W I teaches many different crafts, and leaflets are available on a variety of subjects. Exhibitions and competitions are arranged to stimulate interest and advice and instruction is available.

The following crafts, briefly outlined here, are practised and taught by the WI in the county.

Macrame

Macrame is the art of creative knotting, and is one of most ancient crafts, and it is thought to have originated in Arabia in the thirteenth century. It became popular in Spain and Italy, and was a pastime that was taken up by George III's Queen, Charlotte who, in the 1780's, was making macrame fringes at court. It was revived by the Victorians and again during the 1960's when there was a renewed interest in crafts. Everyone producing macrame uses knots, and the craft needs no more space than an individual's lap. The basic tools are the fingers, and the materials used are ones with which everyone is familiar - string, cord and yarn of all kinds. The variety of texture that can be produced is endless, as are the designs, which range from the strictly practical shopping bag to the most elaborate art forms. The WI has an excellent small leaflet which has clear diagrams and instructions from which beginners will discover that although macrame looks complicated it is a very simple, pleasant craft,

Hand-made toys

These possess individuality and charm sadly often lacking in mass produced counterparts. The most important factor is in the construction, and safety can be carefully controlled. The range of fabrics and colours produced today gives unlimited scope and, provided weak and worn patches are discarded, used materials can make excellent toys.

A range of synthetic stuffing, combined with embroidered features, ensures that a toy is completely machine washable. For the enterprising countrywoman there is an added bonus of a free supply of sheep's wool, which, when collected from hedges and fences and carefully washed, produces a stuffing of the highest quality. For the older child, glass eyes, plastic noses and moveable joints give added attractions, so that toys can stand or sit at their small owner's will.

Home-made wines

Country folk have always made wines, both for the pleasure of the drink and for medicinal purposes, often using recipes handed down for generations. The main ingredients can be gathered from the hedgerow, field or garden, and to which a few other ingredients - yeast, sugar and water - have to be added. Basically a few pieces of equipment are needed, including a large bowl, a wine flask and an air-lock, together with a small corner where the wine can be left to ferment undisturbed. With the help of a good instruction book even a beginner can produce a fair bottle of wine, either for drinking or for culinary purposes, at a very modest cost.

Rushwork

Rushwork is perhaps one of man's earliest known handicrafts, and is a delightful hobby to pursue. The beautiful muted greens and golds of the rushes, or the yellows of the foliage of the Spanish Iris, Tingitana, blend together to make an enormously wide range of articles, from the smallest posy basket to a full size floor covering, which incidentally is very hard-wearing.

The tools needed can be found in and around most homes - a brick, ruler, scissors, mallet and a football lacer. The rushes are worked damp, and after watering are rolled into a blanket and left over-night. The shape of the article to be produced is predetermined by the mould over which the rushes are worked. Having been collected, the rushes are wiped clean and flattened into a soft pliancy and are then ready for the start of a new creation.

Dyeing

Home dyeing can be great fun and not the traumatic experience that some people imagine. There are many commercial dyes on the market, which give excellent results but for the more adventurous plants in the hedgerows and flower border offer many exciting colours. Different parts of the plant give an entirely different colour. For example, when the blossoms of golden rod are used this produces a yellow colour, and a lovely green when the stalks and leaves are used separately. Other easily obtained dye materials which spring to mind are onion skins, elderberries, rose, privet clippings, seaweed and marigolds - but there are many others.

It must be remembered that with home dyeing all material must be clean and made from natural fibres, e.g. wool, pure silk and cotton. This applies for all spinning and weaving fibres and also for 'tie and dye' and 'Batik'.

Pillow lace making

In recent years there has been a revival in the gentle art of pillow lace making, and it is no longer considered to be an occupation for elderly folk. Today a large number of young people are attending classes, thus ensuring the continuation of this ancient craft as a leisure pursuit. Many books have been written with detailed instructions, but it is better for the newcomer to have personal tuition, and the Women's Institutes have helped a great deal to rekindle an interest in this craft by holding classes and exhibitions.

The counties most famous for lace making in this country are Devonshire, Northamptonshire, Bedfordshire and Buckinghamshire. The earliest references to making lace in this country are of the refugee lacemakers who settled in England in the sixteenth century, having fled from the Netherlands and France to escape religious persecution. Most of these made their homes in the counties mentioned above. During her residence at Ampthill Castle in Bedfordshire, Queen Catherine of Aragon, is said to have taught the villagers to make lace, and some of her designs are still in existence today.

The making of lace declined in the second half of the last century when machine lace improved and took the place of the hand-made kind. Cottagers were unable to compete with the new faster machines, and hand lacemaking is now purely a leisure craft.

For many years fine thread was very difficult to obtain, but this has been resolved and a large range of threads are now used - depending on the type of lace required. Bobbins, onto which the thread is wound, were also becoming very scarce as many had been lost or thrown away, but the county now has its own bobbin makers, who are turning out excellent bobbins. Again this is not a very lucrative form of employment and is mainly carried out as a leisure time occupation, but these craftsmen have the added satisfaction of knowing that the craft of lace-making is being kept alive. Antique bobbins are increasing in value all the time.

Patterns used in lace-making are called 'prickings', and many of the old ones were made on sheepskin or calfskin parchment or vellum. Because of the expense present day patterns are made on stiff cardboard. Producing the pattern is a tedious and time-consuming operation, which has to be undertaken with great precision. The pins that are used are made from brass, and although expensive, are easily obtained, The pattern is pinned on to what is called a 'pillow' - hence the name 'pillow lace'. There are various shapes and sizes of pillows, which include round, square and mushroom-shaped. The shape varies depending on the type of lace being made.

Patchwork

Patchwork is a very old 'thrift' craft, which is practised in Northamptonshire today as cheaply as ever. When woollen material was difficult to obtain and very expensive, the housewife saved all her scraps and together with good parts from 'worn' articles they were stitched onto a cotton backing, irrespective of colour, to make warm bed coverings - the patchwork quilt. A modification of this is the 'Log cabin' patchwork in which strips of material are sewn on to cotton squares, using dark and light shades to produce a three dimensional effect. By joining these squares together with the light and dark in varying ways different patterns can be formed.

Much of today's patchwork is made by sewing together patches of different geometrical shapes. In this method two templates are required; a solid one for cutting 'papers' and a window one for cutting material. The material patch is then tacked onto the 'paper'. By careful use of colour, texture, tone and shape, interesting designs or pictures can be made. When a design has finally been arrived at the patches are oversewn on the wrong side. When this is finished, the tacking stitches are removed. The work is well pressed and the papers taken out. The article is then made up.

Pressed flower pictures

This is a method for pressing and preserving summer flowers so that they can be made into beautiful collage pictures. The flowers are freshly gathered, dried and pressed during summer and early autumn, and can then be mounted and framed during the dull days of winter. Flowers need to be pressed as soon as possible after they have been gathered. This is done by placing them between sheets of blotting paper, with a heavy weight on top. Most leaves and flowers can take between three and four weeks to dry, and are then ready to make into pictures.

If the flowers from a special event - like a wedding or anniversary - are pressed the picture provides a lasting memory of the occasion.

Pewterwork
This is a rewarding craft and materials can be obtained from local handicraft shops, including pewter sheets (minimum one square foot), mounts for brooches, pendants, etc., together with filler, peter patina and glue. Other items can be covered in pewter, such as wooden boxes, tins, cardboard, etc. Embroidery transfers and pictures are a source of designs which, when traced onto pewter, can then be embossed before they are stuck onto the article to be covered.

Crochet
A very old craft, crochet has now been revived, and is fashionable. Patterns, wool, cotton and crochet hooks are all readily available at many wool shops and craft centres. Although there are very few stitches to learn, it is the way in which they are put together which gives the different effects. In allied crafts hairpin crochet is worked in strips on a hairpin shape which, when joined in various ways, can be used to make a range of accessories, including attractive stoles and shawls. Tunisian crochet is worked on a long hook in which stitches are collected on to the hook on one row and then worked off on the next row. This method is ideal for producing items like pram covers, blankets and cushions.

Basketry
Basketry is a very quick craft. Natural cane can be obtained from local handicraft shops, together with wooden bases, which are better for beginners before they attempt to make their own woven bases. A range of bases of all shapes and sizes can be made with very few tools.

Corn dollies (contributed by Ron Wilson)
The corn dolly, which was widespread throughout rural Britain, was undoubtedly originally a fertility symbol. It is almost certain that it originates from the ancient Middle-eastern idea that cereal plants would only grow to maturity because the corn spirit protected them. Until the arrival of mechanised harvesting, many people believed right up until the nineteenth century that the spirit of harvest dwelt within the cornfield and had to be protected throughout the winter otherwise next year's crop would not survive. As the corn was cut, the spirit moved away from the scythes until it was 'trapped' in the last remaining stalks of corn. These were collected, and plaited in some way to form a figure, which came to be known as a 'dolly'. During celebrations to mark the end of harvest, the corn dolly had its rightful place on

the table and was then kept in the farmhouse throughout the coming months. It was usually buried in the field with the first seed.

In Northamptonshire the traditional corn dolly takes the form of a horn which, in addition to the 'dolly', was another of the traditional shapes. The Northamptonshire horn is depicted in the picture. It takes the form of a pair of horns, which are decorated, with ears of wheat and barley in the same way as the 'corn dolly'. To form the dolly the corn is plaited or woven, and the way in which this is done produces the characteristic regional variation.

Northamptonshire Horn

More details of how to make corn dollies, which today are no longer seen as fertility symbols, but attractive crafts to give and receive as presents, can be found in most libraries and bookshops.

This brief outline of some of the rural crafts practised in our county has been compiled by members of the former Crafts Committee of the Northamptonshire Federation of Women's Institutes. For further details about crafts, please contact the Crafts Officer, Northamptonshire Federation of Women's Institutes, 11 Albion Place, Northampton, NN1 1UD. Books covering the crafts detailed here, together with many others, can be seen in bookshops, or borrowed from libraries.

COUNTRYSIDE DIRECTORY

This section contains a wide range of information, including organisations involved in the countryside, together with places to visit and things to do. For more information, see *Get Out! Places to Visit and Things to Do in Northamptonshire by Ron Wilson*. Published by Jema Publications and available from all bookshops or directly from the publisher.

Enjoy the countryside and respect its life and work.
Use gates and stiles to cross fences, hedges and walls.
Keep to public paths across farmland.
Fasten all gates.
Avoid fires.
Leave no litter - take it home.
Help to keep all water clean.
Take special care on country roads.
Protect wildlife, plants and trees.
Make no unnecessary noise.
Keep your dogs under close control.
Avoid damaging walls and fences.
Scheduled ancient monuments are protected by law. Respect them and all archaeological sites.

Amenity Reservoirs

Reservoirs not only offer opportunities for relaxation, but most are also good for bird watching and walking, and others are used for a variety of activities such as sailing and windsurfing.

Boddington Reservoir (British Waterways) is used for dingy sailing, cruising and windsurfing, which is under the auspices of Banbury Sailing Club. There are open days for the public, and sailing, etc. is taught. Boddington Meadows Nature Reserve is close to the reservoir - see under Nature Reserves.
Tel: 01926 493368 (Sailing Club), 01788 890666 (British Waterways) or 01604 405285 (Wildlife Trust).

Eyebrook Reservoir was formed in 1939 when surrounding land was flooded, and was established to provide industrial water for, originally Stewart and Lloyds steel works, and latterly British Steel. It is still used with Integrated

Iron and Steel in Corby taking water from the site. Interestingly the reservoir was used by the Dambusters Squadron for low level flying practice before their assaults on the Mohne Dam. There is a great deal of ornithological interest, and some birdwatchers consider that it rivals Rutland Water, not that far distant. It is a good place to watch passage migrants, including redshank, greenshank, ruff, sandpipers and common terns. Birds over-wintering include Canada geese, great crested grebe, mallard, wigeon, shoveler, tufted duck, teal and goldeneye. The birds can be watched from the public road, which goes round part of the site. Access is only available to recognised groups, including the Leicestershire and Rutland Ornithological Society and the Rutland Natural History Society. The site was designated a Site of Special Scientific Interest (SSSI) in 1965. Anyone interested in visiting the site must first obtain permission by writing to The Manager, Eyebrook Reservoir, Corby Water Co, Great Easton Road, Caldicote, Leicestershire, LE16 8RP.
Trout fishing is available from 1 April to end of October.
Situation: Off the A6003 either from Caldicote or Kettering, and then via Stoke Dry.
Contacts: Eyebrook Trout Fishery - 01536 770264, other aspects (Manager) 01536 770256
Web site: www.rutnet.co.uk/eyebrook.

Hollowell Reservoir (Anglian Water) is an almost 'secretive' site hidden away in a valley, and virtually within a stone's throw of its larger cousin, Pitsford Water. Covering an area of 53 hectares (130 acres) it is home to a large number of common duck, with some scarcer species turning up from time to time. During the winter a variety of wildfowl species can be encountered including mallard, wigeon, teal, tufted duck, pochard, shoveler, pintail, gadwall, goldeneye and the ubiquitous Canada geese. Summer passage migrants may include sedge warbler, curlew sandpiper, greenshank, black tern and ruff. Hollowell is a favoured haunt for coarse fishermen, and large fish, including roach, bream, pike and tench, have been landed. Permits are available on site from the hut situated at the west end of the dam, or from Pitsford Fishing Lodge. Hollowell Sailing Club also uses the Reservoir, and the popular club is found at the west end of the dam. There is a clubhouse, which includes a bar and a lounge, overlooking the water.
Situation: Follow the A428 to West Haddon then turn left turn towards Cold Ashby on the B4036. Turn right towards Guilsborough; pass through the village to Hollowell. Car parks are situated at the northern end of the reservoir. The reservoir can also be reached off the A5199 (formerly A50) to the north west of Northampton. Tel: 01604 781350 - Anglian Water); 01604 740328 (weekends only) Hollowell Sailing Club.

Naseby Reservoir (British Waterways). For more details about the reservoir contact British Waterways. Sailing takes place on the Reservoir.
Tel: 01788 890666 (British Waterways); 01858 575711 (Sailing Club).

Pitsford Water (Reservoir) **and Nature Reserve** (Anglian Water) is still one of the county's top bird watching sites, and a number of hides have been built under the auspices of Anglian Water and the Wildlife Trust to enhance the birdwatcher's enjoyment. Bird life varies throughout the year, but by mid September the number of waterfowl visiting Pitsford has generally risen to at least 3,000, and during winter this group is represented by as many as fifteen or more different species. The most abundant of these includes widgeon and teal. Other ducks turn up during succeeding months A range of summer passage migrants also put in an appearance, together with more unusual 'vagrants' that may turn up from time to time. Fishing is available.
In addition recent links with Brixworth Country Park, which overlooks the water, have ensured that additional activities are available, including cycling, walking, etc.
Situation: Pitsford Water is reached from the A43 Northampton to Kettering road through Holcot, or from the A508 Northampton to Market Harborough Road, either through Pitsford or near Brixworth.
Tel: 01604 781350 (fishing). Leisure activities (apart from nature reserve) Brixworth Country Park 01604 883920. For Pitsford Nature Reserve: 01604 781350.
Cycling (hire of): 01604 881777.

Ravensthorpe Reservoir (Anglian Water) is the oldest of the reservoirs in the county, and first 'appeared' in 1890, and it has one of the oldest water treatment plants in the Anglian Water region. Covering an area of 46 hectares (19 acres), and relatively small in size, the area can be a Mecca for a variety of wintering birds, together with a range of summer breeding species. Many of the usual duck species can be seen including gadwall, wigeon, pintail, shoveler, tufted, pochard and goldeneye. Birdwatchers need to obtain permits, and these allow visits to **Hollowell Reservoir** and **Pitsford Water**. Trout fishing is available to anglers either from the bank or by using either rowing or quiet powered motor boats.
Situation: Reservoir is reached from the A428, and then towards Ravensthorpe village. The Reservoir is beyond the village.
Tel: 01604 781350 (Anglian Water - Pitsford).

Stanford Reservoir (Severn Trent)
For more details about this Reservoir, contact Severn-Trent Water on 01926 411412.

Sulby - see Welford and Sulby

Welford and **Sulby** (British Waterways) has a walk between the two small lakes, which supply water for the Grand Union Canal. For more information contact British Waterways on 01788 890666.

Badgers

Brockwatch and North Northants Badgers cover Northamptonshire and the groups encourage members to monitor setts, record/report dead badger sitings, report interference to setts, etc. Both groups monitor and report on setts where various developments in an area are to take place. Details of membership - and how you can help - from Steven Jackson 01327 706349 (Brockwatch) or (01536 510469/761088 (North Northants Badgers).

Books

There are many books published about Northamptonshire, which will enable people to enjoy the countryside. It is worth making use of your local bookshop, and libraries.

Andrews, John (author), and Langham, Mike (illustrator). Birds of Anglian Water Reservoirs. Anglian Water.
Covers all Anglian Water Reservoirs, including those in Northamptonshire. It gives details with colour illustrations of many of the breeds to be seen, as well as clear maps of Anglian Water's reservoirs.

Allison, K J, Beresford, M W and Hurst, J G. The Deserted Villages of Northamptonshire. Occasional papers No 18, Department of Local History. Leicester University Press.
The publication looks at the many villages in Northamptonshire - and there are some eighty - which for one reason or another, have become deserted. The first section covers such aspects as Northamptonshire and its neighbours, Early desertions, Locating sites, etc. This is followed by a Gazetteer, which also includes maps showing the position of the sites.

Belgion, Helen. Titchmarsh Past and Present. Marlow Durndell.
Looks at the past and future of this Northamptonshire village, whose roots go back at least to the beginning of the Bronze Age. As the author reveals there is more to the place than just its early history.

Bishop, Ian. Exploring Oundle and the Surrounding Villages. Jema Publications.

Apart from divulging a great deal about the historic town of Oundle, the author also takes us into the surrounding villages to give an insight into the past and the present.

Blagrove, David. Waterways of Northamptonshire. Northamptonshire Libraries and Information Service.
A fascinating insight into these features of the county.

Blincow, Jeff. The Ornithology of Northamptonshire. Published Privately.
This A4 spiral-bound book contains a comprehensive listing of the birds of Northamptonshire, and also has sections on the history of bird watching in the county. Other chapters cover 'The Development of Habitats in Northamptonshire', and 'An Explanation of the Systematic List'. This is followed by the Systematic List, in which the author gives brief details of the bird species which have been recorded in the county. Each entry is consistent and includes the English and Latin names, together with a note 'Wreck vagrant', 'Regular Visitor', etc., and a few lines giving details of the species. The book also includes tables and graphs.

Brixworth History Society. A Pictorial History of Brixworth.
Perhaps best known for its ancient parish church, which is more than a thousand years old, the collection of photographs shows that there is more to the village than this historic building.

Chapman, Colin, R. Tracing Ancestors in Northamptonshire. Lochin Publishing.
General introductory sections suggest how to set about the study, and specific chapters offer ideas for sources in Northamptonshire.

Collier, Alison, and Thompson, Jeremy. Clipston - A Heritage. Troubador.
This delightful book uses many new photographs, and a lucid text to reveal much about this North Northamptonshire settlement.

Colston, Adrian, Gerrard, Chris, Jackson, Matt, Moore, Linda and Tero, Caroline. Northamptonshire's Red Data Book species to watch in the County. The Wildlife Trust Northamptonshire.
An introductory section explains why the book has been published, and then discusses a variety of habitat types, which are found in the county. Sections cover groups of animals - mammals, birds, insects, etc - noting their status – follow.

Available from The Wildlife Trust Northamptonshire, Lings House, Billing Lings, Northampton, NN3 8BE. 01604 495285.

Colston, Adrian and Perring, Frank (Editors). The Nature of Northamptonshire. Barracuda Books.
Covers every aspect of the nature of Northamptonshire, including geology, changing vegetation, woodlands, grasslands, freshwater, wild flowers, etc.

Gent, G, Wilson, R., et al. The Flora of Northamptonshire and the Soke of Peterborough. Rob Wilson Designs.
This updated Flora, the first published for many years, gives an indication of the distribution of plants around the county. The entries detail the status of individual species, including those that are rare.

Goodwin, Philip. Welton Northamptonshire a sort of History. Goodwin Paperbacks.
A series of historical articles about the village, with some illuminating information.

Gould, Jack. Gothick Northamptonshire. Shire.
Covers a range of stories and legends from around the county.

Gould, Jack. Northamptonshire. (Shire County Guide). Shire.
Covers various aspects of the county, beginning with the 'Lie of the Land', and going on to look at archaeology, industrial archaeology, historic houses, villages, etc. Interesting, but limited within 64 pages.

Greenall, R.L. History of Northamptonshire. Phillimore.

Grimes, Dorothy A. Like Dew before the Storm. Life and Language in Northamptonshire.
The book contains a range of material which covers the following areas People at Home, People at Work, Country People, People at War, Church and Chapel, Children at Play, Song, Dance and Seasonal Customs, Places and People, John Clare, etc. A marvellous pot-pourri of information taken straight from the horse's mouth - and evoking images of bygone Northamptonshire.

Hall, David. The Open Fields of Northamptonshire. Northamptonshire Record Society.
This extensive volume (378 pages) takes a comprehensive look at the intriguing subject of open fields, and topics include 'The Open Fields and their

Records', 'Open Fields Operation', 'Methods of Construction of Open Field Plans', etc.

Henshaw, Ian and Colston, Adrian. Waders in Northamptonshire. An Action plan for Recovery.
The Report, which was commissioned by a number of organisations - English Nature, The Nene Valley Project, Northamptonshire Bird Club, The Wildlife Trust for Northamptonshire and The Royal Society for the Protection of Birds - covers those seven species of waders which breed in Northamptonshire. The sections that follow give an overview of waders in the county, considers individual species, gives details of their breeding sites, etc. Maps are also used to show where breeding sites are located.
More details from Wildlife Trust for Northamptonshire, Lings House, Billing Lings, Northampton, NN3 8BE. Tel: 01604 405285.

Holloway, Roland. Roland Holloway's Northamptonshire. Northamptonshire Libraries.
An interesting collection of images as seen through the eyes of a photographer.

Ireson, Tony. Northamptonshire. Robert Hale.
A good groundwork about the county.

Jenkins, Eric. Victorian Northamptonshire - the Early Years. Cordelia.
An interesting insight into the county in Victorian times.

Jerrams, Leonard. A Brief History of Middleton Cheney, Northamptonshire with Childhood Memories. Privately published.
Written by someone who lived in the village all his life, and who takes a peek back to his childhood.

Key, Russell. Newnham. The Story of a Northamptonshire Village. Published privately.
The late Russell Key spent many years researching the history of this west Northamptonshire village, beginning with the Anglo-Saxons and finishing in the twentieth century. It sheds an illuminating light onto the development and organisation of the village in past centuries.

Martin, R.A. Historical Geology of Northamptonshire. Northamptonshire Natural History Society and Field Club.
Originally published as 'An Outline of the Geology of Northamptonshire', this revised edition begins by discussing the Geological Chronology, and follows it

with a look at the different rocks ages - from The Lias (Lower, Middle and Upper) to The Pleistocene Ice Ages and Glacial deposits. There is a useful book list.

Mee, Arthur. Northamptonshire. Hodder and Stoughton.
The 'classic' book about Northamptonshire, which was produced some time ago, but is still a useful source for information and for research.

Morris, John (General Editor). Domesday Book Northamptonshire. Phillimore.
His translation enables the reader to understand the information, which was collected during the Domesday Survey of 1036.

Noble, Tony. Exploring Northamptonshire. Meridian Books.
Twenty strolls around the county, each based on either a geographical or historical theme, to enable individuals to explore a county which is traditionally known for its 'spires and squires'.

Noble, Tony (Compiler and Editor), Research by John and Vera Worledge. Exploring Parish Churches in Northamptonshire. Jema Publications.
Covers almost all of the churches in the county.

Noble, Tony. Northamptonshire – a Portrait in Colour. The Dovecote Press.
A pictorial view of the county.

Noble, Tony. Waterside Walks. Jema Publications.
The author keeps to the waterways to provide a number of walks that also reveal something of the landscape and history of these areas.

Northamptonshire Bird Report.
This annual publication has articles, together with all the bird records for each year. Further details from R W Bullock, 81 Cavendish Drive, Northampton, NN3 3HL.

Northamptonshire Environmental Education Directory (last edition 1998) lists a range of organisations, which are involved with environmental education in Northampton - and many of these have wider remits in the countryside.

Northamptonshire Federation of Women's Institutes. Northamptonshire Within Living Memory. Countryside Books.
A collection of stories 'within living memory' which gives a clear insight into happening over the past generation.

Northamptonshire Federation of Women's Institutes. The Northamptonshire Village Book. Countryside Books.
Authors from villages throughout the length and breadth of Northamptonshire have come up with vignettes of their villages.

Ottowell, Gordon. Family Walks in Northamptonshire. Scarthin Books.
Takes the family on some interesting walks around the county.

Phillips, David. The River Nene from Source to Sea. The Rivers and Waterways of Britain. Past and Present.
The Nene, which starts its course to the sea on a hillside just outside the west Northamptonshire village of Badby, is the subject of this book. But the author does not forget the other 'source' at Naseby. He chronicles the journey of this important waterway with the addition of a lucid text and plenty of illustrations.

Pipe, Marian and Butler, Mia. Walks in Mysterious Northamptonshire. Sigma Leisure.
The book links walks with legends, stories, etc, and covers a wide area of Northamptonshire.

Rayne, Monica. Geddington as it was. The Social History of a Rural Community. Published privately.
If you thought that the Eleanor Cross was Geddington, then this book will put a completely different slant on the people and happenings in the north Northamptonshire village.

Smith, Judy. Northamptonshire Walks with Children. Sigma Leisure.
This volume provides a series of 20 walks specially prepared with children in mind. There are things to do, to look out for and score points with.

Stainwright, Trevor L. Windmills of Northamptonshire and the Soke of Peterborough. A History of 20th Century Sites. W D Wharton.
Covering windmills, which were so much a feature of Northamptonshire in the not so distant past, the book throws a light on where they were, what they were like, and who owned and operated them.

Tebbutt, Dora. In Summer Meadows. Troubador.
The village of Clipston is the inspiration for the poems in this book, which cover a range of topics – The Trolley Man to V is for Victory.

Wagstaff, Jack. Published privately. The author pulls together a range of material to bring to life the history of the twin villages of Church and Chapel Brampton. For more details contact the author at Brampton Cottage, Chapel Brampton, Northampton, NN6 8AF.

Webster, Brian and Wilson, Ron. Nature Walks in Northampton. Jema Publications.
Covers areas within and on the edge of town, together with a range of useful information - including setting up a wildlife garden and contacting a variety of organisations.

Whynne-Hammond, Charles. Northamptonshire Place Names. Countryside Books.
If you have ever wondered how places got their names, this book will enlighten you. It covers all the places in Northamptonshire, looking at their derivations and, where appropriate, suggesting alternatives.

Wilson, Ron and Johnson, Andy. Walks Around The Three Rivers. Jema Publications.
The book covers more than a dozen walks in and around the Nene, Cherwell and Leam in the west of Northamptonshire and into Warwickshire.

Wilson, Ron. Churches in and Around Daventry. Troubadour.
Provides information about forty of the churches in and around Daventry - most of which are in Northamptonshire, but it also includes two in Warwickshire - Wolfhamcote [which is in the care of the Historic Churches Trust] and Lower Shuckburgh.

Wilson, Ron. Get Out! Places to Visit - Things to do In Northamptonshire. Jema Publications.
Lists a wide range of places to visit in the countryside - from A (Activity Centres and Groups) to W (Woods) and everything in between.

Wilson, Ron. Around Everdon. Wild Boar Books.
Looks at the history in and around the village, covering the deserted villages of Snorscomb and Fawsley. Available from Everdon Field Studies Centre, Everdon, Daventry, Northamptonshire, NN11 3BL, price £2.95 including postage. Cheques to NCC.

Worledge, John and Vera. Wanderers in Northamptonshire/Wanderers in Northamptonshire. The Second Journey. Meridian Books.
Recounts the journeys which George Harrison (1876-1950) made around the county; he was an artist, writer and poet.

Bookshops

The main towns in Northamptonshire have a number of bookshops, of which many are part of countrywide chains. However, there are also a number of independent booksellers and these generally carry stocks of local books, not always obtainable in the larger stores.

Daventry Bookshop, 24 Sheaf Street, Daventry, Northants, NN11 4AB.
01327 703960

Fox in the Pound, The Pound House, Harborough Road, Brixworth, Northampton, NN6 9BX. 01604 880337.

Higham Ferrers Bookshop, The, 3 College Street, Higham Ferrers, Northants, NN9 9DX. 01933 317222.

KK Books, 9 Gold Street, Kettering, Northants, NN16 8JA. 01536 515949

Kingsthorpe Bookshop, 6 Harborough Road, Northampton, NN2 7AZ.
01604 717282.

Old Hall Bookshop, The, 32 Market Place, Brackley, Northants, NN13 5DP.
01280 704146.

Oundle School Bookshop, 13 Market Place, Oundle, Peterborough.
01832 273523.

Mr Pickwick, Lavender Cottage, Shutlanger, Towcester, Northants, NN12 7RR.
Bookfinding service for out of print books. Postal service only.

Towcester Books and Gifts, 211 Watling Street West, Towcester, Northants, NN12 7BT. 01327 358300.

British Trust for Conservation Volunteers

Nationally the British Trust for Conservation Volunteers (BTCV) is the largest practical conservation charity in the country. It encourages people to get involved in practical conservation work within their own environments, and has a large number of offices throughout the country to enable it to keep in touch with local communities. The Trust organises day activities, weekend projects, and conservation holidays. In Northamptonshire it develops conservation volunteering. By running conservation teams it creates volunteering opportunities. These operate at various places on weekdays. Training opportunities are provided for volunteers and it is possible to take NVQ qualifications. In addition residential training courses are organised and practical skills taught. Schools are not forgotten and advice is given about school grounds and other environmental education programmes are provided. Apart from providing practical support, BTCV also offers advice on land management, and where necessary has flexible projects for delivering management schemes. Practical activities, which the Trust provides, include those for coppicing, stone walling, fencing, access, scrub control, hedgelaying, pond clearance and creation, etc.
Further details of activities in Northamptonshire from the BTCV Northamptonshire office, Moulton College, Moulton, Northampton, NN3 7RR. Tel: 01604 643653.

British Waterways is in the business to maintain, conserve and enhance the waterway corridor for the benefit of all - locals and visitors to the area. It is a public corporation that reports to the Department of the Environment, Transport and the Regions (DETR), and nationally receives £58 million from the government each year to help it with its work. In addition to the grant, income is derived from a variety of sources, including property, licences, water sales, freight, partnerships with third parties, etc., which means that over the 2000 mile canal network some £110 million is spent to protect and promote a system which was first put into place 200 years ago.

Locally the Braunston office manages the Oxford Canal and the central section of the Grand Union, and has an annual budget of £4 million. Much of this is spent on ongoing maintenance and operating the canal system. With extra grants from the Government, it is hoped that the Northamptonshire section of the canal network become more attractive and well used due to the careful and sensitive management by the local office.

At the present time the Government has invited British Waterways to find new ways in which to involve a wider range of people in their waterways to enable them to be preserved for community use.
Tel: 01788 890666

Butterfly Conservation was established to save wild butterflies and their habitats and aims to protect these insects for future generations to enjoy. It does this by education through making people aware of the problems which butterflies face, and especially how modern management of the land in general is bringing about their decline. In addition it also funds research into their lifestyle and needs, and where appropriate sets up nature reserves to protect rare species. The local Northamptonshire group of the national organisation is responsible for recording butterflies and for organising work parties from time to time.
Further details from 01582 663784.

Canals

British Waterways (see separate entry)

Inland Waterways Association - Northampton Branch aims to promote the retention and enjoyment of Britain's inland waterways, and membership is open to both boaters and non-boaters.
More details: David King. Tel: 01908 661309.

Old Union Canals Society protects canal heritage, boating, walking and ecology on local canals, together with promoting an interest in canals in general.
More details from Brian Oakley. Tel: 017010 705103.

Churches Conservation Trust

Northamptonshire has many fine churches, the majority of which are still used on a regular basis for worship. However, in relatively recent times many churches have become 'redundant'. One, like that at Newton-in-the-Willows, near Geddington has been turned into a field study centre (see page 171). Others have been taken under the wing of The Churches Conservation Trust. A redundant church is one which belongs to the Church of England, and which is still consecrated, but is no longer used for regular worship. The Churches Conservation Trust, formerly known as the Redundant Churches Fund, was set up in 1969 and preserves churches 'in the interests of the nation and the Church of England'. Where a church is not open, a notice informs the visitor of the opening arrangements and, where appropriate, the name of the keyholder.

Northamptonshire has ten churches, that are cared for by the Churches Conservation Trust. Brief details of these are given here. For more information The Churches Conservation Trust can be contacted at 89 Fleet Street, London, EC1Y 1DH. Tel: 020 7936 2285.

Aldwincle, All Saints

The 15th century of the Church of All Saints dominates the surrounding countryside. Aldwincle boasts two churches, the other being St Peter's. All Saints has not been used for more than a hundred years, but this does not mean that it has been neglected, and has been cared for over that time. With little 'furniture' inside the building, it is possible to appreciate the architecture of a bygone age.

Blatherwycke, Holy Trinity.

With parts dating back to Norman times, Holy Trinity has been added to and altered throughout the centuries. Today, although no longer used it is cared for, and its position close to the lake of the former mansion provides it with a distinctive setting. Unlike many churches, the Victorians did very little to change the earlier appearance of the church. Today, with its memorials to the Staffords and the O'Briens, it represents the work of craftsmen of an earlier age. In addition to well-known local families, there is also a memorial to the Elizabethan poet, Thomas Randolph, who was born in Newnham near Daventry, and who died while staying at Blatherwycke.

Deene, Church of St Peter.

This is the church of the Brudenell family, who have been established in Deene Park since the early part of the 16th century, and whose family members have continuously occupied the site since then. Made from local stone, and capped with Collyweston slates, it has a tall west broached tower which dates from at least the 13th century. A great deal of the interior was re-built at the request of the widow of the 7th Earl of Cardigan, famed for his involvement in the Charge of the Light Brigade. Although some parts of the church can be considered 'austere' as the result of this work, the chancel was given particular attention and is considered to be 'sumptuously decorated'. Members of the family have been buried in the south chapel, the first of these being laid to rest there in 1531 with the tomb to the 7th Earl and his wife taking 'pride of place'.

Furtho, Church of St Bartholomew.

As with other places in Northamptonshire, changes in rural activities left Furtho as a deserted village, not helped by either the diversion of the London to Northampton road or the Enclosure Acts and Awards. The only remains of a once thriving village include the medieval dovecote, a farm - and the Church of St Bartholomew. The chancel is the earliest part of the building, and dates from the 14th century, with the tower and nave being added three hundred years later. Although it escaped the 'ravages' of the Victorians, it did not 'survive' when the village was deserted, finally becoming redundant in 1920. Having been restored by the Friends of Friendless Churches, the Churches Conservation Trust now cares for it.

Holdenby, The Church of All Saints.
Today the Church of All Saints, like so many churches in deserted villages, lies virtually isolated and almost out of sight of the grand Holdenby House. It is sad that such a fine building should have fallen into disuse. Much of the church dates from the 14th century, although Sir George Gilbert Scott made sure that he left his own distinctive mark on it when he rebuilt the chancel during restoration between 1843 and 1845. One of the interesting and unusual features of the building is the series of seven painted texts, which probably date from Elizabethan times and these, together with a number of memorials - the earliest from the 13th century - give the building its own distinctive atmosphere. There is also an interesting alabaster monument to William Holdenby and his wife, and these, together with mesericords, and an impressive screen (which was originally in the house), make this church one worth visiting.

Northampton, Church of St Peter.
Standing in the ancient Marefair, Pevsner considered this to be the most important Norman Church in Northamptonshire. A large building, it has a number of interesting features, including the finely carved arch in the east wall with its knots and saltire crosses. The rather stumpy west tower seems out of proportion to the rest of the building, almost certainly due to the fact that rebuilding work took place in the 17th century. There are a number of memorials including one to William Smith, the creator of modern geology.

Preston Deanery, Church of St Peter and St Paul.
This small, simply constructed church has a Norman arch, and it has been suggested that the stone used to build this may have come from a churchyard cross. Some of the church was demolished in the 16th century and according to some sources was converted to other less spiritual uses. The chancel was used as a dog kennel and pigeons were kept in the Norman tower, although these uses ceased in 1620 when the church was restored. The church has other interesting features, which are worth noting, including a range of carvings on the string course on each side of the chancel arch. The stonemason has included two fan-tailed birds, a snake with its tongue sticking out and a strange

animal, all of which are around one thousand years old. There are also some notable memorials, including one to Mrs Langham and dated 1773.

Upton, Church of St Michael.
This is a strange almost 'ugly' box-shaped Norman church, and like several of the other churches cared for by the Historic Churches Trust, this has become disused because the village disappeared. Signs of the earlier settlement remain only in the mounds, which are nearby. Today, innumerable motorists pass by the church on the A45, and overlooked by Upton Hall, now a private school - the tower having stood at least since the 14th century. In spite of what may appear to many as an 'uninteresting' exterior, the church has an interior character all of its own. There are a number of memorials, together with some hatchments, to the Samwell family, and recumbent alabaster effigies of Sir Richard Knightley (1537) and his wife, the family so much associated with Fawsley Hall some ten or so miles distant. Another interesting monument is to Matthew Harrington, who wrote *Oceana*.

Wakerley, Church of St John The Baptist.
Situated in a prominent position overlooking the Welland Valley, this is a fine example of Northamptonshire's heritage. The tower and spire owe their origins to 14th and 15th century craftsmen, and the other features of the church, including the Perpendicular east window, large north porch, and nave with its splendid clerestory, add to the attractiveness of the building. Inside, the zigzag nature of the chancel arch, reveals its 12th century origins. On the capitals, on which the arch is positioned, there are some beautifully intriguing carvings, which some church historians consider to be equal to the best to be found in any church in England, and date from around 1140. There are monuments to the Cecil family, indicating that Wakerley has a long association with Burghley House, which is a few miles to the SW.

Council for the Protection of Rural England (CPRE) -

Northamptonshire Branch. This national charity, with local branches, aims to get local people involved in protecting their local countryside, to enhance it where the opportunity arises and to not only keep it attractive, but to ensure that it is productive, available and enjoyable to everyone. The aim is to ensure that not only will the countryside be cared for for the present generation, but also for the future. At present CPRE is involved with a national hedgerow survey. There are over 40 county organisation and 200 local groups.
Details from: Council for the Protection of Rural England, Northamptonshire Branch, Hunsbury Hill Centre, Harksome Hill, Northampton, NN4 9QX. Tel:

01604 765888. National Headquarters is based at CPRE, Warwick House, 25 Buckingham Palace Road, London, SW1W 0PP.

Country Eye runs a range of courses on ecology, wildlife, countryside, nature and conservation. Walks are also organised. The aims of the organiser are to get individuals to be environmentally aware and to appreciate the countryside. Publishes a twice-year list of guided walks, together with nature trail leaflets from time to time.
Details from Brian Webster, 49 Broadlands, Brixworth, Northampton. Tel: 01604 881638.

Country Parks are important features of the Northamptonshire countryside, and the county is blessed with a range of these. Although there is some dispute about which is the oldest, Barnwell Country Park was set up as picnic park in July 1971, and was soon followed by Irchester. For more details of these areas see *Country Parks in Northamptonshire* by Ron Wilson, and published by Jema Publications. All country parks organise a range of events throughout the year, and in many cases these include activities for individuals, children and families. Walks are also put on, including those within parks and into the surrounding area. For more details contact individual parks.

The Northamptonshire County Council Country Parks (denoted by NCC in the details, which follow) are part of Countryside Services in the Environment Directorate of the County Council.

Barnwell Country Park (NCC), although originally only large enough to be called a 'picnic park' when it first opened, Barnwell has been 'fully fledged' for many years as one of Northamptonshire County Council's country parks. Covering 15 hectares (37 acres) it is the smallest of the country parks in the county, but nonetheless is no less interesting for that. Based on former gravel workings, one of its boundaries is an arm of the River Nene; it has picnic meadows, waterside walks, and a variety of wildlife. There is a nature trail and an audio cassette, which guides the visitor around. Coarse fishing is available for all. The Visitor Centre sells a range of publications, and has distinctive and changing displays reflecting life in and around the Park. Toilets, picnic areas and car parking available.
The Park in off the A605, 800 metres south of Oundle.
Tel: 01832 273435.

Borough Hill (Daventry) (Daventry District Council) was purchased by Daventry District Council in 1995, prior to which the area was originally owned by the BBC, which had used it as a transmitter site since 1932. Borough Hill Country Park is situated on one of the largest Iron Age hillforts in the British Isles. It is believed that man has lived, worked and played in the area for thousands of years, having made his first appearance on and around the summit some 5,000 years ago. Open to the public as a place of peace and quiet, it consists of a large area of open grassland, which covers around 60 hectares (150 acres). This makes it an ideal area for walking, picnicking, bird watching, and from which to enjoy the wonderful views from this high point across the surrounding countryside. Because the area has not been re-seeded or fertilisers used, the site is species-rich, with both grasses and wild flowers. Such a diversity also encourages a wide range of invertebrates to visit the area, which in turn support a wide variety of bird and mammal life.

In its unique position away from development, it supports many species of birds, including a number of migratory species that nest on site. Insect life is also well represented, with many butterflies, including the widely distributed small tortoiseshell, together with the common blue and small heath.

Situated just off Admirals Way, more information can be obtained by contacting the Rangers on 01327 877173.

Brampton Valley Way (NCC) is different to all of the other country parks in Northamptonshire in that it is a linear park following the line of the redundant Northampton to Market Harborough railway line. Fourteen miles long, the route covers a diverse range of habitats, and thus providing opportunities not only for walkers, but also for cyclists and horse-riders. Car parking and picnic sites are available at various places along the way.
The Park can be reached at various points but 'starts' near Boughton level crossing on the edge of Northampton and completes its 14 mile route close to Market Harborough. Tel: 01604 686327.

Brigstock Country Park (NCC) was formerly worked for sand, and the area has been developed to include trails, and there are links to the surrounding Fermyn Wood. Picnic meadows, car parking and toilets all available on site, with a Ranger service in attendance.
At Brigstock on the A6116 south east of Corby. Tel: 01536 373625

Brixworth Country Park (NCC) is the newest of the country parks and consists of a range of habitats and sites, which have been created. Its 'added value' is that it overlooks Pitsford Water. The Park also has a self-catering

residential centre, an extensive visitor centre, and cycle hire (operated independently). Work continues on this new site, and herb and scented gardens have been provided to cater for a range of visitors.
Off the A508 south of Brixworth. Tel: 01604 882322.

Daventry Country Park (Daventry District Council) centred around a British Waterways canal feeder reservoir, the area provides an interesting range of bird life, including waders and other water birds; hides have been provided to enhance bird watching. In addition there are waymarked walks, which pass through woodland and meadow, including an old unimproved hay meadow. Fishing is available and there is a Ranger Service.
Situated on the B4036 Daventry to Market Harborough road, about a mile from the town centre. Tel: 01327 877193.

Daventry Country Park *Photograph by Ron Wilson*

East Carlton Country Park (Corby Borough Council) covers 40 hectares (100 acres) of parkland with superb views into the Welland Valley. There are ponds and nature trails. The heritage centre gives a glimpse into the long-established steel industry - before modern man came to Corby. There are craft outlets, and a Ranger Service.
East Carlton off the A427, 5 miles from Corby. Tel: 01536 770977.

Hunsbury Hill Country Park (Northampton Borough Council) is set in almost 84 acres (34 ha) there is a nature reserve, hill fort, ironstone railway, playing field, children's activity area and playground, view point, picnic sites with tables and barbecue areas.
Hunsbury Hill Road, Danes Camp Way, off A43 (Towcester Road).

Irchester Country Park (NCC) covers an area of around 90 hectares (220 acres), and has extensive woodlands, which were planted after the extraction of minerals had been completed. There are walks, an audio trail and an interpretation centre, together with a Ranger Service and items for sale.
In Gypsy Lane on the B570, S of Wellingborough on the Little Irchester to Irchester road, and off the A509 SE of Wellingborough. Tel: 01933 276866.

Sywell Country Park (NCC) has the redundant Sywell Reservoir as its most distinctive feature, and which previously provided drinking water for Higham Ferrers. The total area of the park is 58 hectares (143 acres), and the old filter beds have been put into use as a butterfly garden and amphibian area. There is a tree trail, well-marked walks, bird hides, fishing and much more. Car parking, sales, display area and picnic sites, toilets and a Ranger Service.
In Washbrook Lane, about a mile from the A4500 at the Earls Barton crossroads. Tel: 01604 810970.

The Countryside Stewardship Scheme.

The Farming and Rural Conservation Agency, an executive body of the Ministry of Agriculture, Fisheries and Food (MAFF) administers this Scheme, which makes payments to farmers and land managers to improve the natural beauty and biodiversity of the countryside. Its objectives are:

Sustain the beauty and diversity of the landscape.
Improve and extend wildlife habitats.
Conserve archaeological sites and historic features.
Improve opportunities for countryside enjoyment.
Restore neglected land or features.
Create new habitats and landscape.

The project includes the management of both lowland and upland meadows and pastures and chalk and limestone grassland. Grants are also available for re-creating grassland on cultivated land, regenerating suppressed heath and moor, managing lowland heath, re-creating heath, restoring old orchards and managing arable field margins. In addition, grants are also available for access, including open access, footpaths and bridleways.

One of the important features of the scheme is that it allows the public access to some of these areas, including field margins, and land where linear and other paths can - and have - been created. There are many sites that offer educational opportunities for schools under the 'Education Access Initiative'. Northamptonshire is included in the MAFF East Midlands Regional Service Centre, and can be contacted on 0115 9291191.

County Paths - see Long Distance Walks

Cycling in Northamptonshire

Northamptonshire County Council has published a series of Cycletour leaflets, which cover 15 routes in the County, taking in areas such as the Brampton Valley Way and The Nene Valley Way. Titles include 'The Bluebell Line', 'Sulgrave, the Washingtons and the Sheep that 'Eat men', and 'Battlefields and Cattlefields'. Leaflets are available separately or in packs, the latter covering The Nene Valley and the Brampton Valley.

In addition the Great Central Cycle route starts at Stanford-on-Avon and finishes at Syresham. This is Route 70, and marked on signpost, with the number 70 in blue. Route 6 of the National Cycle Network passes through Northamptonshire, from Market Harborough on its way to Milton Keynes. The first stage uses the Brampton Valley Way, and the second stages goes through Northampton to Great Houghton and on to Hanslope.
For more information contact the Environment Directorate at Northamptonshire County Council, 01604 237478/237476.

County, District and Borough Councils

These deal with environmental issues within their locality (see also Local Agenda 21).

Corby Borough Council, George Street, Corby, Northants, NN17 1QB. Tel: 01536 402552.

Daventry District Council, Civic Offices, Lodge Road, Daventry, Northants, NN11 5AF. Tel: 01327 871100.

East Northamptonshire District Council, East Northamptonshire House, Cedar Drive, Thrapston, Northants, NN14 4LZ. Tel: 01832 740222.

Kettering Borough Council, Bowling Green Road, Kettering, Northants, NN15 7QX. Tel: 01536 410333.

Northampton Borough Council, Bedford Road, Northampton, NN4 7NR. Tel: 01604 233500.

Northamptonshire County Council, Environment Directorate, PO Box 163, County Hall, Guildhall Road, Northampton, NN1 1AX. Tel: 01604 236236.

South Northamptonshire Council, Springfields, Towcester, NN12 6AE. Tel: 01327 350211

Wellingborough Borough Council, Swanspool House, Wellingborough, Northants, NN8 1BT. Tel: 01933 229777.

English Heritage is a statutory body which gives grants to thousands of listed buildings, cathedrals, churches, archaeological sites, historic parks and gardens and ancient monuments across the country. By the imaginative re-use of the nation's historic buildings and by working closely with local authorities and other organisations, it seeks to spark the regeneration of the centres of cities, towns and villages. The organisation has nine regional offices across the country and a Centre of Archaeological Excellence at Fort Cumberland in Portsmouth.

It has a turnover of around £150k of which £30k is generated through admissions, membership, retail and catering, sponsorship and fundraising, as well as through publications, survey work and archive services. It manages over 400 of the nation's historic houses and monuments attracting 12 million visitors each year. These include Stonehenge, Dover Castle and Kenwood House. On 1 April, 1999, English Heritage merged with the Royal Commission on the Historical Monuments of England (RCHME) to create a new national lead body for the protection and understanding of England's historic environment and to provide a comprehensive source of expertise, skills and funding.

English Heritage incorporates the National Monuments Record, an archive of over 12 million photographs and records of England's built heritage.
The key objectives of the body are

1 Conserving and enhancing the historic environment for present and future generations.
2 Encouraging physical and intellectual access to the historic environment.
3 Increasing understanding of the historic environment.
4 Maximising resources where they are most needed for the historic environment.

In Northamptonshire English Heritage is responsible for Kirby Hall, Chichele College (Higham Ferrers), Eleanor Cross (Geddington) and the Triangular Lodge (Rushton). For more details see under Historic Houses (page 174).

English Heritage, Historic Properties, Midlands, area office is based in Northampton on 01604 730320.

English Nature was founded in 1991 to replace the Nature Conservancy Council. A government organisation it was established by Act of Parliament 'to advise on wildlife and earth heritage issues, and to achieve and encourage wildlife gain'. It is responsible for providing the government with advice on nature conservation matters in England. It is responsible for promoting the conservation of the wildlife of England, in 'partnership' with a variety of organisations. The English Nature Local Teams have the backing of a range of scientists and experts based at the national office in Peterborough.

English Nature is responsible, on behalf of the Government, for developing and implementing the country's Biodiversity Action Plan, which arose from the 1992 Earth Summit in Rio. Here nations signed up to Agenda 21, which aims at maintaining the world's biodiversity, but at the same time recognises and encourages sustainable development. In addition English Nature also established national nature reserves, and although we do not have any in Northamptonshire, there is one just outside the county border at Castor Hanglands (near Peterborough). English Nature is also responsible for designating areas Sites of Special Scientific Interest (SSSI) and for monitoring these. In Northamptonshire there are many SSSI's. In addition to carrying out its own research the organisation supports other groups. The organisation also publishes a range of leaflets, etc, and a list is available from:
English Nature, Northminster House, Peterborough, PE1 1UA. Tel: 01733 340345.

Farm Centres

The Farm Centres below provide a range of activities, enabling people to have better access to farms and in most cases the animals which are associated with them.

Ark Farm Sheep Dairy Centre is in the village of Tiffield, and is a traditional farm with sheep, cattle and free-range hens. Sheep are also milked between October and November. Farm visits are available for schools and other groups by arrangement. The farm shop sells a wide range of sheep dairy products, together with farm-reared pork and lamb.
Situation: High Street South. The village is signposted off the A5 south of Weedon and North of Towcester. Contact Sue Williams 01327 350202.

The Living Landscape Trust administers the Duke of Buccleuth's estate at Boughton, near Kettering. The Director arranges a variety of courses and activities on the estate farm covering 142 hectares (350 acres), which has cattle, sheep, arable crops, etc. – together with a dairy.
Situation: Off the A43 at Boughton, to the north of Kettering. Contact the Director, Living Landscape Trust 01536 515731.

Northfield Farm and Country Centre is situated at Cransley close to the edge of Kettering, and is housed in a converted barn on a working farm of 30 hectares (75 acres). Arrangements are made for group visits. The farm has various interests, including leisure, conservation, a variety of crops and sheep. Programmes organised take account of requests from teachers. There is a study centre, toilets, a room with seating for 50 people and a small kitchen. In addition to school groups, the centre is also open during the lambing season for people to watch what happens at this time of the year. Open access to farming and countryside subjects.
Situation: Cransley – leave A14 at J7, and follow signs towards Milton Malsor. At the bottom of the hill fork left towards Cransley. Northfield Farm is the first building on the left. Details from 01536 510622.

Rookery Open Farm is a working farm with different demonstrations available. There are cows, calves, lambs, sheep, ducks, rabbits, ponies and tractor and trailer rides. Open March to mid-Nov.
Situation: Rookery Lane, 300m from Stoke Bruerne Lock. Tel: 01604 864477.

The Old Dairy Farm Centre at Upper Stowe, just off the A5 south of Weedon, makes use of a working farm to provide school children with a farming experience. Courses are planned with schools, and a resident teacher organises a range of activities to link to National Curriculum topics. A booklet giving details of the farm and what is on offer is available.
Situation: Upper Stowe, signposted off the A5 south of Weedon. Details 01327 340525.

The Stable Yard Outdoor Activity Centre is not strictly a farm centre, but has two horses (Prince - a rare breeds Dales Pony and Jessie a bay Shire) and it is possible to arrange for hands-on experiences with them, including harness demonstrations. Day courses are also available in which individuals can get involved with Prince who works on a Recycling Scheme pulling a specially adapted waggon for door-to-door collection. It is also possible to see how he pulled canal boats. Jessie works on a round delivering coal and logs. Horse drawn agricultural equipment and waggons are also available for study.

Situation: The Stable Yard, Cosgrove Wharf, Lock Lane, Cosgrove. Tel: 01859 339551.

West Lodge Rural Centre has a wide range of facilities for schools, and the general public. These include access to the farm, trailer rides, crops of the UK, operation on a farm during the year, woods at different ages and stages, flora and fauna, fungi surveys, etc. Orienteering and team leadership courses are also available. Teachers packs (priced) with modules for all Key Stages have been produced. Shire Falconry is also situated at the same address.
Situation: Back Lane, on the Pipewell Road, Desborough. Tel: 01536 760552 (Office)/763762 (Visitor Centre).

Farming and Wildlife Advisory Group (FWAG)

The Farming and Wildlife Advisory Group is the foremost organisation providing conservation advice to the farmer. It was formed in 1969 by a group of farmers and conservationists who were keen to promote environmentally friendly agriculture. Its remit was to consider conservation in its widest possible sense - including wildlife, landscape, archaeology and public access. FWAG has advisers in most counties, and these offer guidance on a range of conservation practices which benefit wildlife and their habitats, without compromising productivity or economic performance. FWAG advisors are available to assist and comment on field margins, wetlands, hedgerows, watercourses, moorland and woodland.

In addition, FWAG also provides updates in technical developments relating to farm operations, and these include the application of agricultural chemicals, waste management and pollution control. Rather than seeing parts of the farm in isolation, FWAG advisors view the farm as a unit, and adopt a whole farm approach when making comments and offering advice. In initial surveys they analyse the whole farm habitat. From this, the farmer receives a detailed report, which will offer suggestions for both short and long-term management. FWAG's Advisory Service is appropriate to all farms, irrespective of size, enterprise, or geographical location. The initial visit is made free of charge, and the fees that are charged for future visits depend on the amount of work to be done. Tel: 01604 491141 (Local FWAG Advisor).

Field Study and other Residential Centres

Badby Youth Hostel - see under Youth Hostels Association

Brixworth Country Park has residential self-catering facilities for up top 24 people (2x12 people units), and the facilities include those for individuals with mobility problems. There is wheelchair access. There is plenty to do within close proximity to the Park, including the nearby historic village of Brixworth, Pitsford Water, Brampton Valley Way, etc. Cycle hire available at the Park. Tel: 01604 882322.

Everdon Field Studies Centre is housed in the former village Victorian school, built in 1879. The two classrooms are now used as dormitories and the main hall serves as a multi-purpose room for dining, working and recreation. A toilet block includes showers and wash basins. The former headteacher's house is also used, and includes kitchen, a staff/resources room, office, staff bedroom and shower facilities for adults. The various buildings in the yard have been modified to provide a drying room/outdoor clothing store, equipment store, washroom, and small classroom.

Everdon is situated in a particularly attractive part of Northamptonshire, some 12 miles (19 kilometres) from Northampton and 5 miles (8 kilometres) from Daventry. The area is ideal for a range of environmental activities, including work linked to the NC and Literacy and Numeracy strategies. Innumerable opportunities for investigative work are possible within the many areas, which are a short distance, from the village.

Everdon has many housing styles, offering a range of studies - from comparing and contrasting localities, to looking at types of building material. An audio trail takes children from the field centre via the blacksmith's to the parish church. Streams offer many ideas, and Everdon Stubbs, a piece of ancient woodland, has unequalled opportunities for looking at many subjects both within and outside the National Curriculum. Transport themes can be included, with the A5, M1, A45 and Grand Union Canal within easy reach. There are also many small, intriguing, and historically interesting villages ideal for comparing and contrasting sites - Farthingstone, Newnham, Stowe Nine Churches and Badby - are all within easy reach of the Centre.

Other study areas include the Old Dairy Farm Centre (Upper Stowe), Daventry Country Park, Daventry Museum and Newnham Mill. The good network of footpaths follow routes which our ancestors used, providing an alternative to road-walking. Here, in this unspoilt part of the county children - and adults alike - can enjoy the peace and tranquillity of a part of Northamptonshire, which appears to have changed little for centuries.

The Centre caters for students between the ages of 5-12 from towns and villages all over the county. Each programme is organised in consultation with staff from schools.

A residential visit allows time for children to learn about the environment, socialise and experience living in a small community. The weekly cost includes the use of the Centre's equipment work/study sheets, minibus and full board. The centre is also open at weekends, for catered and self-catered groups; holiday periods are available, but groups are responsible for their own catering.
For more information visit our website www.daventry-index.co.uk/fieldcentres, or contact Everdon Field Studies Centre, Everdon, Daventry, Northants, NN11 3BL, or tel/fax 01327 361384.

Fletton House is a residential centre situated in the delightful historic Northamptonshire town of Oundle. The Centre offers a catering service, and a range of activities is available close by. Some can be arranged by the centre (for which there is usually an extra charge) others are planned by the groups. Oundle is a fascinating town, which is worth investigating. It has a number of historic buildings, including the mainly 13th century church of St Peter with its 63 metre (203 foot) slender, decoratively carved crocketted spire. Other local sites include Barnwell Country Park, with its lakes, range of habitats, and backwater of the River Nene. Close to Fletton House water meadows lead down to the River Nene, and nearby there are facilities for boating, fishing, bird watching and canoeing. The River Nene is ideal for canoeing, and Fletton House has canoes, which can be used, provided that a qualified instructor is present. Fotheringhay Castle, with its tragic historic association, is also relatively close by. Other facilities include Kettering Leisure Village, Ferry Meadows Country Park, Nene Valley Steam Railway, and Sacrewell Farm Centre.

Accommodation includes dormitories, lounge, large activities games room, and dining room. Further information: 01832 272179.

Grendon Hall The building is a delightful Queen Anne House which stands in 7 hectares (17 acres) of its own grounds, The hall, a residential training centre, has facilities for a range of activities. These include field studies in the surrounding area and outdoor pursuits (arrangements made by the Hall for qualified instructors where necessary). There are facilities for conferences, including two large rooms, which are also suitable for meetings. Other smaller rooms are also available. On site facilities include a swimming pool, playing fields, tennis courts and camping facilities for up to one hundred people. The

site offers a camp kitchen, standpipes, flush toilets, showers and hand washbasins.
Further information from 01933 663853.

Longtown Outdoor Education Centre.
Although outside Northamptonshire, the Centre is part of Northamptonshire County Council's facilities, and caters for groups both within and outside the county. The fully equipped residential Centre is situated in its own grounds covering 6 hectares (15 acres), and has excellent on-site facilities. It is located between the eastern edge of the Black Mountains and the River Monnow. Within the grounds there is a canoe training pool, an abseil tower, a zip-wire, a ropes course, a climbing wall, navigation courses and problem-solving exercises. The Forest of Dean and South Wales are within easy reach. The Centre is a Mountain Rescue Post.

The staff are qualified and experienced to cater for a range of activities and offer safe and challenging activities for groups of young people and adults. Courses/training can be provided for caving, rock-climbing, kayaking, gorge-walking, camping, orienteering, canoeing, navigation, photography, abseiling, painting, nature study, hill walking, industrial archaeology, bivouacs, mountain-biking, Duke of Edinburgh Award, etc. The Centre provides tailor-made courses, or groups can arrange their own activities.

The residential accommodation caters for a maximum of 30 people in various-sized bedrooms, with separate accommodation for leaders. In addition to these facilities, the centre has excellent camping facilities, which include a camping field, car park, showers, drying room, covered cooking area, utility room and shop. Longtown can help camping groups organise and plan their activities.

Courses are also arranged for leaders who wish to gain qualifications, and provides opportunities for such courses with national and local training schemes. Training is also available for business and industry.
More details from 01873 860225.

Knuston Hall, a 17th century country mansion with character, is equipped with modern facilities, Set amidst 16 landscaped hectares (40 acres) of quiet and tranquil Northamptonshire countryside. The facilities include en-suite bedrooms, meeting and conference rooms, together with a high quality catering service. It offers a wide range of courses that will enhance awareness of far-reaching environmental issues as part of a extensive programme of residential, activity courses.

Within easy reach there are many activities and facilities that will be of interest to the visitor. These include towns like Rushden (1 mile), Wellingborough (4 miles), Bedford (12 miles), Northampton (15 miles), with Cambridge and Oxford some 40 miles distant. Within the peaceful surroundings there are many walks, including access onto the Nene Way, and the H E Bates Walk. Skew Bridge has a dry ski slope, and Castle Ashby is within a 'stone's throw'. Country parks include Irchester (2 miles) and Barnwell (12 miles), with Summer Leys Local Nature Reserve 5 miles away with its picnic sites, bird-watching, hides available, which include those for people with disabilities.
Details: 01933 312104

Newton in the Willows Field Centre. Opened in 1975, the Centre is housed in the converted redundant church of St Faith's, in the hamlet of Newton, approximately mid-way between Kettering and Corby. The Newton in the Willows Trust administers it.

The main work of the Centre is to provide field study courses for schoolchildren from both primary and secondary levels in Northamptonshire. Numerous weekend and holiday courses are also organised for adults, and these range from archaeology to landscape painting. In addition there are evening lectures, many of which are aimed at the family.
Details: The Head of Centre, Newton Field Centre, Newton, Geddington, Kettering, Northants, NN14 1BW Tel: 01536 741643.

Footpaths are covered in the main body of the book, where the Ramblers give a resume of the footpaths in Northamptonshire, encouraging people to walk these. In addition the County Council produces a leaflet 'Keeping Paths Open. Public Rights of Way Enforcement Procedure'. This explains why the County Council has this policy because walkers might come across a variety of problems when using these rights of way. It could be that a farmer has planted a crop without making sure the footpath is still accessible, sometimes developments are placed across footpaths illegally, or the finger post indicating the direction of the path is missing. The County Council takes the necessary action where appropriate.

For more details of this, or a copy of the leaflet, contact The Rights of Way Office, Northamptonshire County Council, PO Box 221, John Dryden House, 8-10 The Lakes, Northampton, NN4 7DE. Tel: 01604 237700.

A short rest on a winter's day close to Broughton.
Photograph by Bob Coles

Forestry Commission is responsible for grants and licences, plant health service, and policy and practice. There are national offices in England, Scotland and Wales, and conservancies at area level. These are responsible for implementing Forestry Commission policies, grants and licences at area level.

The Forestry Commission cares for more than a million hectares (24.5 million acres) which is used not only for timber production, but also has multi-purpose benefits, including recreation and public access, and as part of its remit it provides a range of activities, including walking, cycling, horse riding, camping, orienteering, fishing, caravaning, bird watching - and much more. The Commission also has a range of holiday homes in various forests.

The Government's Forestry Strategy for England, *A New Focus for England's Woodlands,* was published in December 1998, and sets out the Government's priorities and programmes for forestry in England for the next five to ten years. It is based on four programmes, which include a range of actions, that the Government intends to take over the next few years to implement the Strategy.

In the Forestry for Recreation, Access and Tourism the document describes what can be implemented to promote more and better-quality public access for woodlands. It also ensures that these woods and forests will continue to be used for a wide range of recreational pursuits, as well as complementing and supporting the tourist industry.

Forest Research is an Agency of the Forestry Commission, and in the main organisation in the UK which is involved with forestry and tree related research. This Agency includes the former Research Division, the Technical Development Branch and parts of the former Surveys Branch of the Forestry Commission. Under one umbrella the Agency will provide research, development, surveys and related services to the forestry industry and provide authoritative advice and support of the development and implementation of the Government's forestry policies.

GB Policy and Practice was set up in 1999 in preparation for devolution, and it will carry out the functions of the Forestry Commission that apply to the whole of Great Britain.

The Forest Enterprise is also an Agency of the Forestry Commission, and its mains aims are, 'To maintain and increase the productive potential of the forest estate; to increase opportunities for public recreation; to increase the conservation value of forests, and to increase the net value of commercial activities'.

Apart from a Head Office and four Regional Offices, the Forest Enterprise has Forest Districts, and these are responsible for managing forests to produce timber for the wood processing industry, other goods, services and environmental benefits for the public.
The Forestry Commission is based in Edinburgh (0131 334 0303). The office for England is a Great Eastern House, Tenison Road, Cambridge, CB1 2DU (01223 314545) or fax (01223 460699), and the Northants Forest District which covers the county is based at Fineshades, Top Lodge, Fineshades, Corby. (01780 443394). The Forest Authority is also based at the same address (01780 444532).
More information can be found at www.forestry.gov.uk.

Friends of the Earth has a local group which supports the national aims of informing and empowering the public, and is involved in local, as well as national, campaigns. For more information contact 01604 513066/0207 5661555.

Historic Buildings, Houses and Gardens

The principle houses and gardens in Northamptonshire are listed below. Because opening times and admission charges may change, these have not been given here, but can be obtained by contacting local Tourist Information Centres, or the establishment concerned.

Aynho Park is a four-period house originally dating from the seventeenth century, with alterations/additions in Carolean, early eighteenth and beginning of nineteenth century.
Situation: Six miles south-east of Banbury on the A41 London to Birmingham road.
Open: Ring for dates.
Tel: 01869 810636.

Canons Ashby (National Trust), an Elizabethan Manor House, which has been the home of the Dryden family since it was first built about 1710. During this time few alterations have taken place to the building. The interior has many wall paintings and some excellent Jacobean plasterwork. The formal garden is also of interest, and an orchard, dating from the 16th century, has some interesting fruit trees. Close by is a fine church, all that is left of the former Augustinian Priory.
Situation: On an unclassified road between Adstone and Moreton Pinkney.
Open: April - end October Wed-Sat. Tearooms and grounds 12 noon; House 1300.
Tel: 01327 860044.

Castle Ashby (Marquess of Northampton) is an Elizabethan House, with a front designed by Inigo Jones in 1635. The ceilings are 17th century, and there is a valuable collection of paintings. The House is used as a Conference Centre, and is no longer open. The gardens are open to public.
Situation: Six miles east of Northampton, one and half miles off the A428, Northampton to Bedford Road.
Open: Ring for times.
Tel: 01604 696996 (Head Gardener)

Chichele College (English Heritage). Henry Chichelle founded the College in 1422, as a college for secular canons. The remains include part of a quadrangle, which incorporates a chapel. There is an exhibition that shows the result of work carried out in the 1980's. The exterior can be seen at any reasonable time. For information about the exhibition contact the area office on 01604 730320.

Coton Manor Garden is a well-maintained old English garden enhanced by the addition of water features, containing many species of wildfowl, including flamingos. There is a delightful bluebell wood in the spring. Garden plants for sale.
Situation: 10 miles north of Northampton off A428 Northampton to Rugby road.
Open: April to October on Thurs to Sun, and bank holidays.
Tel: 01604 740219.

Cottesbrooke Hall and Gardens is a Queen Anne house with an excellent collection of pictures, especially covering sporting and equestrian subjects. There are also good collections of porcelain and some fine furniture. If tradition is anything to go by, this House was the 'model' for Jane Austin's Mansfield Park. There are excellent gardens with a wide variety of shrubs, trees, etc.
Situation: On an unclassified road off the A5199 to the north of Northampton.
Open: Varies – ring for details.
Tel: 01604 505808.

Deene Park has been the home of the Brudenells since 1514. It is of both historical and architectural interest.
Situation: Eight miles west of Oundle and six miles north-east of Corby on the A43 Kettering to Stamford road.
Open: Varies - check local press/TIC.
Tel: 01780 450278/450223.

Geddington - Eleanor Cross is one of nine crosses (only three survive - two in Northamptonshire) put up by Queen Eleanor's husband to mark the stopping points of the funeral cortege on its route from Harby in Nottinghamshire to Westminster.

Hardingstone, near Northampton, has the other example of the Eleanor Cross (see Geddington) erected for the same reason.

Hinwick House is an excellent example of a Queen Anne House. There are fine paintings by Lely, Kneller and C Van Dyck, as well as other notable artists. A good collection of furniture, tapestries and needlework are also on display.

Situation: Six miles south-east of Wellingborough, three and a half miles from Rushden, off the A6.
Open: Mainly by appointment.
Tel: 01933 353624.

Kirby Hall (English Heritage) was begun in 1570. Alterations took place in the 17th century. In many respects the stone-built mansion is one of the most important of its period, and contains local, rather than national, styles. Now only partly roofed. The gardens date from the seventeenth century, and are excellent examples of their kind; there is an exhibition on site.
Situation: Two miles south-east of Gretton village, and reached via an unclassified road off the A43, 4 miles NE of Corby.
Open: All year; closed on Mons and Tues in winter.
Tel: 01536 203230.

Lamport Hall. (Lamport Hall Trust) was the home of the Ishams from 1560. Most of the present house dates from the 17th and 18th centuries. The front is an Inigo Jones design (1635). The gardens have ornamental lakes, wide avenues, flowering terraces and architectural stone buildings.
Situation: On A508 Northampton to Market Harborough road, eight miles from Northampton.
Open: Ring for details.
Tel: 01604 686272.

Lyveden New Bield (National Trust) was begun by Sir Thomas Tresham in about 1595 as a lodge or garden house. It is an unusual Renaissance building. Today it is a roofless shell, but it is still fascinating, because it was built in the shape of a cross, with some interesting exterior frieze work, intended to symbolise the Passion, but unfortunately was never completed. Sir Thomas became involved in the Gunpowder Plot.
Situation: Four miles south-west of Oundle off the A427.
Tel: 01832 205358 (Custodian).

Priest's House (National Trust) is a pre-Reformation Priest's Lodge; its interest is primarily for its architecture. Inside there is a small collection of village artefacts.
Situation: Easton on the Hill, near Stamford, off the A43, and approx. 2 miles SW of Stamford.
Tel: 01909 486411 (Regional Office). Open by appointment only.

Rockingham Castle was a royal residence until 1530, from which date it has been the home of the Watson family. Nine hundred years of English history

can be traced in the building. The gardens are also extremely pleasant, with avenues of fine trees.
Situation: On the A6003 Corby to Uppingham road, two miles N of Corby and nine miles from Market Harborough.
Open: Easter to the end of September on Sundays and Thursday. Parties and groups - including schools - on other days by arrangement.
Tel: 01536 770240.

Southwick Hall is a Manor House which retains some medieval building, dating from 1300. There were additions in the Tudor period and in the eighteenth century.
Situation: Four miles east of Bulwick, three miles north of Oundle.
Open: First Thursday in each month from April to September, as well as on Bank Holiday Mondays. Parties by arrangement on other days.
Tel: 01832 274064.

Sulgrave Manor (The Sulgrave Manor Board). This early English house was the home of the ancestors of George Washington. It is an interesting example of this type of small manor house, with good gardens, which date from Shakespeare's time. Educational visits/material available.
Situation: Seven miles W of Brackley; eight miles NE of Banbury.
Open: Each day (except Weds) all year.
Tel: 01295 760205.

Triangular Lodge, Rushton (English Heritage), is a unique building where everything is in threes to represent the Trinity! There are three floors, three triangular gables and three sides. It has been called 'the purest folly in the country'. Sir Thomas Tresham built this fascinating folly between 1593 and 1597 when he returned after he had been imprisoned for his religious beliefs.
Situation: 1 mile W of Rushton on an unclassified road, and 3 miles from Desborough.
Open: 1 April to 30 Sept 1000-1800 and 1-31 Oct from 1000-1700.
Tel: 01536 710761.

Local Agenda 21

This is an agenda for the 21st century. It has its origins in the 1992 United Nations Earth Summit, held in Rio de Janeiro, and is a 'global plan for sustainable development'. During its various sessions it came up with this statement, 'By 1996, most local authorities in each country should have undertaken a consultative process with their populations and achieved consensus on a Local Agenda 21 for the community'. Many local authorities in the British Isles have taken this initiative on board. In Northamptonshire these include Daventry District Council, Wellingborough Borough Council, etc.

Because it was envisaged that the local population would be involved, the form that the 'group' takes varies from one part of the county to another. In Daventry District the Daventry and District Local Agenda 21 Action Group has been responsible for a number of initiatives. An annual Forum is held, at which community action awards are presented. Submissions are open to any group that falls in with the group's aim 'To help improve everyone's quality of life'. Over the last three years awards have gone to village hall projects, a village walking group, a carers' group, a gardening project for the housebound and lonely, etc. In addition to the Forum, the group has also produced the first of its community directories. This aims to keep everyone informed of what individuals are doing, so that people can network when they need help with a project which someone else may have already been involved with. Leaflets covering wildlife gardens and waste recycling have also been part of the group's projects, and a regular column appears in the Daventry Express. Initiatives at the present include the setting up of a community allotment/garden, and a publication 'Buy It Locally'.

Details of Local Agenda 21 initiatives throughout Northamptonshire can be obtained from the following:

Corby District Council, Environmental Co-ordinator, George Street, Corby, NN17 1QB. Tel: 01536 402552.

Daventry District Council, Local Agenda 21 Officer, Lodge Road, Daventry, Northants, NN11 5AF. Tel: 01327 871100.

East Northamptonshire Council, Environmental Initiatives Officer, Cedar Drive, Thrapston, NN14 4LZ. Tel: 01832 740222.

Kettering Borough Council, Head of Environmental Services, Bowling Green Road, Kettering, NN15 7QX. Tel: 01536 410333.

Northampton Borough Council, Environmental Health Manager, Bedford Road, Northampton, NN4 0NR. Tel: 01604 233500.

Northamptonshire ACRE, Director, Hunsbury Hill Centre, Harksome Hill, Northampton, NN4 9QX. Tel: 01604 765888.

Northamptonshire County Council. Environmental Co-ordinator, P O Box 163, County Hall, Guildhall Road, Northampton, NN1 1AX. Tel: 01604 236236.

South Northamptonshire Council, Environmental Co-ordinator, Springfields, Towcester, NN12 6AE. Tel: 01327 350111.

Wellingborough (Borough Council of), Environmental Co-ordinator, 20 Sheep Street, Wellingborough, NN8 1BJ. Tel: 01933 229777.

Local Associations

Information, telephone numbers and personnel change frequently with many local groups, and details can be obtained from libraries, tourist information centres, etc.

Long Distance Walks

Northamptonshire has several long distance footpaths. Some have been set up on the instigation of the County Council; with others there has been a collaborative involvement with other agencies. The first of these - The Knightley Way (followed closely by The Grafton Way) - were established many years ago. To these early paths have been added the Nene Way, Jurassic Way and Midshires Way, enabling the walker to explore much of Northamptonshire's varying terrain and landscape. Other paths, like the Macmillan Way, pass through the County. All paths are waymarked and signposted along their complete lengths. To these must be added the long distance Grand Union Canal Walk, which starts in Birmingham, and passes through the county on its way to its destination in London - or vice versa!

The Grafton Way was the second of Northamptonshire's long distance footpaths to be established and takes the walker from Greens Norton to Cosgrove, where it links with the North Bucks Way. The Northamptonshire end of the trail at Greens Norton links with the Knightley Way. The Grafton Way is named after the Dukes of Grafton, because much of the walk passes over land belonging to the Duke. The path, some 12.5 miles long, takes the walker over a variety of terrain, using public rights of way, and is well signposted and waymarked. The first section takes the rambler from Greens Norton to Wood Burcote. Passing through fields and over stiles the paths eventually crosses the A43 - the Oxford road. From Wood Burcote the next port of call is Pury End, and thence to Gullet. The A5 needs to be negotiated in a short time, and once Gullet is reached Moor End comes into view, and from this hamlet the winding way takes the walker on to Potterspury. The spire of the church comes into view before the village, and if it is open it is worth taking time out to enjoy this peaceful idyllic church - and the village as well. The final section of the walk leads to Cosgrove where it links up with the North Bucks Way, and if you intend to walk you will need to make your way to Wolverton.

Grand Union Canal Walk links Birmingham and London, Britain's two major cities, and can be joined at various places in the county. A book, showing the route, has a wealth of other information. The towpath beside the Grand Union Canal is accessible along its whole length. There are possibilities for links with walks around villages, and The Grand Union Canal Walk has all the information, together with Ordnance Survey maps to ensure that the long distance walker can complete the 100 mile journey - or simply choose those parts of it in Northamptonshire which appeal. Within Northamptonshire, the towpath starts in the county close to Braunston and passing through a large stretch of Northamptonshire, it eventually arrives at the Buckinghamshire border.

Jurassic Way is a long distance footpath which passes through Northamptonshire linking Banbury (in the south) and Lincolnshire (in the east). On its journey it takes in the county's western and southern borders, starting at Warkworth in the south west of Northamptonshire and ending after its 83 miles journey at Easton-on-the-Hill, close to Stamford. It follows what is thought to be the earlier Jurassic Way. The route goes along a spine of Jurassic limestone, which is believed to have been a trade route linking the Humber and Severn estuaries in medieval times.

The Knightley Way was the first of Northamptonshire's County Paths to be established. Its twelve miles take the walker from Badby to Greens Norton - or vice versa. Although the footpaths are public, the land over which they pass is private and it is important that the walker ALWAYS stays on the path. The Knightley Way has been named after this well-known Northamptonshire family, whose seat was at Fawsley Hall for some 450 years. The path crosses much of the land, which once belonged to the Knightleys.
The first stretch, which starts at Church Hill, Badby, takes the walker to the depopulated twin villages at Fawsley. Passing by the historic Church of St Mary's, with Fawsley Hall to the right (now a hotel). The parkland has seen visits from many 'historic' figures in the past. Queen Elizabeth I stayed at Fawsley Hall on her way to Kenilworth Castle, and Charles I reportedly hunted deer in Badby Wood. In more recent times one of the Lady Knightley's invited Joseph Merrick - better known as the Elephant Man - to stay on the estate.

The path travels past the east end of the church, but if it is open (and leaving muddy boots outside!) it is worth taking a look inside the building, a 'shrine' to generations of Knightleys. Having passed between two lakes - The Canal and Big Waters - the tower of Preston Capes church soon comes into view. From this relatively unspoilt village the route goes past the well-established Woodland Golf Course and then on to Farthingstone, which marks the half way point of the journey. From here the walk crosses pastureland to the delightful village of Litchborough and on to Foxley. The route now winds across undulating countryside at its makes its way to Greens Norton, where the spire of the village church comes into view.

The MacMillan Way, not a Northamptonshire path, but part of the route passes through the county. Starting at Oakham after 230 miles (370 km) it reaches Abbotsbury (on the Dorset coast). The walk enters Northamptonshire near Weston-by-Welland, and passes south through the villages of Braybrooke, Maidwell, Creaton, Holdenby, the Bringtons, Flore, Farthingstone, Canons Ashby and Eydon - and a number of other intermediate villages as well. It leaves the county near Chipping Warden. The route has been set up to raise money for MacMillan Nurses.

Midshires Way long distance footpath starts in Buckinghamshire, and enters the county close to Salcey Forest. Here it makes its way to the Welland Valley, covering a distance of some 46 miles (74 km). The route takes the walker through a series of delightful villages, including Piddington, Bugbrooke, Upper Heyford, Upper Harlestone, the Bramptons, Brixworth, Arthingworth, Braybrooke and Sutton Bassett. Along the way the scenery changes from the undulating nature of the Northamptonshire uplands to the distinctive landscape of the Welland. The Way links with a number of other county paths, including The Nene Way (at Nether Heyford), the Jurassic Way (between Great Oxenden and Hermitage Wood) and the Grand Union Canal walk (between Blisworth and Nether Heyford).

The Nene Way is named after the valley through which it travels. It starts at the village of Badby in the west of Northamptonshire, and close to the 'official' source of the River Nene, near one of Northamptonshire's oldest settlements at Arbury Hill, just outside the village. Having travelled along traditional footpaths, stretches of roads and some permitted footpaths, it eventually reaches the Cambridgeshire border, having left Badby some 70 miles (112 km) behind.

Oxford Canal Walk links Coventry with Oxford along the tow path of the Oxford Canal – or vice versa – and part of the route passes through Northamptonshire. It is fully open to walkers.
Details 01788 890666.

Swan's Way is a long distance bridle route which starts at Salcey Forest in the county and goes 'south' into Buckinghamshire, and ultimately reaches the Thames at Goring.

Moulton College

Has a range of both vocational and academic courses, leading to various qualifications in countryside management. These qualifications are recognised in industry. Skills are enhanced to allow students who leave to achieve employment in a range of countryside-related disciplines/activities.
Tel: 01604 491131.

Museums and Exhibition Centres in Northamptonshire.

Apart from a few larger, 'well-known' museums in Northamptonshire, there are many other 'specialist' collections, which are well worth exploring.

Abington Museum is housed in a 15th century manor house in Abington Park. The house includes a 16th century oak-panelled room and Great Hall. The displays include the social history of the house, together with a Victorian Cabinet of Curiosities, features on Northampton life, the County's military history, and a 19th century fashion gallery. Temporary exhibitions are also staged from time to time.
In Abington Park, one mile from Northampton town centre. Admission: Free.
Telephone: 01604 631454.

Ashton Mill and Fish Museum (near Oundle) is housed in the former mill, which was 'modernised' to produce electricity and supply water. These 19th century features can still be seen. The building also houses a fish museum, and there are exhibitions covering antique farm machinery, basket-making and thatching, together with a forge and tools. On the Ashton Wold estate, N of Oundle. Tel: 01832 272264.

British Waterways Exhibition and Information Centre is housed in the Stop House on the canal towpath at Braunston. The Centre provides a wide range of information about the local canals, and also has a range of exhibitions throughout the year.

Signposted off the A45 (British Waterways) about 3 miles (5 kilometres) west of Daventry.
Tel: 01788 890666.

The Canal Museum (Stoke Bruerne) is in former canal-side warehouses. The two floors of displays give an insight into the canals as they were at the dawn of the Industrial Revolution, and bring to life more than 200 years of the varied history on the canals and waterways.
In Stoke Bruerne. Tel: 01604 862229.

Carpet Baggers Aviation Museum (Harrington) is on an old World War II airfield, which was used by the US 8th Airforce 801st. 492. The group used the code name 'Carpet Baggers' when dropping people and material into Europe. The exhibits cover the history of the airfield, and also include memorabilia and photographs.
Harrington - off Lamport Road. Tel: 01604 686608.

Central Museum and Art Gallery, Northampton. Northamptonshire's main museum it has a wide range of exhibits, as well as 'temporary' displays. It is perhaps most famous because of its internationally acclaimed shoe collection, which also includes decorative items, together with machines introduced to 'mechanise' the industry. There is also a reconstruction of a shoemaker's shop. The Museum also includes many other important aspects of the county's past from earliest Stone Age times to the 20th century. Additionally there is an excellent collection of decorative arts, together with an art gallery.
Guildhall Road, Northampton. Tel: 01604 639415.

Daventry Museum is housed in the historic Grade II* 18th century Moot Hall, and contains temporary and permanent displays, including those covering the social history of the town and district, local trades, rural life and the development of Daventry. Daventry sites, such as the Borough Hill Iron Age Hillfort, and the former BBC Transmitting site, also feature.
Moot Hall, opposite Market Square. Tel: 01327 302463.

Earls Barton Museum of Local Life has displays to show aspects of both work and leisure during the 19th and 20th centuries. The typical ground floor of the home of an early 20th century shoe-worker and his family includes his 'shop'. Additional displays include a parlour and yard with 'traditional' washing kit - dolly tub and mangle. Other exhibits and changing displays are also a feature of the Museum.
Barkers Factory Complex, Station Road. Tel: 01604 811735 (Mrs I Flanagan, Chairman of Museum Trust).

Grandad's Attic Museum is in Draper's Furniture Shop. The eight rooms in this small museum have a fascinating variety of material, and also feature different themes - music, domestic, barn, hobbies, workshops, etc. There is a piano player and scenic railway - and much more.
Location: Draper's. Barrack Road, Northampton. Tel: 01604 638935/639907.

Hannington Vintage Tractor Club Museum has an excellent collection of agricultural and other bygones, including vintage tractors, and 'associated' implements. Other displays feature collections of hedging tools, dairy ware, etc.
Lamport Hall, just off the A508. Tel: 01933 314320.

Irchester Narrow Gauge Railway Museum includes a variety of material linked to the former railway, used during the mining of stone in the area. There are also narrow gauge locomotives and rolling stock - none of which come from this area.
Irchester Country Park, south of Wellingborough. Tel: 01234 750469.

Manor House Museum (Kettering) provides an intriguing 'backward glance' into the town's past. The collections give an insight into social and industrial history, together with archaeology and geology.
Sheep Street, Tel: 01536 534381.

Northants Aviation Museum, The Museum has displays of remains of World War II aircraft, and includes parts of a Junkers Bomber, a Dornier Do 217K Night Bomber and a USAF Liberator. There are also displays of instruments and other equipment.
Off the Lamport Road, Harrington. Tel: 01604 686608.

Northamptonshire Ironstone Railway Museum has a variety of railway engines and wagons from the local iron workings. Exhibits explain how ironstone was carried to the blast furnaces to be made into iron. Diesel-hauled rides.
In Hunsbury Hill Country Park, Hunsbury Hill Road, Camp Hill, Northampton. Tel: 01604 890229.

Oundle Museum has living heritage displays and changing exhibitions, which give a glimpse into the development of Oundle and its environs in Roman times.
Drill Hall Centre. Tel: 01832 274333 (Oundle TIC).

Piddington Museum is run by The Upper Nene Archaeological Society in the former chapel at Piddington and is still being developed. For further information, contact Diane or Roy Friendship-Taylor on 01604 870312.

Rushden Heritage Centre is administered by East Northamptonshire Council, and there are different exhibitions - usually on a monthly basis - throughout the year.
Tel: 01933 412000

Rushden Historical Transport Museum uses the former Railway Station, for its display of many different forms of transport. Artefacts - such as lamps, signs, ticket machines, signal equipment, and other railway relics - can also be seen.
Station Approach. Tel: 01933 318988 (Sat/Sun 1200-1400/evenings 1930-2230).

Sir Henry Royce Memorial Foundation is, as its name implies, devoted to the history of Rolls Royce and Sir Henry Royce, the creator of the car. There are documents, memorabilia and photographs.
The Hunt House, Paulerspury. Tel: 01327 811048.

Steel-Making Heritage Centre is situated in East Carlton Countryside Park, and the Centre traces the history of the excavation of iron and steel making from early times. Displays include equipment, videos, etc.
East Carlton Countryside Park, near Corby. Tel: 01536 770977.

Wellingborough Heritage Centre has displays covering all aspects of Wellingborough's history, the oldest exhibits going back 2000 years. Operated by the Wellingborough Civic Society it is housed in Croyland Hall.
Behind the Hind Hotel. Tel: 01933 276838.

Wollaston Village Museum has a wide range of local material relating to the daily life of the village, including those concerned with archaeology, agriculture and industry, together with photographs, old prints, Victorian family treasures etc.
High Street. Contact Ms I Walker 19 Hookham Path, Wollaston, Wellingborough, Northants, NN29 7PQ.

National Fox Welfare Group

The National Fox Welfare Group has its headquarters in the county and is made up of people interested in the welfare of these often maligned mammals. For further details contact Martin Hemmington on 01933 411996.

National Trust, The

One of Britain's oldest conservation movements, the National Trust for Places of Historic Interest and Natural Beauty - to give it its full title - was founded more than a century ago in 1895. At this time, the three founders realised that there was a need to take care of 'places of historic interest and natural beauty', because of the increasing industrialisation and urbanisation - with the possibility that much of interest would be lost to the nation for ever. A year after it was founded, the Trust acquired its first property, Alfriston Clergy house in East Sussex.

In Northamptonshire the National Trust is responsible for Canons Ashby House (near Daventry) and Lyvenden New Bield (near Oundle), See Historic Buildings, Houses and Gardens section of the Directory, page 174.

Nature Reserves

The majority of the nature reserves in Northamptonshire are either owned or managed by the Wildlife Trust (01604 405285). These are denoted by the letters WT. Full details of all reserves can be obtained from The Wildlife Trust, Lings House, Billing Lings, Northampton, NN3 4BE. Those listed below include a selection. For other open areas see Country Parks and Woodlands.

Ashton Water Dragonfly Sanctuary is unique in Britain, and there are only three others in the world. The sanctuary aims to highlight these extremely attractive and 'ancient' insects, the record of the earliest dating back 350 million years. Apart from being open to visitors, the aim at the 2 hectare (5 acre) site is to provide a refuge for these insects where they are protected and can breed. To date 16 different species have been recorded.
The Sanctuary is at Ashton Wold near Oundle. More information from 01832 272427.

Barnack Hills and Holes National Nature Reserve is an extensive area of limestone grassland covering 225 hectares (555 acres), which was quarried for stone from Roman to medieval times, the material being used for cathedrals and abbeys in the surrounding area. It is considered to be one of the finest pieces of relict (ancient) grassland left in England, and has a range of species,

including pasque flower, cowslip, purple milk vetch, man orchid and squinancywort. Butterflies, which occur, include the marbled white and common blue.
The area is 2 miles (5 kilometres) E of the A1, SW of Barnack village. Wildlife Trust 01604 405285.

Barnes Meadow Local Nature Reserve is managed jointly by the Wildlife Trust and Northampton Borough Council. It was made a local nature reserve in 1990, and covers just over one hectare (2.5 acres), and has a wide range of wildlife interest. The northern arm of the River Nene runs through the area, making most of the site open water, and features a range of plants associated with aquatic habitats. It is also a refuge for dragonflies, and an important area for waterfowl.
Approximately 2 miles (5 kilometres) SE of Northampton town centre, and parking is at the nearby Midsummer Meadow picnic site.

Boddington Meadow Nature Reserve (WT) is situated on the NW bank of British Waterways Boddington Reservoir. The area, covering 2.4 ha (5.57 acres) has been traditionally managed as a hay meadow, and was purchased by the Trust to prevent it from being ploughed. As an area, which has never been ploughed, it is rich in its range of flora and fauna.
The reserve is 1 mile (2.5 kilometres) W of Byfield, and there is a small car park on the Byfield to Boddington road, at the NW corner of the Reservoir, and the Meadow can be reached by foot.

Collyweston Quarries (WT), which is known locally as The Deeps, consists of limestone grassland, which has a wide range of both flora and fauna - and especially insects. Semi-natural, it is the largest area of limestone grassland left in Northamptonshire covering some 8 hectares (19 acres), and is also designated a Site of Special Scientific Interest (SSSI). The Wildlife Trust leases the area from the Burghley Estate.
Situated between Easton-on-the-Hill and Collyweston, it can be reached at two points through kissing gates. There is no car park, but cars can use the layby that is close by.

Farthinghoe Nature Reserve (WT) is in the south of the county, and a good example of an area which has 'returned' to wildlife. Formerly a cutting for the Banbury to Buckingham railway, it was later used as a landfill site, but is now leased to the Wildlife Trust by Northamptonshire County Council, and has become an interesting site with a rare dragonfly being recorded in recent years. The meadowland attracts butterflies and there are many wild flowers.

Off the A422 1 mile West of Farthinghoe, the turning being opposite the bungalow.

Glapthorn Cow Pasture (WT) has been in the possession of the Wildlife Trust since 1968, and covers 28 hectares (69 acres). The name 'pasture' is misleading, because the area is woodland, having grown up on a pasture which was 'neglected'. Blackthorn colonised the site, providing a dense protective thicket for nesting birds - and an important site for the black hairstreak butterfly. The northern end of the reserve consists of high trees forming woodland; the former ridge and furrow farming system can be seen in the undulating nature of the terrain. Designated a Site of Special Scientific Interest (SSSI) the area is a haunt of the summer-visiting nightingale.
Reached from the A604 Oundle to Peterborough road just south of Oundle, there is no car park, but vehicles can be left on the wide verge close to the crossroads.

Great Oakley Meadow Local Nature Reserve (WT) has been saved from urban development in the Corby area, and is managed by the Wildlife Trust. An old established meadow, the area was first mentioned in the Domesday Book of 1085, and although part of the area has been cultivated, the rest is still thought to be natural meadow. The grassland regime is managed by grazing and cutting.
The reserve can be reached from the A6014 and Lewin Road over stiles, or from the Headway. Reached from the roundabout where the A6003 and A6014 converge.

High Wood and Meadow Nature Reserve (WT) is situated in a rural, unspoilt area of Northamptonshire, away from any main road. Consisting of approximately 16 hectares (40 acres) of woodland and meadowland, it is a Site of Special Scientific Interest (SSSI). The woodland part of the site is traditionally managed by coppicing, which not only encourages the cut stools to generate, but allows light through to the woodland floor, so that spring flowers can germinate, flower and seed. More than 80 different birds have been recorded, including wood warbler, redstart, grasshopper warbler, and a number of these are known to breed. The mammal population includes badger, fox, rabbit, stoat, and mice. The mainly acidic meadow is grazed and supports a number of plants, which flourish in these conditions, including cat's ear, sheep's sorrel and heath bedstraw. An information panel at the entrance to the wood provides basic information about the Reserve.
Reached from the gated road between Stowe and Preston Capes, the entrance is along the Knightley Way by the side of Mantles Heath, and then right along

the first boundary hedge, a walk of about a mile (2.5 kilometres), Parking is near Mantles Heath on the roadside verge.

Sheep Grazing in High Wood and Meadow *Photograph by Ron Wilson*

Kinewell Lakes Local Nature Reserve covers 20 hectares (50 acres) of mature gravel pits. A hide provides an opportunity for excellent bird watching. In addition to the expanse of water, the site also covers a further 32 hectares (80 acres).
Reached off the A605 immediately to the W of Ringstead, and car parking is available.

Kings Wood Local Nature Reserve (WT) centres on an ancient piece of woodland, which it was believed was established at least 1600 years ago. The area includes a wide range of tree and shrub species, and the wildlife associated with this diverse plant life. The wood is managed by coppicing, which helps with the diversification process, and the work being carried out will ultimately return the wood to its former state. There is a wide range of bird life including treecreeper, nuthatch, jay, tawny owl, all three species of woodpecker (great spotted, lesser spotted and green) and sparrowhawk.
The wood is 1 mile (2.5 kilometres) from Corby town centre.

Kingsthorpe Local Nature Reserve (WT) takes in some of the area, which was originally known as Kingsthorpe Mill Meadows. Situated beside the Brampton Arm of the River Nene, the 7 hectare (12 acre) site was formerly an

area of flood meadows, and the site of Kingsthorpe Mill, where the old mill race can still just be seen. Large numbers of insects are present, together with a range of wild flowers and mammals.
There are no parking facilities, and the reserve, which is in Kingsthorpe, is off Millway, about 400 metres (400 yards) from the Cock Hotel traffic lights.

Lings Wood Local Nature Reserve (WT) covers an area of 23 hectare (56 acre) and is mainly woodland, with areas of grassland, scrub and wetland. The name 'lings' suggests that the original area was heathland, and during the 16th century it was common land, but by the turn of the 20th century had become deciduous woodland. Some conifers also replaced these earlier trees. There is both a dew pond and a spring pond.
Situated 4 miles to the east of Northampton, the entrance is signed (Wildlife Trust) off Lings Way - from the mini-roundabout on the A4500 (Lings/Goldings).

Mill Crook Hay Meadow Nature Reserve (WT) is in the valley of the River Tove near Towcester, and covers an area of 6 hectare (14 acres). The Reserve is in the care of the Wildlife Trust to prevent it from being developed, and to protect the plants and animals associated with it. Grasses alone are represented by 20 different species, and there are many other wild flowers. The reserve reaches down to the River Tove, which is known to flood from time to time. Here kingfishers also breed.
Close to Grafton Regis, but the nearest parking is 20 minutes from the site. It is therefore advisable to contact the Trust before a visit is made.

Newbottle Spinney Nature Reserve (WT) was a former stone quarry, and when work was finished a range of deciduous trees were planted in the 18th and 19th centuries. These include oak, ash, sycamore, lime and sweet chestnut. Woodland flowers are also well represented and apart from primroses and violets, it is also possible to see twayblade and spotted orchids. The bird population is varied, and includes both tawny and little owls.
Situated 5 miles (8 kilometres) to the W of Brackley, the Reserve straddles both sides of the road from Newbottle to Kings Sutton. There are some parking spaces.

Pitsford Nature Reserve (WT) has been established by an agreement between Anglian Water and the Wildlife Trust. Covering an area of 194 hectare (480 acre), the whole reservoir was designated a Site of Special Scientific Interest (SSSI) in 1971. It has good numbers of wintering wildfowl, and seeding plants provide these with an abundant supply of food. Several hides have been constructed around the reserve, including one specifically for

badger watching. Facilities provide excellent views across various parts of the reserve. Permits are needed to visit the reserve.
Reached from Holcot or from the A508 at the roundabout north of Brixworth Country Park.

Ramsden Corner Plantation (WT), a remnant of a former piece of ancient Stowe Wood, and within the area there are a variety of habitats, including several wet flushes. A number of Northamptonshire's rare plants are found here, including bitter vetch, wood vetch, wood horsetail and golden saxifrage. There is also a good range of birds, including great spotted and green woodpeckers, together with the treecreeper, redpoll, brambling and grasshopper warbler.
The Reserve is on an unclassified road between Preston Capes and Upper Stowe, some 6 miles (9.5 kilometres) to the SE of Daventry.

Salcey Forest is an area owned by the Forestry Authority, but the Wildlife Trust and BBONT have an arrangement to manage 14 hectares (34 acres) of ancient woodland as a nature reserve. The area includes native oak, together with maple, ash, sweet chestnut, turkey oak and sycamore, and a very good mix of shrubs, which include dogwood, guelder rose and Midland hawthorn. In addition the area supports a range of butterflies, including the wood white, and some unusual plants. Nightingales can be heard in the spring.
West of the B526 Northampton-Newport Pagnall road, and 6 miles (9.5 kilometres) S of Northampton.

Short Wood (WT) formerly a piece of Rockingham Forest, was purchased in 1964 to prevent the area from being turned over to agriculture. Twenty five hectares (62 acres) in extent, it has many uncommon plant species, together with a number of woodland types. Mainly mixed woodland coppice of hazel, field maple and ash, there are also some oaks as standards. The variety of shrubs, including spindle and dogwood, together with the relatively rare wild service tree, add interest to the site.
Off the Southwick to Glapthorn road N of Oundle.

Southwick Wood is managed by the Wildlife Trust in association with the owners of the wood, and covers 23 hectares (56 acres). Within the area there are a number of habitats, including woodland, scrub and grassland. An area of ancient woodland, it is known to have been wooded for at least three hundred years, and as such represents one of the few remaining sites in Northamptonshire. Management techniques include coppicing to allow light to penetrate to the woodland floor, thus increasing the diversity of plant life.

The wood is on the Glapthorn to Southwick road, and parking is on the W side of the road between the two villages. The Reserve is then reached by walking N up the road, past the water tower.

Stoke Bruerne Nature Reserve (WT) is adjacent to the Grand Union Canal and has been leased to the Wildlife Trust since 1988. Clay was removed in the past, leaving a low-lying area, which has resulted in several ponds, marshy areas and reed beds. Other habitats include scrub and rough grassland, the whole reserve being surrounded by high hedges. Bird life is well represented with more than 50 species being recorded. Grass snakes are found in the site, and butterflies occur in large numbers, including the common blue, small heath and small skipper. The aquatic areas, which include the Grand Union Canal, entice dragonflies, which feed and rest around the ponds, and which also use these areas for egg laying. Sheep are used to graze the area during the autumn and winter as a means of managing the grassland.
The Reserve is in Stoke Bruerne and on the road to Alderton. Care must be taken when parking, especially in summer when the village is very busy.

Summer Leys Local Nature Reserve has been 'created' from one of the disused gravel pits, and although quite recent it is proving a very important site, particularly for wading birds and waterfowl. A number of islands have been left in the pits, which are valuable for wildfowl, and hides provide excellent sites for bird watching, one hide is specially adapted for wheelchair users. There is ample car parking and places to picnic.
The Reserve is on Hardwater Road between Wollaston and Hardwater Crossing.

Titchmarsh Local Nature Reserve (WT) covers an area of 30 hectares (73 acres), and is an important place for Nene Valley wildfowl. Earlier used for gravel extraction, this is one of the older established sites along the Valley. Scrapes and pond provide sites for waterfowl, and winter visiting provides the birdwatcher with ample opportunities for viewing a variety of species from one of several hides around the reserve to provide different views across several parts of the area.
Reached from either the A605 at Thorpe Waterville (turn off the main road by the public house) or along the A6116 before Islip, following the signs to Aldwincle. Car parking and picnic places available.

Thorpe Wood Nature Reserve (WT) is another of Northamptonshire's few remaining ancient woodland sites, and is an area of coppice-with-standards.

Former management techniques have been reinstated to open up the canopy for the benefit of ground-loving plants.
On the edge of Peterborough, the reserve can be reached from Nene Parkway between Woodston and Bretton.

Nene College

Offers various courses at both undergraduate and MSc level - and full and part-time degree courses. The aims of the courses provided by the School of Environmental Science are to enhance awareness and understanding, intellectual, personal and practical skills and competence. Short courses can also be arranged for a wide sector of the community - from business to local authorities and local groups.
Tel: 01604 735500.

Nene Valley Project (Based at Northamptonshire Country Council - Environment Directorate)

This project has been working to look after the landscape and wildlife of the Nene Valley since 1990. It also works to create and extend opportunities for access to the wider countryside and provide recreational facilities in appropriate places. Guided by the strategic planning document the Northamptonshire Nene Strategy, landowners, community groups and individuals are encouraged to maintain a living and working countryside, and one that people of all abilities can enjoy.

Projects include habitat management, interpretation, production of cycling, walking and canoeing trails, specialist wildlife/landscape advice, including grants advice, and consultation and planning issues.

Long-term and ongoing projects are:

Working with Wellingborough Borough Council on plans to improve Wellingborough Embankment, including provision of cycleways, nature reserve enhancement and recreational activities.

Creation of nature reserve at Abington Meadows, Weston Favell.

Working with the Environment Agency on provision of canoe portage points at each lock along the Nene Navigation (long term).

"Wind in the Willows", a long-term project to restore old pollard willows throughout the Nene Valley in Northamptonshire, and to replace willows where necessary.
For more information contact Cheryl Joyce, Nene Valley Project Officer 01604 236633.

Northamptonshire ACRE (Action with Communities in Rural England).
Northamptonshire ACRE is an independent voluntary organisation working with the rural communities of the county. It is a member of ACRE, the national rural communities charity. Northamptonshire ACRE's purpose is to improve the quality of life for communities and particularly of disadvantaged people in rural Northamptonshire.
The organisation supports and advises rural community groups on a wide range of issues and encourages local action and participation in decision making. The group campaigns to ensure that the interests of people living in rural Northamptonshire are taken into account in policy making and strategic planning for the county. Funding for this work comes from the Countryside Agency, county and district councils, sponsors, donations and membership subscriptions.

The Northamptonshire ACRE team offers advice and support to rural community groups on:

Village Halls and Community Centres; Village Housing; Rural Services; Rural Transport; Health and Community Care; Community Management Plans; Village Design Statement; Local Charities; Fund Raising and Grant Aid; Sport and Play facilities; Village Newsletters and Publications; Community Management Plans; Village Design.

Rural transport is another vital but declining service for people living in rural areas. ACRE offers support and assistance to transport and voluntary car schemes.

Changes in the provision of health and social care are having an impact on where and how people access these. Information or personal references from people with mobility difficulties can back up the representations constantly being made to policy makers.

For more details contact Northamptonshire ACRE at Hunsbury Hill Centre, Harksome Hill, Northampton, NN4 9QX. Tel: 01604 765888.

Northamptonshire Archaeological Society produces an annual journal, and arranges occasional lectures and field visits. Details from Mark Curteis on 01604 238548

Northamptonshire Archaeology is a branch of Northamptonshire County Council that serves both the public and private sectors. It was formed in 1989 when the Archaeology Unit was divided into separate sections: Northamptonshire Archaeology to carry out fieldwork projects, particularly on development schemes; and Northamptonshire Heritage, dealing with planning and policy.

Excavations at Green Street, Northampton

Desk-based studies of maps, documents and other records, together with the use of non-destructive field techniques, such as field-walking, and earthwork and geophysical surveys, are used to assess the likely impact of new development proposals. The first assessment of what actually lies below the ground often comes from trial trenching.

Once development projects are approved there is often a need for further archaeological work, ranging from a simple watching brief during soil stripping or trenching through to the large scale excavation of sites of all periods from the Neolithic to the 19th century, followed by analysis and reporting.

In addition, Northamptonshire Archaeology provides a consultancy and advice service upon matters ranging from individual development schemes to heritage management and restoration projects, including involvement in public promotion and education. Specialist services include buildings recording, covering historic and industrial buildings and churches, and the study of historic garden landscapes.

Although Northamptonshire Archaeology is based in the county, a proportion of the work now takes place in the surrounding counties. Specialist studies, particularly work on historic gardens, have taken place even further afield, including; Hampton Court Palace and Chiswick House, London; Goodwood House, Sussex; Bolsover Castle, Derbyshire; and at Vallery, France.

Recent excavations carried out by Northamptonshire Archaeology:

The majority of the fieldwork projects carried out by Northamptonshire Archaeology take place in advance of development schemes such as new housing, industrial units, new roads, quarrying, pipelines, urban redevelopment and building renovation. They cover all possible types of archaeology ranging from the excavation of prehistoric burial sites to the recording of World War II pill-boxes. Some watching briefs may only involve a few hours work while a trench for drains or a telephone cable is excavated next to a church or across the earthworks of a deserted medieval village. On the other hand, a major excavation project on a new road might run for months, and work on a quarry may take place over several years and the analysis of the records and the finds can take just as long.

There is therefore no typical site, indeed, a major part of the appeal of archaeology is that no two jobs are exactly the same and, despite desktop studies and trial trenching, it is never known exactly what will turn up.

In recent years a number of important sites have been excavated around the county. Work in advance of the new bypass and a housing estate at Warmington recovered prehistoric burials, an early medieval settlement including timber halls, and a medieval windmill mound. At Wollaston Quarry, near Northampton, it has taken five years to investigate a sequence of Iron Age and Roman settlements set alongside a trackway. The major discoveries here were of two Roman vineyards and the grave of a Saxon prince buried with a sword and iron helmet, only the fourth such helmet from this country.

Near the Brackmills Industrial Estate, Northampton, excavation of another Iron Age settlement in the path of a new water pipeline led to the discovery of an Iron Age woman buried face down in a pit with a collar of twisted lead around her neck. This unique collar may have been a mark of rank, but the discovery led to local and national newspaper articles claiming that she may have been a witch.

In Northampton, trenches at Green Street, near the railway station, uncovered the first lengths of the Saxon and medieval town bank and walls to be seen by archaeologists. At Woolmonger Street the remains of late Saxon timber buildings from the earliest town were found beneath the stone buildings of the late medieval street frontage. Most recently, the early 20th century Timber Storage Shed next to the river at Southbridge was recorded before demolition. Work in other towns, such as Towcester and Daventry, has provided further information about their respective Roman and Saxon origins.
Northamptonshire Archaeology, 2 Bolton House, Wootton Hall Park, Northampton, NN4 8BE
Tel: (01604) 700493. Fax: (01604) 702822

Northamptonshire Association for Environmental Education

The Northamptonshire Association for Environmental Education was formed in 1975, and has been working on various initiatives over the years. The first edition of Northamptonshire a Guide to the Countryside was produced in 1977 by County Guide Publication and a completely revised edition was brought out by Jema Publications in 2001. At present the NAEE has contact with other organisations and groups within the county, and has an input where needed, including directories, and local exhibitions, although it is less active than during the early days.
Details: 01327 361384

Northamptonshire Association for Local History

The organisation consists of affiliated individuals and local history groups in the county. It organises regular meetings, and publishes an annual Directory listing members and groups affiliated to it, and the quarterly Northamptonshire Local History News.
More details from Mrs B Hornby, 12 Frog Lane, Upper Boddington, Daventry, Northamptonshire, NN11 6JD.

Northamptonshire Bat Group

The Northamptonshire Bat Group aims to carry out research, and keeps records of the distribution of bats in the County. It offers advice where necessary, especially when bats - which are protected by law - are likely to be disturbed when building work, etc. is carried out. The group welcomes sightings and details of injured bats. More information on 01604 770632.

Northamptonshire Bird Club enables people interested in birds to meet, enjoy a talk and exchange news of latest bird sightings. More details: Mrs Eleanor McMahon. Tel: 01604 880009.

Northamptonshire County Council - Environment Directorate

Within the Environment Directorate are a number of sections covering such topics as Country Parks, The Nene Valley Project etc. Details of these will be found in their appropriate place in this listing.

Northamptonshire County Council - genie

Information about the countryside can be accessed through genie; Northamptonshire Information Exchange, has a range of subjects, the most relevant of which includes Northamptonshire - People and Places, Local Facilities and Services, Transport and timetables and Environment. The service is continually updated and is available via the internet and in most libraries in the county.
http://www.northamptonshire.gov.uk.

Northamptonshire Dormouse Group

The group arranges indoor and outdoor meetings. Most of the outdoor meetings are aimed at enabling people to record dormice populations, check nestboxes, etc. More details from The Wildlife Trust, Lings House, Billing Lings, Northampton, NN3 4BE.

Northamptonshire Federation of Women's Institutes

The county groups are run along the lines promoted by the National Federation of Women's Institutes. The WI offers opportunities for all women to enjoy friendship, to learn, to widen their horizons and together to influence local, national and international affairs. The WI is for the woman of today, the woman who is concerned about the quality of life at home and in the community. The WI is open to any woman, and provides a friendly environment in which women can meet to work, to play and to learn, and it offers its members the opportunity to participate in many areas of learning. With its close contact with other voluntary sector organisations, together with the media, and the government, it is possible for members to make a difference

on matters of concern locally, nationally and internationally. Established in 1915 to voice women's concerns, be they simple, complex or controversial, the organisation is now the largest and most influential voluntary women's organisation in the country. It has a long history of campaigning which has included the following issues - breast and cervical cancer screening, child benefit, consumer rights, environment, - local and international - equal opportunities, food safety and healthy living, HIV/AIDS education, pollution, public transport, and support and recognition for carers.
In Northamptonshire there are WI groups in many villages. For more information contact the Northamptonshire Federation of Women's Institutes, 11 Albion Place, Northampton, NN1 1UD. Tel: 01604 638378.

Northamptonshire Gardens Trust, The

Aims to encourage an awareness of historic gardens and landscapes from all periods – and to preserve them. Carries out surveys, researches and records gardens of all sizes - from the largest (including parkland) to the smallest. Also includes modern garden designs.
Details: Mrs Norma Pearson 01604 843552.

Northamptonshire Heritage (Northamptonshire County Council - Environment Directorate) is responsible for the management of all aspects of the County's historic environment. As part of the Environment Directorate of Northamptonshire County Council it is made up of a small team of professionals with expertise in the conservation and management of archaeology and historic buildings.

The main source of information on the archaeological sites, historic buildings and landscapes of the county, is the Sites and Monuments Record or SMR. The SMR is available for members of the public to use for research. It contains reports, aerial photographs and other information about every part of the county. Anyone interested in the history of the county should contact Northamptonshire Heritage to arrange a visit to view the SMR.
Northamptonshire Heritage, Northamptonshire County Council, PO Box 163, County Hall, Guildhall Road, Northampton, NN1 1AX. Tel: 01604 237246. Fax: 01604 236696.

Northamptonshire Industrial Archaeology Group

The group has regular indoor meetings, but is also working in the field to record Northamptonshire's Industrial Archaeology.
More information from Mr G Starmer, 34 The Crescent, Northampton, NN1 4SB.

Northamptonshire Local History News is a quarterly A5 publication, featuring a range of subject matter, including articles about people and events in Northamptonshire, together with original research (eg The Blackshirts of Wellingborough). Published by the Northamptonshire Association for Local History, subscribers and others contribute the features that appear in each issue. Titles of recent articles include 'Our new VC War Hero', 'Gretton Memories', 'Concealed Shoes', 'Echoes of the Civil War', 'Earth Structures', 'Boughton Green Fair', 'Memories of Granny', 'A Brave and Gallant Gentleman', 'Theodore Payne', 'The January Sales', 'Findings of St Luke's Archaeological Group', 'Caring for the Navvies of Woodford Halse', 'Research by Ringstead Anchors Aweigh Youth Group', etc. These and many more articles have appeared in the last eighteen months. In addition there are regular book reviews, news, and details of meetings of local history groups.
For more details contact Ron Wilson, Darby House, Welton, Daventry, Northants, NN11 5EJ.

Northamptonshire Master Thatchers Association

Thatching was one of the traditional crafts of the countryside. In recent years there has been a renewed increase in the craft. There are a number of thatchers in Northamptonshire, including those which are members of the Master Thatchers Association. Details of this, and services to thatchers, can be obtained from Roger Scanlan on 01604 499555.

Northamptonshire Natural History Society and Field Club

The Northamptonshire Natural History Society and Field Club was founded in 1876 by George Claridge Druce, who was a pharmacist, and also one of the county's eminent botanists. He was later curator of botany at the Ashmolean Museum at Oxford. The objects of the Society are to provide interest and research in natural history and allied and natural science, particularly relating to Northamptonshire; to provide facilities for the reading of papers; exhibitions of specimens; the maintenance of a library and collections; the recording of research and field work, and the extension of knowledge by such other means as the Committee may further determine from time to time.

The Society has one of the finest - and most complete - collections of sands in the world, and regularly receives requests for information. In addition, it has weather records which go back more than a century, and which have proved of interest to students studying for their degrees.

To cover such a wide spectrum of interests the Society has twelve sections, although some are more active than others. Membership of the Society is open to anyone who wishes to widen or gain a more intimate knowledge of natural history and its allied subjects. Although not all are active, the twelve sections of the society are as follows: Archaeology and History, Astronomy, Botany, General Section, Geology, Meteorology, Microscopy, Ornithology, Photography and Natural History Walks. Photography, Saturday Walks and Zoology. Other sections cover Conchology, Entomology, Ichythology, Ornithology and Natural History Walks.

A quarterly programme of meetings and excursions is made available to members. Evening and daytime meetings are held throughout the year, and these include lectures, talks, study sessions and exhibitions. In addition, the Society has a small observatory, which is situated some distance from the meeting rooms. The Society publishes a journal, which includes a range of articles and information.

Meetings are held at the Humfrey Rooms, Castilian Terrace in Northampton, and these rooms were given to the Society by Dr and Mrs Humfrey some time ago.

For more details of the Society, its membership and the Rooms, contact the Secretary, The Humfrey Rooms, Castilian Terrace, Northampton, NN1 1LD.

Northamptonshire Otter Group

Linked to the Wildlife Trust and arranges surveys, etc. of otters.
Tel: 01604 405285.

Northamptonshire Record Office

The Northamptonshire Record Office holds a wide range of records and in many different formats. There are charters, court rolls, deeds, parish and non-conformist registers, maps, letters, diaries, accounts, minute books, wills, photographs and films. These include the official, judicial and administrative records of the county and other local government authorities, records of the Diocese of Peterborough covering Northamptonshire, the Soke of Peterborough and Rutland, probate records covering the same areas, together with records of local families and estates, business and professional firms and societies. Microfilm copies of census returns are also available.

There is also a small reference library, and the office also has a large collection of pamphlets to which there are separate indexes.

Visits can be made to the Record Office for those who wish to consult documents and reference works. A personal visit is always preferable, although it might be helpful to write first. In certain circumstances searchers may be required to provide a letter of introduction.
Northamptonshire Record Office, Wootton Hall Park, Northampton, NN4 8BQ. Tel: 01604 762129.

Northamptonshire Record Society

The aims of the society are to edit and publish original documents and other material relating to the history of Northamptonshire. It also aims to stimulate interest in the history of the county by arranging lectures from time to time. The Society also maintains a library for the use of members. It publishes the annual *Northamptonshire Past and Present*, and an annual book covering some aspect of the history of Northamptonshire.

Northamptonshire Spinners, Weavers and Dyers

The group arranges courses, runs groups, etc.
For more information ring 01604 890534/01908 542898.

Northamptonshire Studies Room, Central Library, Abington Street, Northampton. A varied and interesting collection of material from around the county, which is available for study. Any items, which were produced before 1850, are now in a closed area to prevent their deterioration, but they are still available. The stock is now on a computerised library catalogue, which has enhanced access to the collection.
For further information contact the Local Studies Subject Specialist on 01604 626711.

Northamptonshire Women's Environmental Network

Northamptonshire Women's Environmental Network aims to educate and empower and inform women who care about the environment. It arranges meetings and seminars. For details of the local groups contact 01604 810647.

Northamptonshire Federation of Young Farmers Clubs

The Young Farmers' Club movement was established in 1932 with the aim of meeting the needs of rural young people through various means, including educational, training and social programmes. These are planned in such a way that they encourage community involvement and a concern for the environment. The groups are organised to enable young people to participate and make their own decisions both within the YFC movement, and independently, based on issues which affect them.

Further details of local groups from Lodge Farm, Pitsford Road, Moulton, Northampton NN3 1SX.
Tel: 01604 760562.

Orienteering

Orienteering involves using maps to get from one place to another. There are a number of orienteering opportunities at various places in Northamptonshire. These are listed below. Further information can be obtained from the contact number.

Barnwell Country Park Tel: 01832 273435.
Brigstock Country Park Tel: 01536 373625.
Brixworth Country Park Tel: 01604 882322.
Daventry Country Park Tel: 01327 877193.
East Carlton Country Park Tel: 01536 770997.
Irchester Country Park Tel: 01933 276866.
Salcey Forest Tel: 01780 444394 (Forest Enterprise).
Wakerley Great Wood Tel: 01780 444394.

Orton Trust

Situated in the disused church at Orton, the Trust organises courses for stonemasons, which include weekend courses on all aspects of the stonemason's craft.
Further information from 01536 761303/710692.

Pocket Parks (Northamptonshire County Council - Environment Directorate). Northamptonshire was the pioneer in setting up these areas which are, as the name implies, 'pockets' of land, and there are now more than seventy of these areas 'scattered' around Northamptonshire. Each park 'belongs' to the people and is managed by them. If there is an area of land close to you which you think would make a suitable pocket park, contact the Pocket Parks Officer on 01604 237222.

Ramblers Association has campaigned for a long time using its national status, and with the help of large numbers of local groups, to enable people to enjoy the countryside. It aims to foster a greater knowledge and love of the countryside, and to help protect it for the use and enjoyment of all - and not just its members. Locally there are well-established groups in many parts of the county, and one of these has successfully campaigned for a bridge across the busy A14, where a number of 'footpaths' cross it. In Northamptonshire the groups also keep watchful eyes on their local rights of way, and work with the

County Council to effect the removal of obstructions and the replacement of stiles and bridges, thus enabling the local authority to meet the Government's targets, to ensure continuity of the rights of way. Not only do groups organise walks, but may also be involved with the removal of obstructions and undergrowth. In addition social get-togethers are also arranged, and programmes of activities produced.

When joining the national group, Northamptonshire members are entitled to belong to their county group, and participate in events without additional membership charges. Everyone is welcome, and there are no age barriers or walking experience. Walks, which are arranged, vary but are usually between eight and twelve miles, and consideration is given to families as well as individuals when programmes are arranged.
Ramblers Association, 1-5 Wandsworth Road, London, SW8 2XX. Tel: 020 7339 8500. www.ramblers.org.uk.
Further details of the Northamptonshire group can be obtained from the national group.

Rockingham Forest Trust, The, is a registered charity, and was formed 'to promote a thriving countryside in Rockingham Forest'. The main thrust of its work consists of environmental management, and it does this by offering an insight into what makes Rockingham Forest special. This is achieved by working with local people so that the landscape, local traditions and the rural way of life will be conserved.

The Trust fulfils its objectives in a variety of ways. One of these is to produce a booklet called 'Rockingham Forest Products - Woodland Skills Directory', which takes the form of a logbook and is regularly updated. This contains details of 'craftsmen' with a range of skills - planting trees and hedges, managing woodland, carrying out tree surgery (including pollarding), supply and production of woodland products (including charcoal, rustic poles, firewood), etc., in addition to those who are involved with training, demonstrations and teaching. The Trust is situated at the Drill House Hall, Benefield Road, Oundle, Peterborough, PE8 4EY. Tel: 01832 273278.

Royal Society for the Protection of Birds, which was founded in 1889, is Europe's oldest conservation organisation, and has more than a million members. The Society owns or leases a wide range of nature reserves around the country, and these are open to visitors - some to members; others to the general public. The RSPB has no reserves in Northamptonshire, but it has a number in surrounding counties, including The Lodge, Sandy, Bedfordshire (The RSPB's HQ) and the Ouse Washes in Cambridgeshire.

The 42 hectare (104 acre) site at Sandy is the setting for the work of the RSPB, and the many departments - including the Young Ornithologists Club - operate form the site. School parties are catered for at the Reserve during certain seasons, and will benefit from direction from a teacher-naturalist.

In contrast to this woodland, the 515 hectare (1,275 acre) Ouse Washes is more open, and at certain times of the year less hospitable, although it is equipped with hides, to enable the visitor to gain as much as possible from a visit. During the winter the reserve has some of the most spectacular gatherings of wildfowl in the country. The Reserve is open throughout the year.

Apart from managing its reserves, the RSPB is also engaged in a wide range of research, and sets up projects to enable it to understand changes which are taking place in the wild bird population. It also organises the Garden Bird Watch for young members. Other duties include protection of vulnerable sites, prosecution where laws are being broken, and especially with regard to thefts of eggs and young birds.

As an expert in this field, the RSPB is often called upon to provide evidence to a wide range of bodies, and also co-operates with other organisations to mount campaigns and publish research.

The Charity produces its excellent Birds Magazine, sent free to members, and also Bird Life and Phoenix, which are for younger members. The organisation produces a range of educational material, and a free catalogue can be obtained from RSPB headquarters, The Lodge, Sandy, Beds, SG19 2DL - 01767 680551. Information about membership is also available from The Lodge.

Royal Society for the Protection of Birds (local groups)
There are two groups in the county. For details of the Northampton Group contact Liz Wicks - 016904 408717; for the Mid Nene Group Michael Ridout - (01933 355544 - evenings).

Severn-Trent Water Authority
Is responsible for the administration of the Stanford Reservoir.

South Court Environmental is made up of workers who form a co-operative and has twin aims:

(1) Supports wildlife conservation and ecological work for the benefit of communities

and (2) Supports communities in benefitting wildlife conservation.

Members of the group have various skills, which are employed in the above

in practical conservation
in wildlife survey work
in ecological research
in research methodology and computing related to the environment.
in fund-raising for the community and wildlife.
in networking and publishing.

The group operates STORES, which has a number of strands, including the buying and selling of books from members/member groups, it supports nature conservation in Northamptonshire, and helps support overseas communities working in co-operation with Tools for Self-Reliance. For more details contact 01604 630719 or 01604 250856.

Tree and Landscape Officer (Northamptonshire County Council - Environment Directorate) organises a range of tree planting schemes, and also works in liaison with the education service. In addition, there is the opportunity for specific skills training and also for schools ground development, linked to tree and woodland aspects.
Tel: Tree and Landscape Officer 01604 236236.

Upper Nene Archaeological Society

The Society arranges meetings, excavation work, visits, etc. It is also responsible for excavations at Piddington, and manages the museum there. It publishes a variety of documents and reports.
Details from Roy or Liz Friendship-Taylor, 'Toad Hall', 86 Main Road, Hackleton, Northampton, NN7 2AD. Tel: 01604 870312.

Wildlife Trust for Northamptonshire

The Wildlife Trust is a consortium covering the counties of Northamptonshire, Bedfordshire and Cambridgeshire. In Northamptonshire it is the main organisation working to conserve and enhance the wildlife environment in the county. It manages a range of nature reserves throughout the county, and in Northampton works with the Borough Council to manage reserves like Lings Wood, Barnes Meadow and Kingsthorpe Local Nature Reserve. In addition the charity also consults, and is consulted on a variety of topics by a range of

groups and organisations, and offers advice to both voluntary, statutory and commercial organisations. Apart from offering support by joining the organisation, it is possible to volunteer and get involved with practical conservation work.
Details: The Wildlife Trust, Lings House, Billing Lings, Northampton, NN3 8BE. 01604 405285.

Wildlife Watch is the junior arm of the Wildlife Trust, and runs a variety of groups for young people across Northamptonshire.
Details of both organisations from The Wildlife Trust, Lings House, Billing Lings, Northampton, NN3 8BE. 01604 405285.

Woodland Trust, The, was founded by Kenneth Watkins in 1972, and is the UKs leading charity dedicated solely to the protection of the country's native woodland heritage. And almost without exception the Trust's woodlands are open for everyone - not just members - to enjoy. The Charity now owns some 1000 sites, covering 16,600 hectares (41,000 acres) of woodland - and in addition has planted more than a million trees. The rapid growth in the 1980's and 90's makes The Woodland Trust a major contributor to broad-leaved woodland in Britain by planting in the region of a quarter of a million trees annually.

'The Objectives of the Trust are to conserve, restore and re-establish trees and in particular broad-leaved trees, plants and all forms of wildlife in the United Kingdom of Great Britain and Northern Ireland and thereby to secure and enhance the enjoyment by the public of the natural environment of those territories'. (Taken from The Woodland Trust's Memorandum of Association).
The Trust owns a number of sites in Northamptonshire (see under woodlands).
Tel: 01476 581111.

Woodlands

When visiting woodland sites it is important that the Code is followed.

Guard against all risk of fire.
Protect trees, plants and wildlife.
Leave things as you find them, taking nothing away.
Keep dogs under control.
Avoid damaging buildings, fences, hedges, walls and signs.
Leave no litter.

Bucknell Wood (Forest Enterprise)
A 200 hectare (500 acre) mixed woodland, there are waymarked trails, picnic places and car parking.
Situated off the A43 Silverstone to Abthorpe Road. Tel: 01780 444394.

Charter Wood (Northampton Borough Council)
The broad-leaved woodland was established by the Mayor of Northampton (Malcolm Lloyd) to mark the 800 Anniversary of the granting of the Charter to Northampton by Richard I. Covering 8 hectares (20 acres), it consists of 800 oaks planted during 1989/90. Each tree was sponsored.
Situated in Delapre Park, behind Delapre Abbey, and maintained by Northampton Borough Council. Tel: 01604 233500.

Cherry Lap/Mounterley (Forest Enterprise)
Woodland covering 124 hectares (300 acres), there are woodland walks.
Tel: 01780 444394.

Everdon Stubbs (Woodland Trust)
Although this ancient piece of woodland has been there for at least 300 years, it was not recorded during the Domesday Survey. Covering 30 hectares (72ha) it 'straddles' the Everdon to Farthingstone road, and consists of a mixture of hardwoods, and has both sessile and penduncculate oak, together with a range of other species including hornbeam, rowan, hazel, sycamore, silver birch and some very old beeches. A Site of Special Scientific Interest (SSSI), the wood is also well-known for its display of spring bluebells. Small car park and well worn paths (not waymarked). A booklet about the wood (price £1.25) from Everdon Field Studies Centre, Everdon, Daventry, Northants, NN11 3BL (01327 361384).
Situated on an unclassified road reached from the A45 at the Everdon/Upper Weedon turn at Dodford. At the t-junction - approximately 2.5 miles (4 kilometres) - take the left turn towards Farthingstone, and the wood is about half a mile along this road.

Fineshades Woods (Forest Enterprise)
A large wood of 475 hectares (1174 acres), it was once part of the extensive Rockingham Forest. Rich in plant and animal life - including birds, it is also home to the wild service tree. Deer include fallow and muntjac, and woodland butterflies are also common. Woodland walks, parking, picnic areas and toilets. Special cycle route.
Situated off the A43 Stamford to Corby road near Duddington. Tel: 01780 444394.

Grafton Park Wood (Living Landscape Trust/Boughton Estate)
Used for shooting and game rearing, it is also available for visitors, and includes picnic areas, waymarked walks and car parking. Group visits can be booked at least seven days in advance. Open by appointment only. Roadside notice board gives details of when walks can be taken.
Situated NE of Kettering off the A43. Tel: 01536 515731.

Harlestone Firs (Althorp Estate)
Mainly consisting of coniferous plantations, it is a worked wood and the timber is harvested regularly. The area has many footpaths and bridleways, although there is only one official right of way through the Firs.
Situated off the A428 Northampton to Rugby road before Harlestone village. Parking in layby opposite the entrance and by the Garden Centre. Tel: 01604 751346.

Harry's Park (Forest Enterprise)
Area covering 186 hectares (460 acres).
Situated near Brigstock. Tel: 01780 444394.

Hazleborough Forest (Forest Enterprise)
This mixed woodland was originally part of the once-extensive Whittlewood Forest, and is 407 hectares (1005 acres) in extent. Parking, walks and picnic places. There is a 1.25 mile (2 kilometre) forest trail.
Situated off the A43 S of Silverstone. Tel: 01780 444394.

Irchester Country Park (Northamptonshire County Council)
In addition to other areas within the park there is an 81 hectare (200 acre) area of planted woodland. Walks and leaflets available - see also Country Parks entry.
Situated on Gypsy Lane on the B570, Little Irchester to Irchester road, and off the A509 SE of Wellingborough. Tel: 01933 276866.

Lings Wood (Wildlife Trust)
This area of mixed woodland forms part of Lings Wood Nature Reserve (see separate entry under Nature Reserves) and is managed by the Wildlife Trust for Northampton Borough Council. There are walks (not waymarked). Car parking at entrance. Various activities arranged during the year.
Situated off Lings Way, off the A4500 Northampton to Wellingborough road, at the mini-roundabout 4 miles (6.5 kilometres) from Northampton town centre. Tel: 01604 405285.

The Nuttery (Woodland Trust)
Originally a commercial cob nut orchard, The Woodland Trust is now returning it to its original state by managing it by coppicing. In spring the area is covered with snowdrops - and care should be taken when visiting at this time.
Situated in Manor Lane, Newnham, not far from the Nene Way.

Rotary Wildlife Corridor (Rotary Club)
This long narrow strip of woodland covers 4 hectares (10 acres) and was planted during National Tree Week 1993, on Lord Northampton's land. Instigated by the Rotary Club, assistance came from Northamptonshire County Council, the Nene Valley Project and South Northamptonshire Council, together with 400 members of the public. Trees planted included crab apple, field maple, oak, birch, hazel, alder, ash, and hawthorn, the latter to provide a roadside hedge. Car parking available.
Situated on the Cogenhoe road between Cogenhoe and Grendon.

Salcey Forest (Forest Enterprise)
Formerly part of an ancient hunting forest, the 500 hectare (1235 acre) area has some very ancient oaks. Waymarked walks - Lesser Spotted and Great Spotted Woodpecker Trails - car parking, picnic area, play equipment, toilets, information board and Ranger Service.
Situated off the B526 between Northampton and Newport Pagnell. Tel: 01780 444394.

Southey Wood (Forest Enterprise)
The area has been continuously wooded for many centuries, and it includes a range of wild flowers.
Situated on a minor road from Helpston and the A47 near Wansford. Tel: 01780 444394.

Stoke Wood (Woodland Trust)
A remnant of the once extensive Rockingham Forest, the remaining 11 hectares (27 acres) has a wide range of trees, together with many wild flowers, birds and butterflies.
Situated between Stoke Albany and Desborough, off the B690.

Wakerley Great Wood (Forest Enterprise and Marquis of Exeter).
An area, which was once part of Rockingham Forest, the 361 hectare (890 acre) site has waymarked walks, car parks, toilets, an orienteering course and picnic places.
Situated near Wakerley and NE of Corby, and off the A43. Tel: 01780 444394.

Whistley Wood (Forest Enterprise)
As a remnant of the once much larger royal hunting forest of Whittlebury - which covered some 8100 hectares (20,000 acres) - it is an excellent place for birds and to hear the dawn chorus (interrupted by traffic!).
Situated off the A43 0.75 miles (1.2 kilometres) from Syresham - take the turning for Crowfield. Tel: 01780 444394.

Youth Hostels Association (YHA) has been providing cheap accommodation in the form of hostels for many years, having been set up in 1930. Its principle aim is 'to help all, especially young people, of limited means to a greater knowledge, love and care for the countryside, particularly by providing Youth Hostels or other simple accommodation for them in their travels, and thus promote their health, rest and education'. The 240 hostels are situated in a range of locations throughout Britain. The organisation has always encouraged people staying at the hostels to see the countryside on foot. However, anyone wishing to use a hostel is welcome to stay. Hostels are closed during the daytime to encourage people to be out and about exploring the countryside. There is a maximum period at which a person may stay at a hostel.

Individuals wishing to use a hostel must be a member of the national association, and this facility is available to both individuals and families. Having read through the pages of Northamptonshire a Guide to the Countryside it is to be hoped that readers will want to explore the landscape, and make use of the facilities offered by the county's only YHA Hostel at Badby. Situated in the village of Badby, just off the A361 Daventry to Banbury road, the village is 4m (6.4 kilometres) S of Daventry - and the hostel is signposted off the main road. Take Main Street through the village and travel up Vicarage Hill to the hostel on Church Green. There is limited parking. Map Ref: 561588 (Landranger 152) or Pathfinder 999.

Postal address Badby Youth Hostel, Church Green, Badby, Daventry, Northamptonshire, NN11 6AR. Tel: 01327 703883.
For details of YHA membership contact Youth Hostels Association, Trevelyan House, St Albans, Herts, AL1 2DY.